The
Twilight of
Democracy

The
Twilight of
Democracy

PATRICK E. KENNON

DOUBLEDAY
New York / London / Toronto / Sydney / Auckland

PUBLISHED BY DOUBLEDAY
a division of Bantam Doubleday Dell Publishing Group, Inc.
1540 Broadway, New York, New York 10036

DOUBLEDAY and the portrayal of an anchor with a dolphin
are trademarks of Doubleday, a division of
Bantam Doubleday Dell Publishing Group, Inc.

Library of Congress Cataloging-in-Publication Data

Kennon, Patrick E.
    The twilight of democracy / Patrick E. Kennon.—1st ed.
        p.   cm.
    1. Democracy.   2. Democracy—Developing countries.
    3. Postcommunism.   I. Title.
    JC421.K46   1995
    321.8—dc20   94-14566   CIP

ISBN 0-385-47539-X
January 1995
1   3   5   7   9   10   8   6   4   2
FIRST EDITION

This book is dedicated to my wife, Jo.

Contents

Introduction

Wall Street has an adage that says, whenever stocks become so universally popular that they can "only go up," the wise investor will sell short. In the last decade of the twentieth century, democracy is the hottest stock on the board. Communism has been defeated, history has ended, and from now on it is clear sailing. Contrarians, if any there be, have yet to call their brokers.

In this era of democracy victorious, it is hard to remember that for Plato, and even for Tocqueville, democracy was a political system like any other, with its own special virtues and faults. It was not the presumed end of political and social evolution. It was not Heaven on Earth. It had open and articulate enemies, many of whom were men of honor, intelligence, and social conscience. Serious arguments were heard for Catholic traditionalism, for monarchy, for the dictatorship of the proletariat.

But that was then, and this is now. Now everyone is a democrat. Generals seize governments to protect democracy. Terrorists detonate powerful bombs in crowded markets to bring about democracy. Governments regulate private morals in the name of democracy. We have "People's Democracy," "economic democracy," "social democracy," "racial democracy," and "sexual democracy." Most of these new "democracies," while often worthy of support, have little to do with customary definitions of the word.

The very completeness of democracy's victory as an ideology, however, constitutes a threat. In the past, as many thoughtful observers recognized,

Democracy (with a capital *D*) was something to be achieved against strong counterforces of left and right. Like the Communist paradise that was to be the end point of Marxist socialism, Democracy (with a capital *D*) was something that lay in the future. In the present, it could only be approximated. It was something to fight for, not to have.

In time of relative calm, the approximation was fairly good. Voters voted their preference, within a very limited range, and elected officials ran the government, also within a very limited range. In time of crisis, however, the approximation was not as good. Voters and elected officials alike temporarily ceded their rights to the experts of the bureaucracy. The national interest—indeed, the interest of Democracy itself—demanded that the collective ignorance of the citizens give way to the expertise of the generals and the economists. Any other course would risk losing the battle against domestic depression or foreign aggression.

Now Democracy has won—it has no serious competitors as an ideology —but individual democracies continue to have their problems. To many observers, it seems that Washington is in perpetual gridlock, that Bonn is kowtowing to the skinhead right, that Rome is sinking under corruption, that Tokyo has been sold to the highest bidder, and that Paris and London are intent upon proving that neither capitalism nor socialism can work. The newly democratized Soviet Union is in shambles, and Hungarian wags note that "democracy was able to do in three years what Communism had not been able to do in forty-five—make Communism look good!"

At the same time, other governments appear to be solving their problems by methods that bear little resemblance to those of traditional democracies. Taiwan, South Korea, and Singapore pull their peoples out of poverty under thinly disguised dictatorships. Authoritarian Mexico successfully copes with economic problems far greater than those that seem beyond the capabilities of the United States to resolve. President Alberto Fujimori overthrows his own gridlocked and guerrilla-besieged government in Peru and becomes wildly popular. Liberal elements in Russia and Algeria take grossly undemocratic actions in their efforts to forestall less liberal elements—and are quietly applauded in the West.

In response to these contradictions of democracy victorious—the macro success and the micro failures—a new and less rigid definition has come to the fore. Many in the West now appear to define democracy by form alone. Under this definition, a democracy is essentially any government that has the external characteristics of the democracies of the past. Under this definition, one can cheer the bureaucratic authoritarian successes of Lee and Salinas with good conscience. One can even contemplate using their methods.

The less-than-democratic methods that served Democracy so well in the past are being called upon to protect democracies in the present. Today, when the stakes for individual countries are as high as—or even higher than—in the past, the voters are coming to recognize that the best course is not always the most popular, that one person's view is not as good as another's, that the opinion of the expert is worth more than that of the layman. In the post–Cold War world of repeated economic and ecological crises, the politicians are beginning to realize that what was once the exception has become the rule. They see—but are reluctant to admit—that they are inadequate to the problems of the day. As patriotism struggles against pride, they keep the democratic form but cede the power, hang on to the word but abandon the content.

In its victory as an ideology, Democracy has become marginal as a system of government. The politicians, even as they deny to themselves and others that anything has changed, relegate themselves to making speeches while unelected experts make policy. To the extent that the politicians do not cede their position, to the extent that they uphold democracy in fact as well as name, they risk perpetuating and deepening their nations' problems. This situation is unlikely to change.

THIS BOOK WAS many years in the writing, and I have made some adjustments, but no major changes, to reflect the evolution of the world situation, and my own thinking, since the book was begun. To the extent that my reasoning is valid, the reader will find that my structure allows him to gain a better understanding of recent events and of events yet to come; to the extent that my reasoning is flawed, the future will make obvious those flaws.

PART ONE

The Triad and the Developed World

The relationship among the bureaucracy, the political leadership, and the private sector has largely determined the effectiveness and the form of political and economic life from the beginnings of civilization to the present.

CHAPTER 1

The Ideas of 1776
and the Road to 1789

The eighteenth-century Enlightenment ended the monopoly of the old authoritarian state and ushered in two unique political forms: deliberately limited government and deliberately unlimited government. Although both forms stemmed from many of the same sources and both could claim—accurately—to be democratic, they reflected very different ideas about the perfectibility of humankind. Conflict was inevitable.

It is only partially coincidental that the year 1776 saw the publication of both the Declaration of Independence and *The Wealth of Nations*. These two works were the reflection and, in many respects, the culmination of a unique and relatively short-lived *Zeitgeist* in France, England, and the colonies. On both sides of the Atlantic there was a widespread feeling, at least among intellectuals, that government—any government—was more of a danger than a help and that it should be circumscribed rather than made more powerful. As Tom Paine wrote in *Common Sense*, also published in 1776, "Government, even in its best state, is but a necessary evil; in its worst state, an intolerable one." Both Adam Smith and Thomas Jefferson could agree with that statement.

To advocate deliberately weakening government in favor of the governed required a historically unusual optimism about the workings of human nature and human society, because democracy—no less than laissez-faire capitalism—could only be justified on the premise that the net result of individual selfishness was the collective good. Any effort to tip the scales against an imposed order in favor of "natural rights" presupposed that the blind selfishness of the individual, as represented by the voter or the "economic man," was superior to the rational selfishness of the authoritarian and mercantilist state. The men of 1776, like the good deists that most of them were, replaced an anthropomorphic God with a benevolent Natural Law that was only slightly more believable.

Having been brought up on the ideals (if not always the reality) of Jeffersonian democracy and Smithian capitalism, Americans have trouble realizing how revolutionary the concept of limited government was. Although the men of 1776 may have had a few precursors in Republican Rome and elsewhere, most men in most societies equated strong government—and the stronger the better—with civilization. Only strong government made possible the irrigation systems upon which civilization had been built in Egypt and Mesopotamia. Only strong government could build granaries against periodic famine, enforce true weights and just trading in the market, and protect the average citizen from criminals within the city and foreign armies outside the walls. Not least, only strong government made a rule of law possible (though far from inevitable). Heavy taxes, great social and economic inequalities, and brutally intrusive administration seemed a small price to pay for such benefits.

MERCANTILISM

The economic doctrine and practice of mercantilism were essential to the development of the strong nation-state. Although certain mercantilist practices date back to ancient Egypt, if not before, the earliest versions of modern mercantilism arose in what were arguably the earliest true nation-states—fifteenth-century Portugal and Spain. Iberian mercantilism—though only a crude form of what later developed in Holland, England, and France—has come to characterize the doctrine in the modern mind. This primitive version of mercantilism, the idea that exports should always exceed imports in order to accumulate gold for the greater power of the state, has been termed "bullionism" by Shepard B. Clough to differentiate it from more refined versions of the same doctrine.[1]

Spanish and Portuguese bullionism had three principles in common with the trade-centered mercantilism of Holland and the production-centered mercantilism of England and France: (1) the goal of economic policy was to strengthen the nation and only incidentally to increase the welfare of its citizens; (2) the state had the right and duty to regulate all aspects of the economy; and (3) economic gains by one state almost inevitably came at the expense of some other state or states. These three principles constituted a good working definition of the doctrine and the practice. Nothing else was essential. Dutch mercantilists, for example, advocated free trade and low tariffs. For their part, some French and English mercantilists doubted the wisdom of maintaining a favorable balance of trade or accumulating bullion.

Nationalism and mercantilism complemented each other. The rising states needed counterforces to check the still strong medieval powers of Catholic universalism and aristocratic localism. If Rome and the nobles were the enemies of the king, his natural allies were those who depended upon his direct or indirect favor—the army and the bureaucrats falling into the first category and the merchants and manufacturers into the second.

Thus was born—or rather reborn in modern form—the political-bureaucratic-business triad that has been with us ever since. Long before there was a "Japan, Inc." of the LDP, MITI, and the *keiretsu*, there was a "France, Inc." of Louis XIV, Colbert and his minions, and the French East India Company and similar monopolies. This triad was repeated—with variations—wherever nations were being built from the England of Elizabeth to the Russia of Peter. Although the success of the combination varied according to the personal qualities and institutional strengths of rulers, bureaucrats, and businessmen, in country after country it represented a remarkable step forward. Rarely, if ever, had governments been stronger, material progress more rapid, or economies more prosperous than under mercantilism.

Mercantilism and nationalism brought together king and people and created a "we-they" attitude with regard to foreign nations. While men had long been willing—on rare occasions—to sacrifice themselves for a feudal lord or a religious faith, now they were willing—on rare occasions—to make sacrifices for the nation. Crops still failed, diseases still raged, rulers were still arbitrary, justice was still rare, and war became more terrible than before. Yet now there was a feeling of unity and pride that had not been seen in the individual nations of Europe since the absorption of the barbarian tribes.

This did not mean, of course, that any segment of society willingly accepted low living standards in the interests of strong national government—any more than any segment willingly accepted administrative tyranny. Indeed, *particular* governments were often blamed—justly or unjustly—for public misery. Discontent and social violence were never far beneath the surface. Taxes were protested, ministers were decried as incompetent, royal courts were characterized as extravagant and immoral. The remedy, however, was always to change policies or ministers, to let the "good king" know what was happening behind his back, and to hope for the best. It was to replace bad government with good government, not strong government with weak government.

THE ENLIGHTENMENT

The first systematic challenge to the idea that strong government equaled good government came as a part of the intellectual atmosphere of the Enlightenment. During this period, thinking men were greatly impressed by the orderly world of nature as revealed by Newton and his colleagues. Some of these thinkers made the by-no-means-logical jump from the natural realm to that of society and economics and postulated a Natural Law that would work for the benefit of all mankind—if only the kings and priests and mercantilist busybodies would get out of the way.

Strong government, far from being a guarantee of life, liberty, and property, came to be seen as their enemy. Bloody "national" wars, oppressive state monopolies, brutal taxation, antiscientific religion, press gangs, *lettres de cachet,* and Star Chambers cast a bad light upon established authority in all of its forms. Solutions ranged from "utopian democratic" to "totalitarian democratic" (complete with censorship, neighborhood spies, brainwashing, and forced obedience—in the name of the general will).

Most solutions were more moderate, however. The men of the Enlightenment—men such as Locke, Montesquieu, Hume, Petty, Smith, Quesnay, and Voltaire—were indeed enlightened. As men of some property and position, they sought not to abolish the monarchy, but to bind the king to a "democratic" constitution; not to suppress religion, but to disestablish the Church; not to eliminate the state, but to remove its dead hand from the economy. The last issue was perhaps the most basic: should a person's, or a nation's, livelihood be guided by the heavy hand of the government or by the invisible hand of laissez-faire? Indeed, many of the political ideas of the Enlightenment are simply glosses on John Locke's dictum that "government has no other end but the preservation of property."

THE AMERICAN REVOLUTION

The American Revolution was one of the few internal conflicts fought largely for economic reasons. It was concerned with trade and taxes and the expenses of quartering troops. It was fought to redress economic grievances and to secure economic rights and to change as little else as was consistent with these first two goals. Indeed, the political aims of the Revolution—true to the spirit of Locke—were little more than to achieve the independence necessary to secure economic rights against all future kings and Parliaments.

The men of 1776 saw the danger of homegrown as well as foreign tyranny. Their first response to this danger was the establishment of the Articles of Confederation, a uniquely democratic document and, according to some, the high point of the movement against strong government in Europe and America. Under this regime, central government was almost nonexistent; there was no federal executive, and such centralized power as existed was lodged in a one-house congress in which each state had one vote. It was clearly spelled out that each state retained its "sovereignty, freedom, and independence." Real power, such as it was, was held in the state legislatures, which were considered to be more subject to direct popular influence than federal institutions.

The Articles of Confederation, however appealing they might have been to radicals such as Sam Adams and Patrick Henry, were soon seen as unnecessary to—and ultimately destructive of—the economic goals of the Revolution. Although federal tyranny was effectively eliminated, the tyranny of the majority in individual states might over time become an equal threat to life, liberty, and property. Moreover, even an Adam Smith would agree that some government functions, such as improving education and transportation or restricting monopoly, would help rather than distort economic life.

The Constitution, though not as radically democratic a document as the Articles of Confederation, is perhaps the true high-water mark in the movement against strong government. It recognized that state governments, beholden to the mob, could also become "strong" and thereby threats to the life, liberty, and property of the minority. (Jefferson himself worried about "elective despotism.") Strengthened federal powers provided a mechanism to keep the states under control. Yet the federal government itself was weakened through the separation of powers among the branches and by the still substantial powers retained by the states. Finally, the Bill of Rights provided a check on both the states and the federal government in favor of the individual.

The Constitution, and especially the Bill of Rights, clearly spelled out the idea that strong government—even strong government in the service of democracy—was an evil to be avoided. The ratification of this document marked the culmination of the libertarian current of the Enlightenment.

THE ROAD TO 1789

The American Revolution, though, was an anomaly in world history. It was, and remains, the only successful attempt to radically reduce the power of the state through military means. The fact that the American Revolution had no successor reflects a certain disappointment with what was achieved. The Revolution had shown that the old authoritarian state could be defeated by the "people," but there it had stopped. The Revolution had given power to the people, but then it had demanded that they do nothing with it. It had opened the door to Utopia, but at the same time had forbidden the people to pass through. What in 1776 had seemed revolutionary seemed entirely too modest by 1789. The world, though it did not yet realize it, was ready for the first modern totalitarian state.

Totalitarianism, which is defined here as a system of government that attempts to control its subjects' thoughts as well as their actions, did not spring fully formed into the collective French mind in 1789, or even in 1793. Most of the French revolutionaries thought they were following in America's footsteps, and, indeed, Tom Paine and the Marquis de Lafayette were early supporters. When the time came, however, the French, unlike the Americans, did not fear to grasp for Utopia.

The French Revolution, though it took some of its ideas and much of its impetus from America, was not at all what the men of 1776 had in mind. While the Americans wanted to change as little as possible commensurate with settling their economic grievances, the revolutionaries of France ultimately wanted to create a whole new world, where injustice would be a thing of the past, where men and women could achieve their full potential, where privilege would give way to brotherhood, and the "general will" would be omnipotent in both government and society. The revolutionaries of France, unlike the self-serving merchants and planters of the thirteen colonies, wanted nothing of any so-called freedoms that would leave the old structure in place. Tom Paine and the Marquis de Lafayette soon became personae non gratae.

The French Revolution reflected a second, more mystical current of the Enlightenment. For the Enlightenment embraced not only the rationalism of Locke but also the antirational and quasi-religious romanticism of Jean-Jacques Rousseau. Unlike Locke, who thought that the state should be limited to protecting property, Rousseau called for a police state to establish a "reign of virtue" in accordance with the "general will." In this state, the rulers would determine the general will on the basis of the public interest as they defined it. In the words of Bronowski and Mazlish:

> In Rousseau's formulation, the state is all-powerful and must be given total allegiance. It is not the individual who is possessed of inalienable natural rights, but the sovereignty of the people which is inalienable. And this sovereignty is simply another word for the general will. Thus all rights belong to the state, for it is the state which embodies the general will.[2]

For the revolutionary followers of Rousseau, it was not enough to free men's minds; it was also necessary to change men's souls. Perfection was possible and Utopia was at hand, but first error had to be stamped out and virtue had to be enforced. Truth was not only knowable but known, and the free mind was not really free if it was allowed to believe a lie. As Rousseau himself had noted, "to permit vice, when one has the right and the power to suppress it, is to be oneself vicious." Religion had been laughed out the front door by Voltaire only to be sneaked in the back under the cloaks of the Jacobins.

It should be emphasized that the totalitarianism of the French Revolution, like all later totalitarianisms, was democratic and therefore a legitimate child of the Enlightenment. It was democratic in the same sense that all great revolutions are democratic, that new religions are democratic, that the lynch mob is democratic. It was democratic in the sense that, at the outset, it owed nothing to established authority and everything to popular enthusiasm. It was democratic in that it cared more for people than for law or justice and more for passion than for reason. It was democratic in that it allowed the majority to run roughshod over the minority. It was democratic in a way that had nothing to do with the ideas of 1776.

THE NATURE OF TOTALITARIANISM

France's "Republic of Virtue" has the distinction of being the first modern totalitarian state, because it was able to enforce ideology through an effective and well-armed bureaucracy. Some other states—indeed, all theocracies—had had totalitarian aims but had been unable to implement them. Some leaders, such as John Calvin, had come close but were ultimately defeated by the divided nature of their followings. The tyrannies of the past, though they had their totalitarian elements, were essentially authoritarian in that they pragmatically put security above principle and made no serious claims to represent higher abstractions. The Spanish Inquisition, for example, was a totalitarian organization; the Spanish state, which gave it its power and ultimately controlled it, was not.

Totalitarianism has its origins in what might be called the religious or moral mind-set. This is simply the belief that in any given circumstances there is an absolute code of right and wrong, that this code has been revealed to or deduced by a certain group of people, and that this group has the duty to enforce this code on itself and on the rest of the world to the best of its ability. For the totalitarian, as for the true believer, there are no shades of gray and a thought can be as evil as a deed.

Totalitarianism, like new religion (but quite unlike established religion), has no use for pragmatism. Indeed, pragmatism—doing what is expedient rather than what is moral—is among the greatest sins. The good totalitarian is more than willing to cut off his nose to spite his face, to pluck out his eye if it offends God, to divert trains from moving munitions to the front to bringing Jews to extermination camps. The good totalitarian would rather fight the good fight and lose than compromise one jot of the Truth. The good totalitarian has no stomach for fence-sitters, believing firmly that those who are not with him are against him. The good totalitarian has a list.

Totalitarianism, like new religion, is ambitious, not satisfied with the way things are. Unlike authoritarianism, which guiltily seeks to preserve an unjust status quo and is too hard-pressed trying to control people's actions to even worry about their thoughts, totalitarianism recognizes no limits to its authority. It seeks what it perceives as a radical good and is willing to take radical measures to achieve it. Whereas totalitarianism, like new religion, is the war chariot of the young, the pure, and the intolerant, authoritarianism, like old religion, is the foxhole of the old, the corrupt, and the tolerant.

Perhaps R. H. Tawney captures the relationship between totalitarianism and new (or newly reformed) religion best in his description of Calvinism: "That it should be as much more tyrannical than the medieval Church, as the Jacobin Club was than the *ancien régime,* was inevitable. Its meshes were finer, its zeal and its efficiency greater. And its enemies were not merely actions and writings, but thoughts."[3] Elsewhere, he notes that Calvin "made Geneva a city of glass, in which every household lived its life under the supervision of a spiritual police . . ." and in which a child could be executed for striking its parent.[4]

SIDESHOWS AND MAJOR TRENDS

The political history of the two centuries that followed the American Revolution and its French counterpart—on the surface, at least—is largely the story of the conflict between an adulterated form of the libertarian current and a relatively pure form of the totalitarian current of the Enlightenment. In the last decade of the twentieth century, it appears that the libertarians have won. But, while these two trends were locked in combat, something that very much resembled pre-Enlightenment mercantilism took over the battlefield. The strong but limited state was back, more powerful than ever, in a form that owed little to either libertarianism or totalitarianism. Before we can understand how that happened, however, we must examine a much older and more basic current in human history: the movement toward specialization.

CHAPTER 2

The March of Specialization

To a very large extent, the ideas of 1776—indeed, the Enlightenment itself in both its libertarian and totalitarian currents—were a sideshow to an older and more enduring trend: the relentless march of specialization. This trend, entailing as it does the erosion of military, political, and entrepreneurial authority by technical competence, has dominated political and social life since at least the Middle Ages, overshadowing the disappearance of absolute monarchy and the varying fortunes of democracy and totalitarianism.

In the beginning, we were all amateurs and generalists. In its essence, the history of the human race is the story of amateurs and generalists becoming professionals and specialists. Out of a relatively undifferentiated mass of humans (or perhaps prehumans) rose hunters and builders, farmers and soldiers, shamans and priests, witches and thieves, kings and merchants. Society became possible. Specialization—or division of labor—was clearly advantageous in the struggle for life. Over time those groups in which specialization was honored advanced, and those that distrusted specialization stagnated.

Yet, despite its advantages, the march of specialization was resisted in most societies. People with specialized trades—blacksmiths, merchants, moneylenders, tanners, *curanderos*—were more often scorned than honored. Heroes, average men and women who "rose to the occasion," were valued over those whose training allowed them to meet the occasion as a matter of course. "Citizen armies" were considered superior in some moral sense to professional armies. Small family farms raising a variety of crops and livestock were good, whereas commercial plantations raising a single crop were bad. Household crafts were wholesome, while factory manufactures were not. And so on.

On any given occasion the antispecialists might be proven right. Sometimes citizen armies did defeat professional soldiers, and sometimes diversified farms did cope with climate change better than specialized plantations. Sometimes heroes won the day. Sometimes—but very rarely. Over time the specialists always triumphed: the factories beat out home crafts, the commercial farms beat out the family plots, and the pros beat out the heroes. At best, the antispecialists won a few glorious battles; the specialists won all the wars.

THE MILITARY SPECIALIST

Nowhere has the prejudice against specialization been more ingrained than in the military. Nowhere has the hero been more glorified, from David and Ajax and a horde of noble Romans down to Sergeant York, Audie Murphy, and Rambo. And nowhere has the prejudice against specialization been so costly in terms of life and property. This prejudice, incidentally, is not lessened by the fact that many of the most prejudiced are themselves military "specialists."

Of course, even in the darkest Age of Heroes, the military had its specialists. Armorers made shields and lances, quartermasters fed the troops, engineers threw bridges across rivers and undermined walls. There were even a few strategists and military theorists. But, by and large, battles were still won—or believed to be won—by the courage, strength, and martial skills of gifted amateurs.

In his excellent book on the development of the military, *The Pursuit of Power*,[1] William H. McNeill gives much of the credit for professionalizing European armies to Maurice of Nassau, who, in order to fight the Spanish armies in the Netherlands with less than spectacular human material, was forced to rationalize the art of war. Unable to create a band of heroes, Maurice formed an army of bureaucrats with muskets. That is to say, he created an army of men with the bureaucratic virtues of discipline and duty, rather than with the older martial virtues of valor and personal loyalty. Through incessant drill, he transformed the dregs of the city and the countryside—men who were no match for the battle-hardened Spanish soldiers in courage, strength, or versatility—into specialists who could be depended upon to follow orders or to give the right orders almost without thought.

Maurice's specialists were the antithesis of heroes. Their individualism had been stamped out. They won battles not by death-defying deeds, but by being able to load and fire a matchlock a fraction of a second faster than the enemy. They were easily substitutable; when one fell, another similarly trained man took his place with no loss of efficiency to the machine as a whole. They were less interested in glory than in staying alive. For them, war was a job, not a calling. And generally they won.

Those countries that were unwilling or unable, usually because of the opposition of their military caste, to take fighting out of the hands of sportsmen and patriots and put it into the hands of specialists began to lose wars. It is ironic that those soldiers who, in the sixteenth and seventeenth centuries, were best endowed with the heroic values of courage and individual fighting ability—the Spanish and the Italians—came to be considered militarily inept cowards because their countries lost wars. It is even more ironic that those countries that began to win wars because they had better bureaucrats with muskets assumed that their success was due to their soldiers' superior courage and martial spirit.

In the nineteenth century, when the European powers began to consolidate their position in Africa and Asia and their American cousins began to move across the plains, the bureaucrats with muskets came into their own. The Europeans' enemies, whether Afghans or Apaches, had all the conventional advantages in terms of courage, derring-do, fighting skills, knowledge of the land, nationalistic or tribal feeling, and numbers. Moreover, their initial disadvantage in modern weapons was soon remedied through capture, purchase, or gift from rival powers. What they did not have was specialization.

Thus, a tiny group of specialists was able to take over three-quarters of the world. Empires greater than any dreamed of by Alexander or Caesar were acquired almost as a matter of "office routine" by these military bureaucrats. They found conquest to be so little strain that they had plenty of time left over for dabbling in languages, exploration, and natural science. It became easier to enforce one's will on a million nonspecialist Malays or Bengalis than to move a European border a few kilometers against other specialists.

The bureaucratic army survived because it won wars, not because it was loved. Indeed, the pseudo-specialists, abetted by civilian romantics, never ceased their battle against the true specialists. They fought rearguard actions against every improvement in weapons and tactics from the crossbow to the foxhole, usually on the grounds that such improvements made war less sporting and gave shelter to cowards. To keep war in the hands of "gentlemen"—that is to say, amateurs—and out of the hands of "mechanics"—that is to say, people for whom war was a job like any other—they demanded family or property qualifications for officers and lobbied for more cavalry and less artillery. The lance was still used in World War I.

The professionalization of the military was antidemocratic as well as antiaristocratic. Although democracy is not usually seen as a military trait, in past ages a good deal of rough equality characterized the raiding party (even the raiding party on a grand scale) going back from Pancho Villa's División del Norte, Geronimo's Apaches, and Quantrill's Raiders to the Vikings, the Huns, and the pirates of the *Iliad*. As recently as the American Civil War, some units elected their officers. Moreover, the mutiny—that ultimate form of military democracy—has been a constant threat to military organizations until very recent times.

The bureaucrats with muskets are concerned with ends not means, and these ends, dictated from above, are only rarely questioned. Win the war, capture Vicksburg, open up Japan for Western trade, hold Stalingrad, pacify the Zulus, map the coast of Australia, suppress the slave trade, round up the Jews in Poland, make school integration work in Little Rock, conserve your men at all costs, fight to the last man—any legitimate order is not only obeyed but in time is made to work in a good specialist army. Hierarchy rules. The good specialist army is a machine, not an organism, a finely tuned Rolls-Royce, not a thoroughbred Arabian steed. Both the car and the horse must have drivers, but the horse occasionally has a mind of its own.

Although the good bureaucrats with muskets accept the goals of their legitimate superiors and, somewhat more reluctantly, any parameters that these superiors may establish (don't overspend your budget; obey the Geneva Convention; promote more women), they have a professional pride in choosing the means to achieve the given goals. By definition, they are the experts and they resent micromanagement by civil officials. A president or a legislature that tries to dictate strategy is seen as a wrench in the machine, a threat to the very goals that the government itself has set. Civilian leaders who fancy themselves military geniuses—Lincoln, Churchill, and Hitler come to mind—are always resented by military specialists. On occasion, this resentment can reach such levels that, in the name of achieving government goals, it comes to threaten the civilian government's very existence.

Usually, however, in times of crisis at least, the civilian authorities are only too ready to bow to the expertise of the specialists. When an elected official believes that his nation's life is at stake, he is not going to insist that the military buy the plane made in his district or put highest priority on liberating the homeland of his grandfather. While he may recognize that gifted amateurs sometimes have insights that the specialists lack—Lincoln, Churchill, and Hitler once more come to mind—he also knows that wars are won or lost by specialists. Neither the politician nor the voters whom he represents want him to second-guess the experts on matters of importance.

THE ADMINISTRATIVE SPECIALIST

From the very beginnings of government, leaders have had advisors. These advisors—tribal elders, sages, cronies, relatives—were not true specialists. Although many were men of talent and experience who greatly aided the process of governing, they had no formal position or qualifications other than the ear of the ruler. Like the military heroes of the age, they were gifted amateurs.

As tribes developed into city-states and then into empires, true administrative specialists came into being. Men with special skills in writing, mathematics, hydraulics, or astronomy were needed to keep track of taxes and tribute, to partition irrigation water, and to set dates for planting or feasting. Most of these early specialists were priests, but their value to their ruler and their nation lay in their administrative rather than their religious function.

From the very beginning, rulers had a love-hate relationship with their advisors. On the one hand, they feared the true specialist, whose skills and dedication to his profession seemed a constant challenge to their position. Ancient and not-so-ancient history is a recital of the exile, imprisonment, and murder of skilled ministers by fearful kings. On the other hand, in times of crisis—which were frequent—the survival of kings and realms depended on having the best man in the right job. Thus, during periods of prosperous calm, the king paid a premium for the loyalty of cronies; when disaster loomed, however, he had to call back the specialists.

As government became more complex, the number and variety of administrative specialists grew and kings learned to play off generals against viziers, viceroys against governors, majordomos of the royal palace against high priests. It was a government of checks and balances long before

Montesquieu—but in this case it was to protect the freedom of the monarch rather than that of the citizens.

With the breakdown of centralized authority in medieval Europe, the true administrative specialist almost disappeared. The king became little more than a noble among nobles, the only difference being that the king had more expenses and more pretensions. Monarchs and high nobles held widely scattered possessions inhabited by subjects of widely varying language, customs, and history. Loyalty and responsibility were as uncommon as expertise and specialization. Rarely had so many (and so diverse) been ruled so poorly by so many.

This situation couldn't last, and it didn't. In their effort to reclaim political supremacy from a perennially disloyal nobility, the kings re-created the specialists. Replacement of a quasi-voluntary collection of noble "knights in armor" and their retainers with a paid standing army was an obvious place to start. But raising the funds to pay professional soldiers eventually required the establishment of a civilian bureaucracy to collect taxes and foster economic growth. It also required an alliance, based to an increasing extent on nationalism, with the manufacturers and merchants who were willing to create taxable wealth in exchange for protection and special privileges.

The king/bureaucracy/private sector triad, in an atmosphere of rising nationalism, eventually overcame the threat from the nobility. Over time, kings came to be replaced in function, if not in name, by presidents, prime ministers, and dictators, but the other legs of the triad remained much the same.

THE PRIVATE-SECTOR SPECIALIST

The private sector, like the military and political sectors, has both its gifted amateurs and its specialists. The "merchant princes" and "captains of industry" were amateurs; their accountants and managers and foremen and engineers and sea captains and chemists were specialists. The Wright brothers were amateurs; the CEOs of Boeing and Lockheed—and all their underlings—are specialists.

Specialization was what allowed "business" to become "big business." The inventor or entrepreneur who was willing to take the risk of breaking out of his circle was able to hire experts who could compensate for his deficiencies and expand his business far beyond the range of his direct supervision. And the inventor or entrepreneur who refused to professionalize his operation always lost out. The history of business is replete with examples of geniuses who were unable to market their quite worthy inventions and tycoons who built companies from nothing only to drive them back into nothing because they refused to delegate authority to specialists.

In business, even more than in government and the military, the specialist has largely usurped the authority of his nominal leader. In a new company, where the entrepreneur is still very much on the scene, the specialist may do no more than set limits. The engineer, the marketing man, the lawyer, the accountant, tell the entrepreneur what he can and cannot do. In older, more established companies, the professional managers have taken almost complete control from the stockholders or other owners. Although "founding families" may throw their weight around and stockholders may revolt from time to time, the professional managers almost always win and they are almost always right.

Specialization in the private sector extends beyond business. Churches, universities, research institutes, criminal organizations, and political parties have replaced the gifted amateurs, the hot partisans, and the Renaissance men with specialists. Indeed, as Max Weber has noted, specialization, or bureaucracy, came into its own in American political parties long before it did in the formal American government. This perhaps reflects the fact that Americans take winning elections much more seriously than governing. In short, wherever achieving a goal or meeting the competition (however defined) was important, the citizen called in the specialist.

SPECIALIZATION AND BUREAUCRACY

Specialization demands bureaucracy. Unlike generalists, specialists by themselves tend to be useless. While an hourglass may be inferior to a watch, it is far superior to a spring or a cog or a stem taken alone. The specialist is the precision part, and the bureaucracy is the machine. Unlike true machines, however, a bureaucracy may be considerably better or worse than the sum of its specialists.

CHAPTER 3

The Nature of Bureaucracy

Max Weber has said it best: "In a modern state the actual ruler is neces-sarily and unavoidably the bureaucracy, since power is exercised neither through parliamentary speeches nor monarchical enunciations but through the routines of administration. . . . Just as the so-called prog-ress toward capitalism has been the unequivocal criterion for the mod-ernization of the economy since medieval times, so the progress toward bureaucratic officialdom . . . has been the equally unambiguous yard-stick for the modernization of the state, whether monarchic or demo-cratic. . . ."[1]

In his excellent primer on the subject, Martin Albrow has pointed out that "two incompatible concepts—bureaucracy as administrative effi-ciency and bureaucracy as administrative inefficiency—compete for space in twentieth-century theory."[2] This apparent confusion, which goes far beyond political science professionals to encompass everyone who thinks about government, is not based on a simple misunderstanding or a conflict in definitions. Rather, it is based on the fact that bureaucracy does have two distinct faces. Bureaucracy put a man on the moon, won World War II, wiped out a thousand diseases, and raised Japan from postwar poverty to world-class economic power. It has also, in certain times and places, sabotaged the welfare state, smothered economic progress in red tape, made postal systems and railroads almost unworkable, and unjustly deprived men and women of life, liberty, and property.

BUREAUCRACY DEFINED

To quote Max Weber once again—and no one can write about bureaucracy without quoting Max Weber at every turn—bureaucratic administration is "domination through knowledge."[3] According to Weber, the characteristics of bureaucracy are "formal employment, salary, pension, promotion, specialized training and functional division of labor, well-defined areas of jurisdiction, documentary procedures, hierarchical sub- and super-ordination."[4] An American authority on the subject, Carl J. Friedrich, characterizes bureaucracy by "differentiation of functions, centralization of control and supervision, and qualifications for office," and notes that individual bureaucrats are circumscribed by rules to enforce "desirable" behavior patterns of "objectivity, precision and consistence, and discretion."[5] In a word, bureaucracy is professionalism.

Bureaucracy is also the machine that brings professionals—that is to say, specialists—together and regulates their relationship with each other. At its best, it is an impersonal mechanism to assure that a hammer is not used where a screwdriver would be more appropriate, that a biologist is not sent to do a chemist's job. It is intended to ensure that each is tasked— and rewarded—according to his or her abilities and that the tasks are carried out. Due to bureaucracy, and to bureaucracy alone, battles are no longer lost for want of a horseshoe nail.

As is made clear by the definitions of both Weber and Friedrich, bureaucracy includes much more than drones in government hives. Wherever professionals work together in a single organization, bureaucracy exists. The automobile plant, the Ranger platoon, the hospital, the law office, the research institute—even, in many cases, the criminal enterprise, the terrorist organization, and the guerrilla army—are all bureaucracies in the Weberian sense. (Clearly not all professionals are bureaucrats. The doctor, lawyer, plumber, or master pickpocket working alone is not a bureaucrat— and probably not nearly as successful as his peer working in an organization.)

BUREAUCRACY AND CIVILIZATION

Bureaucracy—the organization of specialists—was, and is, the backbone of civilization. It was what separated the city-state from the tribe. In the earliest empires it was the "enabling technology" that allowed individual insights and lucky accidents to become part of culture. As the inventor of writing and mathematics—indeed, as the only group to understand the *need* for writing and mathematics—the bureaucracy made sure that nothing of perceived importance was lost.

The earliest bureaucrats—almost certainly priests—differed from both the rulers and the common people in that their personal well-being involved long-term goals. Their full bellies and their place in society depended upon their being able to convince the ruler that taking an inventory, building a temple, or calculating an eclipse was important; that the ruler's time horizon was not limited by death and thus that he had an interest in projects that would not be completed in his lifetime; and that they, the priestly bureaucrats, were the people to organize the civilization-building process.

Then, as today, neither rulers nor ruled saw any particular advantage in civilization, in giving up present consumption for a future glory that they might not live to see. Why should the ruler live in a mud palace, while his tomb was made of polished stone? Why should the peasant leave his fields for half a year every year in order to construct roads and canals that he would never use? Why should the priestly bureaucrats be lining their pockets through expensive projects that no one could understand, when the ruler was short of concubines and the peasant was short of grain? Or, to put it in more current terms, why build a superconducting supercollider or send a man to Mars, when there are wars to be fought and hungry people to feed?

Then, as now, civilization was a construct of rules and laws and constraints. It was, by definition, not only unnatural but antinatural. It had no use for the savage, noble or otherwise. It valued work over leisure, construction over war, thought over emotion, saving over consumption, organization over freedom, society over the individual. Civilization frowned upon coveting thy neighbor's wife or life or goods. It was pure killjoy. And its custodian and creator, the priestly bureaucrat, was the Serpent who lured Adam out of Paradise and the Aunt Polly who made Tom Sawyer wash behind his ears. It is no wonder that the bureaucrat was and is hated.

Civilization had its costs, and those costs were borne by everyone except the bureaucrats, who alone profited directly from the process. (Everyone, of course, profited indirectly.) They alone were comfortable with goals and rules. They alone could turn goals and rules into a paying job. Thus, it should be no surprise that throughout history the bureaucracy has been the most consistent builder and maintainer of civilization. Civilization was and is the iron rice bowl of the bureaucrat.

WHAT BUREAUCRACY DOES WELL

Bureaucracy works best when it has a single goal, to which all else is subordinated. Tell the bureaucrats to design an atom bomb, and chances are they will do so, be they Americans or Russians or Israelis or Indians. Tell them to design an atom bomb and stay within budget, and chances are they will end up doing neither. Task them with ending inflation or unemployment or the trade deficit, and they will do so. Task them with ending all three or even with ending one while not letting the others "get out of control," and they will do a miserable job on all counts. Few if any tasks—from stopping the drug traffic to finding a cure for AIDS—are clearly beyond the abilities of a strong, well-financed national bureaucracy so long as it has no other priorities.

This means that contrary to the stereotype, bureaucracy works best in a crisis situation. In time of popular war, for example, when all segments of government and the public are agreed upon the major goal, bureaucracy is in its element. Taxes can be raised, wages checked, food rationed, men and women drafted, civil rights trampled, and the environment degraded with little more than a peep from business, labor, or the general public. And it seems to matter little whether the bureaucrats are American or British or Russian or German.

Bureaucracy can respond equally well to lesser crises, provided the solution of such crises is the clear priority of the relevant group. Creating a new alloy, fighting a forest fire, cleaning up after an earthquake, catching the "Son of Sam," or ending legal segregation are examples. Less admirably, in the past, bureaucracies have been just as efficient in responding to perceived crises by putting Japanese-Americans into concentration camps and German Jews into gas chambers.

WHAT BUREAUCRACY DOES POORLY

Bureaucracy is at its worst—once again, contrary to the stereotype—in coping with routine, noncritical matters. This is because routine issues are numerous and conflicting, with no clear priorities. In time of popular war, to use our previous example, a base can be sited under the sole criterion of winning the war. In peacetime, however, questions of employment or ecology may be as important as military efficiency. Bureaucracies may find themselves pitted against each other, and politicians and the public may also be split according to their prejudices and perceived advantages. It is a recipe for failure. To the extent that the military, labor, and ecology bureaucracies do their job well, they run the risk of canceling each other out and frustrating progress toward any of their goals.

Moreover, because of its goal orientation, bureaucracy resists change. If, for example, the long-term goal given to the military by the political leadership is to prepare for World War III, the military will continue to prepare for World War III even if a new political leadership decides that it should be preparing for "low-intensity conflict." The generals will salute, organizational changes will be made, but years later the resources, the men, and the best brains will still be intent on accomplishing the old goal. In a similar fashion, an agricultural bureaucracy dedicated to preserving the family farm will resist new orders to let the market weed out the weak, and a government laboratory dedicated to finding a cure for cancer will resist switching to AIDS research. In the bureaucrat's eyes, such shifts in response to policy, however rational and necessary, seem close to dereliction of duty.

Given that there is no substitute for bureaucracy in routine as well as critical matters—that, for example, the only alternative to a bureaucratic mail system, public or private, is not a nonbureaucratic mail system, but no mail system at all—two strategies have been devised to cope with bureaucracy's limitations. The preferred strategy of politicians (and high-level bureaucrats who think like politicians) is to increase the size of bureaucracy in an effort to increase their control. New layers of bureaucracy are instituted to oversee and coordinate bureaucratic actions, and new bureaucracies are established to provide competition for existing bureaucracies. The preferred strategy of most bureaucrats, by contrast, is to increase the efficiency of individual bureaucracies through decentralization and the extension of more resources. These bureaucrats always want more funds and less micromanagement.

To the extent that the politicians get their way, the bureaucracy will be more responsive to policy change and individual bureaucracies will be less likely to fight each other to a standstill. At the same time, the expense of government will be increased and the efficiency of government reduced. To the extent that the bureaucrats get their way, the individual goals of individual bureaucracies—whether finding a cure for cancer, reducing inflation, or exterminating Jews—are much more likely to be achieved. (Throughout the world and throughout history, it is always those bureaucracies with the most funds and the least outside control that achieve the breakthroughs. They dug the Panama Canal, built the atom bomb, saved postwar Europe, and put a man on the moon.) Finding the right balance is difficult. In general, the military does a better job than the civilian bureaucracies in combining central control with small-unit initiative. But even the military is far from perfect.

BUREAUCRACY AND THE MARKET

It is often assumed that there is a natural incompatibility between bureaucracy and free-enterprise market economics. This is not the case. The real natural enemy of the market is the politician and in many cases the broader public that the politician represents; the bureaucracy is only the politician's more or less willing agent. In those rare cases where the politician tries to support the market, by establishing laws to prevent monopoly, for example, the bureaucrat is equally willing to work toward that goal.

Most of the goals of any government—which, except in rare cases, automatically become the goals of the bureaucracy—entail some limitation on the rights of citizens to maximize their perceived utility, what the layman would call happiness, in economic interactions. A citizen may prefer to spend his or her money on cocaine or alcohol or handguns or pornography or abortions. He or she may not want to pay taxes to support Star Wars or welfare. He or she might rather work in a gas station than go to war. In such cases, the government may decide to nullify the citizen's freedom of the marketplace and use the bureaucracy to enforce its decisions. It is ironic that many "free market" governments that would never think of attempting to protect their citizens from routine economic risk are the most shameless in their attempts to thwart the market to protect their citizens from moral risk!

The experience of the Communist bloc—and many other countries as well—clearly shows that the bureaucracy is inferior to the market in satisfying the short-term wants of the average person. This is the kind of routine matter that bureaucracy finds most difficult to handle. Even the best bureaucracy cannot mimic the market; bureaucracy always seems to produce blue shoes when the customer wants only red.

In times of crisis, however, when no one is worried about the color of shoes, the bureaucracy is clearly superior to the market. Herbert Hoover's relief efforts in Europe after World War I are an excellent example of bureaucracy stepping in where dependence on the market would have resulted in massive starvation. And, of course, if the United States had tried to fight World War II without replacing the market with a command economy, the war would have been lost.

When it comes to the question of long-term economic prosperity, the relative virtues of the market and the bureaucracy are more difficult to determine. Command economies instituted in time of crisis do not work well after the crisis is over. Even "democratic" socialist countries, such as the United Kingdom during much of the postwar period, have generally done a poor job in looking after the long-term prosperity of their citizens. Yet the example of Japan and the newly industrialized countries shows that a large dose of bureaucratic dirigisme need not be harmful. Indeed, the record of the neomercantilist nations has generally been superior to that of their laissez-faire competitors.

BUREAUCRACY AND POLITICS

Max Weber postulates three sources for governmental legitimacy: tradition, charisma, and law, which he equates with bureaucracy. If we stretch these categories somewhat and allow for their combination, this three-way division seems a reasonable method to characterize past and present governments. Roughly, the choice is between a monarchy, a popularity contest, and a bureaucracy, or some combination of the three.

Traditional government is essentially government based on inherited status. (Traditional rulers who do not inherit their positions—the pope and the Dalai Lama come to mind—are already well on their way to becoming bureaucrats.) In its pure form, it is more of a caste system than a class system. The legitimate ruler cannot be removed for stupidity or cruelty but can be removed if the rains fail to come or the "Mandate of Heaven" is lost or the local god is defeated by a foreign god in tribal war. In the real world, of course, stupid and cruel rulers were often removed on some properly traditional pretext.

Charismatic government is rule by the "Man of Destiny," chosen by God or History or the People to lead the nation. It is the *Führerprinzip* pure and simple. Yet, at the same time, it is the most democratic form of government, because, while the charismatic leader may think that his people depend upon him, the reverse is actually the case. The charismatic leader can do no wrong, is bound by no law or custom, and is even exempt from the norms of morality—but only so long as he has the support of the people. Once he loses that support, he is very liable to end up hanging from a lamppost or a cross.

Outside of East Asia, few examples exist of bureaucratic national government in a relatively pure form, although bureaucratic rule is the norm in the private corporation, the university, and the nonprofit foundation. Perhaps France during the Fourth Republic constitutes the best recent Western example of nearly pure bureaucratic rule. Between 1946 and 1958, there were twenty-four changes of premier. Each of these weak parliamentary regimes was too busy with politics to provide even a minimum direction to the day-to-day running of the government. Because of France's superbly trained and organized government bureaucracy, the politicians were never missed.

Most governments clearly depend to a greater or lesser extent on all three sources of legitimacy. The Ayatollah Khomeini's revolutionary Islamic state depended—and still depends to some extent, though it is being rapidly bureaucratized—on charisma and tradition. Generalissimo Francisco Franco's Spain depended on tradition and bureaucracy. The revolutionary states of Vladimir Lenin and Adolf Hitler, like Franklin Roosevelt's New Deal, were based on charisma and bureaucracy, though all three found it necessary to destroy, or attempt to destroy, some of the bureaucratic structures of older regimes. Fidel Castro bases his right to rule Cuba on almost pure charisma, with very little admixture of either Cuban or Marxist tradition and even less of law.

In a mixed government, when charisma fades or tradition proves inadequate, bureaucracy fills the void. The reverse is never the case; when an Andrew Jackson or a Ronald Reagan declares war on the bureaucrats, he finds that bureaucrats can only be fought with bureaucrats, regulations with regulations, big government with big government—and the result is almost always an expansion in the size and cost of the bureaucracy. Thus, there is a continual, largely unintentional encroachment of bureaucracy on the other forms of government.

The religious leader—the archetypical charismatic ruler—is a case in point. When a Christ or a Muhammad or a Gautama dies, he is not replaced by another equally charismatic figure, but rather by the embryo of an organization. If the religion is successful, the organization grows. Other charismatic figures—saints and the like—may come along, but, unlike the founder, they will always be subordinate to the organization. In place of the charismatic leader, we now have the professional, largely interchangeable bureaucrat. All properly ordained priests have the same powers, quite without regard to their intelligence or even their morals. A pope dies and a new one is selected; law replaces charisma and the machine rolls on.

The same is true of the charismatic dictator. Joseph Stalin, Kemal Atatürk, Ho Chi Minh, Mao Zedong—those dictators lucky enough to live out their rule—generally passed it on to "faceless bureaucrats." If history had been different and Napoleon's Empire or Hitler's Reich still existed, who can doubt that it would now be ruled by laws—perhaps bad laws—and bureaucrats and not by megalomaniacal whim? It is happening in post-Khomeini Iran; it will happen in post-Castro Cuba.

Charisma is much diluted in democratic society—not because democratic leaders are necessarily less charismatic than dictators (though often they are), but because the bureaucracy has already taken over most of the field. A charismatic president like Roosevelt or Reagan finds that no matter how great his popularity with the people, he must still play by the rules —and playing by the rules is the bureaucrats' game. Individual bureaucracies and bureaucrats may rise or fall, but the bureaucracy as a whole wins. The president ends up following the law rather than his mandate from the voters, and his charisma is cut down to size.

Neither democrats nor autocrats like to admit, even to themselves, that for some time important matters have been left to the specialists and that the field of politics is being increasingly narrowed to the trivial. The Supreme Court, the Federal Reserve, even the Joint Chiefs of Staff—and their equivalents in other nations—are safeguarded by law or custom against political pressures. This is not the result of some plot by the bureaucracy to expand its power, but rather an admission on the part of politicians and the public that certain things are too important to be allowed to fall into the inept hands of the elected official. The politicians pretend, of course, that these matters of justice, prosperity, and security are secondary issues "best left to the specialists," while they deal with important issues like the designation of National Grape Week.

Modern politics, as distinct from government, has also been bureaucratized. Political parties themselves have become giant bureaucracies, and many of them are among the most efficient bureaucracies around. The party's skill in raising funds, devising strategy, courting the media, and getting out the vote is often more important in electoral success than the candidate or the platform. Once elected, politicians in the legislature (or the opposition) who have little or no opportunity to make use of the established government bureaucracy create their own mini-bureaucracies. These staffs take over much of the politician's duties with respect to "governing," such as writing laws, so that the politician will have more time for "politics," such as passing laws.

BUREAUCRACY AND LEADERSHIP

The administrative bureaucracy, despite its large and growing importance, has not replaced the other elements of the triad. Private business and the political leadership—both increasingly bureaucratized themselves—continue to play vital roles in government.

CHAPTER 4

Political Leadership

If bureaucracy is often made out to be an evil, which it is not, leadership is rarely recognized for what it is—an ancient virtue that has long since become a vice. Leadership is a thing of the tribe, and its function essentially ended when the tribe ceased to be the dominant form of political organization. When man came out of the caves, the leader's position was taken by the manager. And yet the leader refused to go away. Like the reptile brain that remains buried deep beneath the human cortex, the leader has hung on, maladaptive and dangerous, re-creating tribal thinking behind more advanced forms of political organization.

L eadership is a form of aggression. The leader cannot be a leader unless he dominates his fellows. The leader's goal is to maintain and if possible to expand that domination. In the true leader, all other goals, all other loyalties, all other principles, are subordinate to this. Thus, David on occasion joined the Philistines against his fellow Jews; Themistocles, the great Athenian leader during the Persian War, ended his days in the court of Artaxerxes, while Alcibiades, who led the Athenians against Sparta in the Peloponnesian War, changed sides several times before that conflict ended; El Cid, the champion of Christian Spain, was quite ready to lead the Saracens against his fellow Christians; Muslim princes united with Crusaders to fight other Muslim princes, and vice versa; Lenin was willing to turn Marxism on its head with his New Economic Policy in order to stay in power; and Churchill was quick to change parties when his leadership was not properly appreciated.

The leader would of course argue that such stratagems were justified because only by maintaining himself in power would he be able to do the great things that he was meant to do. Only by dominating Europe would Napoleon be able to spread the benefits of the French Revolution. Only by making himself dictator would Oliver Cromwell be able to protect England from popery. Only with a third and fourth term would Franklin Roosevelt be able to carry America out of the Depression and through the war. And only by selling himself to the polls, or the PACs, would the local political hack be able to do wonderful things for his constituents.

IN THE BEGINNING

The tribe is a peculiar institution. Specialization is limited. Indeed, although there is some division of labor by sex, the tribe has only one true specialist—the shaman or witch doctor. The tribal leader, far from being a specialist, is little different from the other males of the tribe, perhaps a bit older, a bit more experienced, a bit more successful in war or the hunt. In this Darwinian democracy, all males are potential tribal leaders. The actual tribal leader is well aware of this fact and spends most of his waking moments trying to ensure his continued dominance.

The tribal leader maintains his dominance—to the extent that he does maintain it—in two ways: (1) by convincing the other members of the tribe that he can do things for them that none of his potential rivals can; and (2) by killing or otherwise getting rid of his potential rivals. From the dawn of history to the present, these two tactics (or strategies or instinctive responses) remain the sum total of leadership. These two tactics, exercised in varying proportions, characterize the professional lives of all leaders from Moses to Muhammad, from Genghis Khan to Hitler, from Pizarro to Al Capone, from Washington to Thatcher, from Gompers to Gandhi.

In the tribal situation, leadership was beneficial. Tribes with strong leaders—those who were quick to slaughter their peers outside the tribe and to dominate their potential peers within it—lasted longer. Although the unity and cohesion of the tribe often depended in part upon totemic kinship myths and grisly initiations, effective cooperation in war or the hunt depended almost entirely upon the strength of the leader's domination. In the dog-eat-dog world of primitive man, one lived longer and better if one ran with the meanest dog around.

FROM TRIBE TO EMPIRE

It should be emphasized that the tribal leader was not seeking power, but domination. Indeed, the concept of power—the ability to achieve goals—hardly existed. To the extent that anyone in the tribe had power, it was the shaman, who could bring game and cure disease and ward off sorcery. True power would have to await the rise of the specialist and the creation of new forms of political organization.

Sometime around 9000 B.C. the Paleolithic gave way to the Neolithic, hunting and gathering gave way to agriculture and herding, the camp gave way to the village, and the magician's cave gave way to the priest's temple. In hundreds of Near Eastern sites from the southern Caspian to the Nile, favorable geography and human invention combined to allow tribes to settle and create the surpluses that would enable specialization to begin.

With specialization, true power—in contrast to mere domination—became possible. It now became feasible to set and achieve goals, to amass, enjoy, and bequeath wealth. It seems probable that the organizers of specialization—the first bureaucrats—were the priests and priestesses of the new religions. These religions, although clearly evolving out of the magicians' animistic cosmology, had a very different spirit. They were open, social, and imperial, rather than hidden, personal, and restrained.

Above all, they were goal-oriented. Working through—or, if necessary, around—the political leadership, the priests organized the population to build temples and pyramids, granaries and canals. They solved a thousand practical problems in geometry, architecture, mechanics, hydraulics, and astronomy. They convinced rulers and people alike that they held the fate of the nation, if not of all mankind, in their hands. At that time, they were the cutting edge of civilization.

With the beginnings of civilization, the leader's position became more secure but less pervasive. He no longer had to worry about every young male in the tribe; imprisoning or executing his brothers, sons, and uncles, as well as the occasional vizier or high priest, was generally sufficient to provide an acceptable level of security. But, at the same time, he could no longer hold the same sway over his subjects. His power—and now he had real power—depended upon the metalworker, the merchant, the mason, the farmer, the soldier, and especially the priestly bureaucrat in a way that it had never depended upon the undifferentiated tribesman.

Pampered and flattered by the priests, the leader (whose mind was still stuck at the tribal level) justified his honors by expansion. Bored with rituals he valued but did not understand, having no specialized skills himself except the aggressive skills of leadership, now having power but still lacking goals, he set out to conquer the next city-state. He had no concept that power could be used in any other way. If the bureaucracy behind him was good enough at marshaling resources and fighting battles, he became a Menes or a Sargon and an empire was born.

Despite the occasional utility of an Alexander or a Caesar in spreading superficial aspects of one or another civilization, the political leadership of the great empires has always been reactionary. By its very nature, it had to try to re-create the anticivilization of the tribe in the midst of civilization. Its whole reason for being was domination—internal security and external expansion. Thus, we are continually presented with the juxtaposition of great civilizations and petty rulers, of great advances in art, science, medicine, and city planning coexisting with barbaric cruelty, naked aggression, and paranoid suspicion. The good ruler—and they were rare indeed—was the one who got in the way of civilization as little as possible.

POLITICAL LEADERSHIP IN THE MODERN WORLD

The tribes are dead and the great empires are dying, but political leaders linger on, pampered and flattered by the public as they once were by the priests. In truth, they are not quite the living fossils that they seem. Most of the time, in most countries of the modern world, political leaders are irrelevant: their small virtues offset their small vices for no net gain or loss. In rare cases, however, they are capable of leading nations into great evil. In even rarer cases, they are capable of achieving a good that would not have been possible in their absence. The world of politics, past and present, is made up of a multitude of hacks, a much smaller number of worldshakers, and a handful of saints.

Let us first consider the hacks, the great majority of political leaders whose net contribution for good or for evil is nil. These deputies and congressmen and presidents and prime ministers and party chairmen and dictators are like constitutional monarchs: they reign but do not rule. They are risk-averse. They love the trappings of power but are terrified of the real thing. They have no goals aside from the tribal goal of remaining in office. Occasionally they like to stir things up—ape-men beating their chests in front of the campfire—just to scare the bureaucrats and show that they are forces to be reckoned with. But essentially they don't want to make waves.

Despite their occasional braggadocio on the stump and in the halls of government, these men and women know—at least, subconsciously—that they are not equipped to govern. They recognize that they lack the specialized knowledge to decide arcane questions of military posture or economic strategy. This is not to deny that some politicians may have been specialists in a previous incarnation and may retain much of their specialized knowledge, that some may acquire a respectable amount of specialized knowledge in the course of practical politics, and that some may even go on to use that knowledge productively—as cabinet members, for example—after they leave elective politics.

The point is that, unlike the bureaucrats, the few politicians who have specialized knowledge cannot use it as it should be used. They must think first and foremost of remaining in power, and popularity and good policy rarely go hand in hand. Thus, we have the frequent example of distinguished economists and the like who, having been elected to the legislature, vote not on the basis of what is good for the economy, but rather on the basis of the voters' short-term perceptions of that good. Like the proverbial "teats on a boar," even the most profound specialized knowledge is no more than useless adornment in the professional politician. (Those legislators credited by the public with profound knowledge of and influence over military or financial affairs are generally those who slavishly follow the promptings of the military and financial bureaucracies. This is, quite correctly, considered a sign of wisdom and patriotism.)

While these petty leaders may hate the bureaucrats for their power, they have no desire to share it when matters of importance are at stake. Fed by their own staff specialists, they make wise-sounding speeches, enforce minor changes here and there to show that they are on top of things and to protect the perceived interests of their voters and financial supporters. But they have no mind to change the course of history.

The second category of political leader, the world-shaker, is far more dangerous. These leaders are not at all afraid of power, and they have goals that far transcend merely staying in office. They want to do what mere managers and bureaucrats could never do: they want to create a revolution, to turn history in its tracks! They want to conquer or to liberate. They want to destroy capitalism or slavery or the Jews. They want to spread a splotch of British pink from Cairo to Cape Town or to extend Imperial German influence from Berlin to Baghdad. Unlike run-of-the-mill politicians who promise more change than they have any intention of delivering, these leaders hide the full extent of the change they envision.

Both categories of leaders remain captives of the tribal mentality. Both see problems in terms of enemies and solutions in terms of domination. Paranoia goes with the territory. The hack—like a small-time mugger—demands your vote and then lets you go your way in peace. He is an amiable type, whose only real enemy is the man or woman who wants to take his place. The world-shaker, in contrast, demands your soul; he enlists you for a crusade that will end only in victory or in death. Unlike the hack, who is the heir of the court sycophant, or the bureaucrat, who is the heir of the priest, the world-shaker is the heir of the utopian prophet, the man with a program that *must* be put into operation for the good of us all. And his enemies are all who sin against the light. Such a leader is never far from totalitarianism.

THE EXCEPTIONAL FEW

A third category of leaders is made up of those who—in their best moments at least—are able to achieve benefits for the nation that would be impossible for conventional leaders or even for skilled and dedicated managers. These "saints"—some of whom are also world-shakers in their less admirable moments—do more than just counteract other great leaders. At some point in their careers, they come out of the cave and renounce the domination game in whole or in part. In so doing, they help create the conditions of political stability that allow the bureaucracy and the private sector to foster civilization and prosperity.

Such leaders, though often ambitious, rarely claw their way to the top with tribal ferocity; some literally have greatness thrust upon them. These men, often with no real ideology and remarkably little attachment to office, happen to be in the right place at the right time. George Washington, Lázaro Cárdenas, and Charles de Gaulle come to mind. These three men were true leaders in the sense that they were capable of domination and saw the utility of domination. Their early careers were based on little else. Yet, paradoxically, their long military experience may have allowed them to see the limits of domination. In any event, these notoriously proud men turned out to be unusually modest in their goals when it mattered most.

I am not concerned here with Washington the general. He was a competent but not brilliant military bureaucrat, a good but not great strategist. With considerable help from abroad, he did what any good military leader has to do. He dominated his men, he dominated the civilians in Congress, and eventually he dominated the enemy. Even as a president, he was in some ways mediocre. Yet his conduct of the presidency and the example it left for future American politicians were crucial for the success of the political system. He did not think himself indispensable, he had no broad program, he sought to establish no Utopia. Most important, he was willing to step down while he was still able to rule. If our first president had been an Alexander Hamilton or a Thomas Jefferson—an "indispensable" man with an ideology or a plan—the future of American democracy might have been quite different. The example left by Washington's South American counterparts—the brilliant and painfully honorable José de San Martín, who withdrew from politics rather than compromise, and the equally brilliant Simón Bolívar, who appeared to believe that the salvation of the continent depended upon his continued domination at all costs—may explain many of the problems that trouble Latin American political life to this day.

Lázaro Cárdenas played only a small part in the military aspects of the great Mexican Revolution of 1910. He was first and foremost a political general, who slowly worked his way up in the Revolutionary elite by carefully choosing his mentors and hedging his bets. He had little charisma, apparently no strong principles, and no obvious sense of destiny. He followed orders, was reasonably honest, and, compared with other Mexican politicians of the day, had few enemies. He was a fairly obvious choice as another puppet president in ex-President Plutarco Calles's ongoing "Maximato."

In office, he turned out to be more of a leader than Calles had expected. One of his first acts was to exile Calles to the United States. This act, like many others for which he is revered in Mexico, such as the great extension of land reform and the nationalization of the foreign oil companies, was essentially an act of necessary domination. He was showing the *políticos*, the landowners, and the gringos who was boss. As beneficial as some of these actions were in clearing the path for progress, they were still acts of domination; the petty political general was showing himself to be a world-shaker, of which Revolutionary Mexico already had more than enough.

Cárdenas's moment of true greatness, like that of Washington, came at the end of his term as president. Although relatively young, vigorous, popular, and certainly powerful, he chose to leave office. Completely and totally. His last act was to "appoint" the new president (the election was only a formality once the presidential *dedazo* had been given), after which he bowed out. Nothing quite like that had ever happened in Mexican politics before. But it set an example that stands to this day: for well over sixty years now no Mexican president has seriously tried to retain power beyond his legal term. This is almost without precedent in the third world, and the "circulation of elites" that it allows is one of the strengths of the Mexican political system.

Charles de Gaulle, much more than Washington or Cárdenas, was your typical world-shaker, recognizably kin to Roosevelt and Churchill, Stalin and Hitler. Soldier, scholar, historian, teacher, author, the son of a philosophy professor, de Gaulle was a man with a program. He knew what was best for France and what was best for Europe. He was willing to dominate allies and enemies in order to make his vision reality (although, unlike his four world-class contemporaries, he had only a moderate amount of personal ambition; he was not particularly interested in ruling for its own sake).

It is not de Gaulle the world-shaker who is most interesting, however. Europe, like Mexico, has always had far too many great leaders for its own good. Rather, it is the de Gaulle who, at risk to his life, his reputation, and even his vision of France, chose to get out of Algeria. This act was not part of his plan and not part of his character, nor was his hand forced by events. Lesser French rulers would have hung on until they were defeated. Indeed, lesser French rulers had done just that in Vietnam some eight years before.

To renounce power was one thing—he had done that before and he would do that again—but to give up a *département* of France ("as French as any other," according to the apologists for the war) was the exact opposite of conventional great leadership. By going against the leadership ethos at a crucial moment, de Gaulle freed the nation from the deadweight of empire and allowed France to become a major power of postwar Europe.

I could give other examples not only of exceptional leaders but also of exceptional leadership in more conventional leaders. Just from recent American history, we have Truman choosing to rebuild Europe with the Marshall Plan, Nixon choosing not to contest the 1960 election, Johnson choosing (for perhaps the first time in American history) to go beyond minimalism in pushing civil rights for blacks. What all of these cases have in common is a renunciation of the leadership ethos. To be in a position to maintain or extend one's domination and to choose not to in order to achieve a higher goal is civilized. A leader who takes such a step turns his back on thousands of years of tribal imperatives.

THE BENEFITS OF CONVENTIONAL LEADERSHIP

More conventional world-shakers, without the vision to renounce the tribal ethos, may also benefit society on rare occasions. Just as the suspicious and aggressive reptile mind behind the human cortex can occasionally be the salvation of the modern urbanite, so the aggressive instincts of the tribal leader in political pinstripes or military khaki can occasionally be the salvation of the modern nation. This usually happens when another troglodyte is on the loose. Hitler calls forth a Stalin and a Churchill and a Roosevelt. Richard the Lion-Hearted calls forth a Saladin. Billy the Kid calls forth a Pat Garrett.

Without the challenge, the response is unnecessary—and probably harmful. The very traits that made Stalin, Churchill, and Roosevelt great wartime leaders made them dangerous peacetime managers. Admittedly, trying to pack the Supreme Court is not the same as establishing a gulag. Both acts, however, reflect the counterproductive personification of problems that is typical of tribal thinking. Richard and Saladin, like Billy and Pat (or, for that matter, those heroes of Lancaster and York, the Crips and Bloods of their day), were essentially charismatic delinquents, whose main contribution to civilization was to act as a check upon each other. The real function of the world-shakers, in contrast to the saints discussed above, is to protect us from others of their own kind.

The benefits of not-so-great leadership—of the hacks rather than the Hitlers—are considerably more profound. First and foremost, political leadership legitimizes the bureaucracy. The elected president, the hereditary monarch, even the leader of a successful coup or revolution, is considered in some sense to represent the people. Although this representation is largely spurious (even in the most effective democracies, the national leader rarely gets much more than half of the votes of the half of the electorate that chooses to go to the polls, which in turn may constitute considerably less than half of the people who actually reside in the country), it does constitute a useful political fiction that the vast majority has agreed to accept. By appearing to do the will of the politicians, the bureaucrats also appear to do the will of the people.

The benefit that the run-of-the-mill politician bestows by legitimizing the bureaucracy is to a large extent offset by the harm that this same politician does by saddling the bureaucracy with incompatible or contradictory goals. In this regard, bureaucracy usually works better under a world-shaker who has a clear hierarchy of goals and who values an efficient bureaucracy as a means of achieving those goals. The hacks, who have no goals beyond staying in office, do their best, consciously or unconsciously, to sabotage the rational achievement of goals.[1]

Second, the run-of-the-mill politicians, depending as they do on their constituents for their continued employment, have the incentive to act as effective ombudsmen. Both good bureaucracies, because they play strictly by the rules, and bad bureaucracies, because they don't, may on occasion commit grave injustices against particular individuals. In any government that has even a slight claim to being a democracy, the politician can, should, and usually does prevent this from happening.

Finally, the political leadership can arbitrate among the different bureaucracies with their different agendas. Only the political leadership is in a position to balance the guns bureaucracy against the butter bureaucracy, the labor bureaucracy against the environmental bureaucracy. Being in a position to call the shots, however, does not mean that the shots will actually be called. It is common, even in strong governments, to let the boundaries of bureaucratic power fluctuate from day to day in response to special pleading and public clamor.

CHAPTER 5

Freedom and the Private Sector

The private sector[1] is the guardian of choice, both economic and political. Without a strong private sector there can be civilization, prosperity, even justice, but there can be no freedom.

The merchants, possibly the merchants of Sumer, were the first private businessmen. Before the emergence of the merchant class, the private sector as such hardly existed. The kill of the hunt belonged to the tribe, the harvest of the fields belonged to the village, the produce of the mines and quarries belonged to the pharaoh. Although private property existed, the allocation of goods was on the basis of political, not market, criteria.

In the self-contained world of the tribe and the village, it could be no other way. Distribution belonged to the leader, and arguments about distribution took the form of political revolt. The skilled flint chipper or toolmaker, like the shaman, might have goods or services that were in demand, but those goods and services only served to establish his niche in the society. Even at somewhat later stages of societal development when skilled metalworkers and others apparently wandered from village to village "selling" their services, they did so as part of a cultural rather than economic pattern, much like the tinkers and other skilled nomads of more recent times.

This was largely the situation in the early empires as well. What the ruler wanted he commanded if it was inside his empire and conquered if it was outside. Yet, as civilization advanced in different places in different ways, the attraction of foreign novelties and luxuries grew. And it was not always practical to lead an army into distant conquests just because one lusted for cedars or incense or blond slaves from the Caucasus. Sometimes even a "living god" was forced to embrace the very human concept of cost-effectiveness.

International traders—perhaps originally outlaws or pirates who operated along the edges of the great empires—were quick to take advantage of the situation. Although "official" trading missions were an early development, most merchants were to some extent outside the political system, as much parasites as citizens. They did their business—whether raiding or trading—in the free space between empires. Although they were often the subjects of one empire or another and "their" ruler could take their goods or even their lives, he could not command them. If he wanted a steady supply of the novelties and luxuries he craved, he had to "deal."

Dealing, however, implies equality, and the living gods and their successors, down to the present day, have found this intolerable. Equality, no matter how well disguised—and the early merchants went to great and fawning lengths to hide the functional equality of their relationship with the rulers—goes against the entire leadership ethos. The merchants were in the state but not of it, men of independence who could not be commanded, potential fifth columnists against the empire, potential heretics against the living god.

This fear of the merchant class as a potentially disruptive element in the smooth course of government, which gripped not only the ruler but also his civil and religious bureaucracy, is the basis for many attitudes about the private sector that still obtain. The man with no fixed place in society, who may be your inferior today but your superior tomorrow, is seen as a threat to all who value the "natural" or "God-given" order. Thus, Old Society hates the parvenu, the "natural aristocrat" hates the "plutocrat," the proletarian masses hate the "kikes" and the *"turcos,"* and the ghetto black hates the Korean grocer. Philosophers and religious leaders from the Old Testament prophets to Veblen and Marcuse rant against the rich and would-be rich, while fearful and jealous politicians from ancient China to modern Africa enact sumptuary laws to keep merchants in their place.

This hatred by the forces of order, including modern Communist order, is justified, because the true merchant is subversive in a very profound sense. He pursues profit but achieves tolerance. He deals across the boundaries of caste, class, nation, and religion. He sells to the enemy in time of war, thereby undermining the concept of the "just" or "necessary" or "patriotic" war. He considers anyone he can make a nickel from to be his brother, thereby undermining the concept of racial or religious superiority. And he will supply anything people will pay for, thereby undermining the concept of morality. In his mind, he may be as patriotic, ethnocentric, and moral as the other citizens of his nation. But, by his actions, he reveals himself as a citizen of the world.

AGRICULTURE AND INDUSTRY

Unlike trade and crime, which were private-sector endeavors from the beginning—and which, even now, remain linked in the popular mind—hunting, herding, agriculture, and manufacturing were functions of the tribe or state. This is not to say that they were communal efforts, though often they were. It merely means that the state, rather than the market, controlled the factors of production and allocated the output. Even in the case of the "family farm," the land often belonged to the state, irrigation water was controlled by the state, and the farmer's surplus was taken by the state according to some combination of bureaucratic rules and leadership whim. Manufacturing often took place in imperial workshops, while construction and mining were carried out by corvée labor during the agricultural off-season.

The ruler might assign vast estates to favored generals, priests, or other high bureaucrats, but these gifts were tenuous and often revoked. Lands controlled by the religious establishment as a whole, rather than by individual religious bureaucrats, were somewhat more stable. However, because the religious establishment was an integral and almost always subordinate part of the government, these lands could not be considered private property. The means of production were as completely in the hands of the state in ancient Egypt as in Stalin's Russia or Mao's China. And, as in these more recent command economies, markets—though they existed—were marginal to the economic life of the country.

This situation changed, even as it has now changed in Russia and China, as empires crumbled and rulers lost their strength. On the one hand, rulers—eager to hang on to power or at least to a luxurious lifestyle—traded land for warlords' support or traders' goods and farmed out manufacturing or tax collection to private persons. On the other hand, strong individuals—generals, provincial bureaucrats, traders, and outlaws—seized lands and peasants for their own use. Bureaucracy and civilization declined, and aristocracy and chaos rose.

In the so-called hydraulic societies of Egypt, Mesopotamia, China, and India, this situation could not last for long, and Karl Wittfogel's "oriental despotism" usually reasserted itself after a generation or two.[2] Indeed, such societies, perhaps again like modern Russia and China, may well have required centralized direction in order to function efficiently enough to support their large populations. Private enterprise, while not abolished, was returned to a secondary position. Only in areas such as Greece and Asia Minor, where nature and a still strong tribal tradition favored small groups—city-states or semifeudal estates—did the private sector become a continuing political and social force.

Greece and parts of Asia Minor in some ways resembled medieval Europe more than the modern capitalist West. Politics and economics were hopelessly mixed. States were merchants, pirates, or colonialists as opportunities presented themselves. War was often waged for profit. Absolutist tyranny was rare, but corruption was rampant. Justice could be bought and sold, and one private individual could own another as an economic asset.

Although Greece and Rome derived much of their culture from earlier, more original hydraulic states, they gave it an individualistic twist that was largely alien to the mother civilizations. To the civilized Asiatic observer, it must have appeared that religion was out, philosophy was in, community was out, egoism was in, morality was out, art was in, family position was out, new wealth was in, absolutist government and unthinking obedience were out, democracy and corruption were in. The observer might even have realized that all of these social, political, and intellectual changes were, at least in part, the result of the enhanced position of the private sector.

By the time Republican Rome had evolved into Imperial Rome and absorbed many hydraulic traits from its Asiatic and African empire, another change was in the works. Authority was being strengthened and individualism was being weakened. Merchants, though in some ways more secure than before, were once again seen as a possible threat to the state. Trade was something vaguely dishonorable, best left to Greeks and Levantines. In contrast, the "productive classes," especially farmers, were beginnning to be exalted—in word, if not in deed. This division between "parasitic" merchants and moneylenders on the one side and "productive" farmers and artisans on the other has continued to influence popular and elite opinion ever since. From the Church Fathers, to the Physiocrats and Jefferson, to the latest crop of ecologists and folksingers, this relic of Oriental despotic thought continues to undermine economic rationality.

THE PRIVATE/GOVERNMENT INTERFACE

As we have seen, the boundaries between the private sector and government are constantly changing and often unclear. Was the medieval manor a political unit with an economic function or an economic unit with a political function? Was the medieval city a political unit that sheltered certain rising economic groups or was it merely a front for those groups? Was the Massachusetts Bay Company or the East India Company an enterprise or a government? Was Sir Francis Drake's crime syndicate really only a joint stock company in which the queen held shares, or was it an arm of the regime? Is the great wealth of the king of Saudi Arabia or the queen of the Netherlands national or personal?

Moreover, a recognized function of government in one country or age may seem unnatural in another country or age. European princes once contracted war out to the private sector, just as some American communities have contracted out police protection or prison administration. Government employees have produced major works of art in ancient Egypt, Renaissance Italy, and Revolutionary Mexico, while in other countries private individuals have collected trash, delivered mail, manufactured arms, printed money, and rendered legal judgments. A circus clown, a plastic surgeon, a ballet dancer, or a clergyman may work for the state, while a private think tank may dominate government decision-making with regard to military strategy or economic policy. Socialist nations, in Scandinavia, for example, may host billion-dollar private industries, while capitalist nations may own and operate everything from railroads and oil companies to grocery stores and gambling casinos.

It is not clear that certain industries belong in either the private or the public sector. Some government-run airlines, railroads, and hotels give efficient, attentive service, while some private railroads, airlines, and hotels do not. Some private hospitals do an excellent job of taking care of patients too poor to pay, while some government hospitals do not. Some government-owned manufacturing firms operate according to the market and produce quality goods and services at low prices, while some private firms take advantage of monopoly situations to produce shoddy goods at high prices.

In general, the private sector is at its best in providing for the everyday needs of the great mass of people. Where the free market holds sway, the invisible hand does a very good job of supplying the public with the relative quantities of Toyotas and Buicks, concerts and prizefights, churches and universities, black shoes and brown shoes, cocaine and beer, heart transplants and tummy tucks, leisure and work, that it desires. In this ideal laissez-faire world, capital, labor, research, and entrepreneurial genius are automatically allocated in the quantities needed to fill these desires in the most efficient manner possible.

Even in the real world—where, as Adam Smith has implied, it often seems that all politicians, most businessmen, and many bureaucrats are doing their best to thwart the market—a strong private sector will do a reasonably good job of bringing prosperity and choice to the masses of people. The United States is a prime example. Despite a number of market-eroding laws and practices that prevent the U.S. public from obtaining the amount of Japanese cars, South African Krugerrands, Colombian dope, Mexican vegetables, Cuban sugar, and Iraqi oil that it desires and is willing to pay for, the people are generally well served. Indeed, even in this day of presumed American economic decline, the prosperity of the average American is celebrated around the world.

To the extent that the government exerts a force in the market, individual prosperity and choice are threatened. It is not necessary to go to the Communist world to see blatant examples of this. In Japan, a brilliant bureaucracy has built national economic might on the basis of high prices, limited choice, long hours, and poor working conditions for the average Japanese. In Sweden, an intrusive welfare state, while guaranteeing a minimum standard of living for all, has so limited choice as to make quiet desperation a national characteristic. In the United States during the Reagan years, corrupt appointees, far from supporting the market, joined with equally corrupt politically favored businessmen to misallocate resources on a grand scale.

But this is not the whole story. The market also has a dark side. The invisible hand is better at catering to consumer whims than at building civilization. In a laissez-faire world, the pyramids of Giza and Tikal would never have been built, nor would the cathedrals of Paris and Cologne. If they had had to depend totally upon the market, Michelangelo would never have decorated the Sistine Chapel, Columbus would never have sailed the ocean blue, Teddy Roosevelt would never have dug the Panama Canal, governments and government-supported tycoons would not have spanned the world with railroads and telegraph lines. Yellow fever, malaria, and polio would be endemic, and atomic energy would still be untried. Man would never have reached the North Pole, much less the moon. The market encourages the modest ambitions that bring short-term contentment and comfort, but it discourages the grandiose dreams upon which civilization is built. It is all Panza and no Quixote.

In the ideal laissez-faire world, there is little incentive to build for the future. The time horizons of stockholders, entrepreneurs, consumers, and workers are typically short—a few months, a year or two, rarely if ever more than a lifetime. Had the early tribes been made up of market-oriented businessmen instead of self-aggrandizing leaders and would-be leaders, sufficient capital would not have been accumulated to construct either civilization or even simple material prosperity. If, by some quirk of fate, market individualism had come to rule in the Paleolithic, mankind would never have reached the Neolithic.

It is hard to escape the suspicion that, in the perfect laissez-faire world, living humans would combine optimum consumption with optimum choice, while future generations would be left with nothing. The invisible hand would dole out beer and champagne in the proportions required but would exert no discipline on the drinkers. Wealth would be equalized as the poor worked hard to get the things they wanted and the rich retired to avoid accumulating wealth they could not spend in their lifetimes. The rising poor would make only short-term investments, while the rich would disinvest. Capitalism itself would wither, and the only long-term savers would be a few sociopathic misers who loved money more than anything money could buy.

What prevents this from happening in the real world is a combination of altruism and egotism—what might be described as a lust for immortality that works to defeat the logic of the market. Despite appearances, even in late-twentieth-century America time horizons stretch beyond a single lifetime. The altruist wants to provide a good life for his children or his nation, so he works and saves and invests. The egotist wants to dominate, to have wealth far beyond human needs, to put his name on a building or a company that will last for generations, so he works and saves and invests. Both egotist and altruist, however, fear that the free market will sabotage their efforts and that their dreams of their own glory or their children's prosperity will be slapped down by the invisible hand.

So both turn to the government. The altruist wants a subsidy—for schools, roads, health, and security—because he knows that all his hard work and saving cannot provide these things for his children. The egotist wants protection—a monopoly would be nice—so that his hard work and investment will flourish, and he is willing to accept a certain amount of government direction to achieve this. Both recognize that they need the government to allow them to extend their time horizons without putting themselves at a disadvantage relative to others. And the government bureaucracies are only too happy to harness the needs of egotists and altruists for their own, usually neomercantilistic, goals.

The bias of the market that heavily discounts the future in favor of the present and the community in favor of the individual—the very factor that makes it such a superb instrument for assuring prosperity and choice in normal times—limits its response to crisis. The typical market response to disaster is abandonment—witness the hundreds of ghost towns in the U.S. West. If World War II had ended in a Smithian world without the planners from Monnet to Marshall, without the great "misallocation of resources" constituted by U.S. aid, without the scores of international bureaucracies created to prevent economic chaos, Europe might still be in ruins. While the private sector clearly had the capacity to rebuild Europe, there was little market incentive to do so.

LEADERS AND BUREAUCRATS IN BUSINESS

Leadership is not quite as harmful in the private sector as it is in government. Although in business, as in government, it is only under exceptional circumstances that a strong leader does more good than harm, these exceptional circumstances do arise more frequently in the private sector.

The exceptional business leader is one who creates something beneficial that did not exist before. In some cases, he may be the inventor of a new and needed product or service; more often, however, he is an organizer. The nineteenth-century robber barons, who organized banking, steel, oil, railroads, and the like, were just as important as the tinkerers who invented the steamboat and the telegraph. More so, perhaps. The inventions of the nineteenth century, like those of the twentieth, were more products of their time than of the genius of a particular person. This is shown by the frequency with which independent inventors came up with the same device at almost the same time. If Thomas Edison had never lived, we would still have electric lights, phonographs, movies, and voting machines. If Andrew Carnegie and John D. Rockefeller had never lived, the United States might today be a much less developed industrial power on the order of Canada or Australia.

Most of these exceptional business leaders, be they inventors or organizers, are entrepreneurs. Most ordinary business leaders, as differentiated both from exceptional business leaders and from managers, came up through the company bureaucracy or were hired away from another company's bureaucracy but imbibed very little of the Weberian bureaucratic ethos. These men, the bane of American business, are like their political counterparts in that their self-esteem requires the domination of others. These are the men, and more and more women, who "don't get ulcers, but give them." And that is their entire claim to fame. Unlike the exceptional business leaders, who want power for a purpose, these men shun power for perquisites. While they are willing, luckily, to leave the hard decisions to the company experts who thrash out recommendations that they rubber-stamp, they are quite unwilling to accept a lower salary or a smaller office or a less extravagant bonus than that of their rival in the other department or the other company. American business, for the most part, is ruled neither by autocracy nor by plutocracy, but by timocracy.

Nowhere has the disease of private-sector leadership been more harmful than in the United States. Although the U.S. private sector has its share of competent managers, American business leaders—unlike the vast majority of their peers in Europe, East Asia, or even the third world—are often outlandishly paid do-nothings. Their loyalty to their companies is transitory at best, and their goals are entirely personal. Their vision of the future ends at the next stockholders' meeting. Their achievements rarely outweigh the disasters they create. They are a major cause for the decline of U.S. business relative to that of East Asia and parts of Europe.

The glory of the private sector is its bureaucracy, the managers and other specialists who avoid the temptations of leadership. As James Q. Wilson has pointed out, the private-sector bureaucracy is generally more efficient than that of the government. He gives several reasons for this, but they all boil down to the idea that business leaders and business bureaucrats are allies, whereas government leaders and government bureaucrats are enemies. Indeed, in most companies (especially foreign companies), the CEO is simply a manager—the top bureaucrat—not a leader or entrepreneur at all. He has no desire to dominate or to give ulcers, but rather to cooperate with others for a purpose. In a good private bureaucracy, the single overriding goal of manager and managed alike is to make the highest profit possible, because everyone's wages, salaries, and bonuses depend upon the size of that pot. Everything else is secondary.

In the government, except in cases of war, crisis, or rare national purpose, the situation is very different. The bureaucrat's goal may be to find a cure for AIDS, or to administer subsidies for tobacco farmers, or to keep a certain number of bombers ready to fly at a moment's notice. These goals are rarely high priorities for the Congress or the president, because the jobs and salaries of the political leadership rarely depend upon whether or not the bureaucrat is successful. Rather, their reelection depends upon showing that the bureaucracy has the proper numbers of minorities and women, that contracts are being properly handled, that no one is overpaid, that procurement is spread among the states, and that nobody is "getting away with something."

In the business world, no manager is going to spend $1,000 to guard against the possible theft of a few hundred, or write a multivolume set of regulations on how to purchase office supplies, or demand that a factory be located in the state where he votes. These things are common in government. The example of efficient business bureaucracies shows that red tape is not inherent in bureaucracy. Indeed, the truth is that legislatures—and occasionally executives—create red tape and that government bureaucrats, even more than ordinary citizens, suffer under it.

THE PRIVATE SECTOR AND FREEDOM

The private sector is a monument to and refuge for the individual. By its very existence (in the developed world, at least) the private sector proclaims that the individual counts, that he has rights and powers that do not derive from government, that his preferences have to be taken into account, that he can make choices, that he can rise and prosper without kowtowing to any leader. Although an authoritarian government and a strong private sector can coexist—witness Japan and the East Asian NICs (newly industrialized countries)—a totalitarian government, by definition, has no room for anything private.

This is a point worth emphasizing. Most governments in most parts of the world during most of history have been neither democratic nor totalitarian. Under these governments, a large amount of private enterprise and personal freedom has coexisted with authoritarian rule. And the two tended to go along together. Under strong governments where the market for goods flourished, so did the market for ideas—in Holland, in England, in pre-Revolutionary France, in the Italian city-states of the Renaissance, in the Islamic world of Avicenna, Averroës, Ibn Khaldun, and Omar Khayyám. Wherever there was trade, there was also freedom—even if under a dictatorial queen, king, shah, or caliph.

Totalitarian states are very different. Such states are, without exception, theocracies or would-be Utopias. Their purpose is to change people, not simply to control them. For Robespierre or Lenin, Torquemada or Calvin, Khomeini or Castro, Mao, Mussolini, or Mather, nothing was innocent, nothing was private, nothing was outside the purview of the state. In the tradition of religions everywhere, a desire was as evil as a deed, an impure thought as much of a sin as an action, a book as bad as a bomb. Sedition was a form of pornography, and pornography was a form of sedition. Literature, which had thrived under the czars, dried up under Lenin. Art that had been appreciated by the Stuarts and their court became an offense to God under the Puritans.

In the end, however, Mammon and freedom always win out over God and enforced virtue. The market works its subversive way under, through, and around even the most absolutist economies and governments. In state-dominated economies, smugglers, black marketeers, and bribable officials, with no other aim than a slightly better material life for themselves and their families, strike blows for political as well as economic freedom. Even true believers *who continue to believe* come to see the preachers, priests, and party bosses as impractical idealists who don't understand the real world. The heaven-oriented somberness of the Elect and the nation-oriented abnegation of the Stakhanovites become tiring. A man may still respect God or Lenin, but he's not so sure about their Vicars on Earth. After a few generations, private life is once again private and even the threat of eternal damnation or the gulag fails to sway businessmen from the bottom line. The Puritan oligarchy was destroyed by New England merchants and sea captains who never stopped thinking of themselves as good Puritans.

CHAPTER 6

The Triad in the
United States

Through most of recorded history, the political sector has dominated the triad. In the post–Civil War United States, however, the private sector achieved a dominance unprecedented in other nations and other times. Politicians and bureaucrats became the handmaidens of big business in apparent fulfillment of the Marxist prediction. Successful, corrupt, antimarket, yet in some ways democratic, the system put into place by the Radical Republicans made the country the greatest economic success of all times. It proved inadequate to cope with the challenges of the twentieth century, however, and the politicians and bureaucrats made their comeback.

We all see the present through the eyes of the past. Thus, at each period of history, thinking men and women attempt to push contemporary institutions and forces into categories inherited from earlier times. Given that all but about 10,000 of the some 200,000 years that *Homo sapiens* has been on the scene were spent in the caves, it is no wonder that our ancestors so often looked at the triad and saw only the political leadership.

The political leadership was, of course, justly dominant through prehistory. Leaders made the difference between survival and extinction, while bureaucrats and businessmen had no place in the caves. But, by the time that civilization had advanced enough for the names of leaders—Menes, Gilgamesh, Sargon, and the like—to come down to later generations, leaders were already a drag upon civilization and a menace to the safety and prosperity of their subjects. Once the Paleolithic had ended, the specialized knowledge of the bureaucracy and the hard work of the farmers and artisans were responsible for most if not all progress; the leaders—at best —only served to hold others of their own ilk at bay. Yet, they were seen then—and are seen now—as the embodiment of their age, nation, and civilization.

The continuing dominance of the political leader was based on the fact that while he could not exist without the bureaucracy and the peasantry, he could exist very well without any particular bureaucrat or peasant. The individual bureaucrat or peasant, for his part, had no doubt as to who was in charge; he was eager to extol—and perhaps even to believe in—the glory of the leader. Despite the fact that the leader was essentially a parasite on society, his dominance was real. When he gave an order, the bureaucrat and the peasant obeyed—even if it meant abandoning the construction of a needed irrigation canal to build an unneeded palace or leaving crops unharvested to march to war.

THE TRIAD IN EUROPE

Long after the leadership had largely ceased getting its way by cutting off heads, it remained the foremost element of the triad and an object of profound envy. Farmers and businessmen, military officers and tax collectors, artists and inventors, administrators and scholars, clergymen and guildmasters, all longed to have a title of nobility or at least to live the life of a member of the political elite. If that were beyond their possibilities, they would do their best to ape the manners and ideas of the leadership class. By and large, this meant avoiding all useful work, spending beyond one's means, cultivating ostentation, and thinking a great deal about one's personal pride and possible affronts thereto.

In this situation of reverse Social Darwinism, the most talented and hardworking citizens abandoned their talents and hard work as soon as they had progressed enough to be able to do so. These newly minted gentlemen taught their children that the only acceptable way to obtain money was to inherit it, thereby sterilizing—from the viewpoint of economic progress—any superior genes that they might have passed along. All meaningful work—as opposed to politics, war, the court, and similar trivial or harmful occupations—devolved onto those least able to do it, and the material conditions of society suffered. The Renaissance Church reinforced this perverse ethic. Catholic doctrine was interpreted to mean that although wealth was acceptable, striving for wealth was a sin and thrift was another name for avarice.

Forces, however, were at work to undermine this leadership-centered culture. Within the Church itself, some monastic orders honored hard work and innovation even as they scorned the luxury of the prelates and the sloth of the mendicants. The production of these monasteries—not only cheeses and liqueurs but a variety of other products—was sought after for its quality. At the same time, many international merchants and financiers, Jews and Lombards, found the adventure of primitive capitalism far more rewarding than the petty political contests that occupied the leaders of Europe. They could barely hide their amused disdain for the kings and popes who depended upon them for funds and exotic luxuries.

The most important force undermining the dominance of the political leadership in the triad was Calvinism. As Max Weber has shown in *The Protestant Ethic and the Spirit of Capitalism,*[1] the Puritans of England, Holland, and Massachusetts had a very different view from that of the Catholic Church and the secular political leadership. According to Calvinist thinking, most of mankind was predestined for Hell from the moment of creation by a God who evidently found his amusement in the sufferings of his creatures. The small group of the Elect, saved through no virtue of their own, could be recognized and, more important, could recognize themselves by the constancy of their morals.

Unlike the Catholic or Lutheran, who could sin, repent, and still be saved through some combination of good works and faith, the Puritan who sinned even once knew that he was not one of the Elect. In order to prove to himself, even more than to others, that he was one of the Saints, the Puritan had to live a perfect life. This meant honesty, hard work at one's calling, extreme thrift, and sobriety in all things. In a reversal of the Catholic ethic, the sin was not in making money, but in spending it. The simple life of long hours of work, very little sleep, church, and the occasional witch burning did not require great expenditure; the money saved was plowed back into the business. Amusement, art, beauty, tolerance, sex (if any pleasure was obtained therefrom), and even excess sleep were all beyond the pale.

Weber finds the roots of modern capitalism, especially industrial capitalism, in this Puritan ethic. Unlike the primitive capitalists, who made their wealth by lending at interest, by buying low and selling high, by traveling great distances to obtain exotic goods in exotic lands, an increasing number of Puritan businessmen made their wealth by providing high quality at low prices, by expanding markets, and by technical innovation.

European Puritanism eventually lost much of its religious character while retaining the work ethic. Even at their high point in the Industrial Revolution, however, the secularized Puritans were never strong enough to allow the private sector to dominate the triad. That would only happen in America.

COLONIAL AMERICA

Like the later New England missionaries who went to Hawaii to do good and ended up doing "well," the first Calvinists went to America to create a totalitarian state and ended up creating American capitalism. "New England Democracy," to the extent that it existed before the Revolution, owed nothing to the Puritans. John Winthrop himself considered democracy "the meanest and worst of all forms of government." If all had worked out according to the Puritan plan, Massachusetts would have resembled later totalitarian states like Nazi Germany and Communist Russia, with the government subservient to the "party"—in this case, the Church. Freedom of conscience, the most basic of all freedoms, was anathema. Only the Elect could vote, and the range of issues that could be voted upon was extremely limited.

The Elect were select, a vanguard party rather than a mass party, a ruling class with a patent direct from God. They saw it as their duty to enforce God's way on everyone they came into contact with, although the non-Elect, by definition, could not avoid damnation by even the most virtuous life. In true totalitarian fashion, they encouraged neighbor to spy upon neighbor and decreed harsh physical punishment for private moral lapses. By and large, however, like the Old Testament Jews whom they modeled themselves upon and like their coreligionists in South Africa, they preferred apartheid to the direct contact that domination required. They drove out or murdered Baptists and Quakers. They distrusted their neighbors in the other colonies. Indians, obviously not part of the Elect, were always fair game.

The New England Puritans also had the more admirable traits of their British and Dutch fellows. They were industrious, ingenuous, thrifty, sober, and honest. Moreover, they valued education—they were remarkably well educated themselves—and often showed an interest and aptitude for both theoretical and practical science. They were favored by having settled a land that by its nature encouraged trade through fine natural ports and industry through swift-running rivers made to turn mill wheels, while its

climate and soil discouraged plantation agriculture. Soon they were prosperous.

There are a number of reasons why totalitarianism failed in colonial
America. The inability of John Cotton or another to knock heads together
in true Hitlerian or Leninist fashion; the influence of the crown; the need
to cooperate with the non-Elect of other colonies; disputes among theologians within the fold; antagonisms between church and civil officials; de-
centralized authority; and the beginnings of religious doubt all played a
part in undermining the Puritan oligarchy. The most important factor,
however, was the growth of the private sector. In the words of Thomas
Jefferson Wertenbaker:

> With the development of trade and industry . . . a separate merchant
> class had developed. Between the merchant and the clergyman there
> was a distinct and growing divergence of interests. The former looked
> out upon the whole world, his vessels wandered from the West Indies to
> England, and from Chesapeake Bay to the Mediterranean; he learned to
> know the Catholic Spaniard, the Anglican Virginian, the Quaker of
> Pennsylvania, and found good in them all. He had no sympathy with the
> policy which would make of New England a Zion, walled against the
> contagions of a sinful world.[2]

America's sole serious experiment with totalitarianism ended with the
end of the seventeenth century. Despite relapses from the Great Awakening down to the "banned in Boston" incidents that made Massachusetts
synonymous with censorship earlier in this century, the merchants held
the upper hand and to an ever greater extent the government responded
to them and not to the preachers. The Congregational churches began to
play down their Calvinist doctrines and—in an ironic vindication of
Servetus over Calvin—the heirs of the cream of the Puritan oligarchy
drifted into Unitarianism.

If we strip the Puritan of his religion, his morals, his racism, his intolerance, his hatred of beauty, his scorn of any form of pleasure, his self-
righteousness, and his desire to be a "city upon a hill" and leave only his
honesty, his thrift, his respect for learning, his industry, and his practical
and scientific bent, we see a man with an uncanny resemblance to Benja-
min Franklin. It is no coincidence that Max Weber considered the ideas of
Boston-born Franklin to be American capitalist thinking at its most typical.

THE EARLY REPUBLIC

The Founding Fathers—considering that they were revolutionaries—seemed to have had a remarkably static view of things. They saw themselves as tinkering around the edges of an essentially fixed order, protecting ancient rights rather than creating new rights, removing burdens that never should have been placed on the colonial economy, putting things back into order. They talked a good deal of freedom and inherent rights but very little of progress or change. By and large, they looked east across the Atlantic and not west across the mountains.

Government, of course, might slowly be perfected, but society was largely fixed. To the extent that the Founding Fathers thought about it at all, they assumed that there would always be planters along the Potomac, patroons along the Hudson, merchants along the Charles, yeomen farmers in the Piedmont, and wild Indians west of the mountains. Despite the admirable theories of Locke and Montesquieu and Smith, which they were endeavoring to put into effect, there would still be rich and poor, slave and free. They could conceive of progress only in terms of a return to Republican Rome or Periclean Athens.

Alexander Hamilton was the major exception. Virtually alone among the Founding Fathers, Hamilton had a realistic view of America's future. Like some MITI bureaucrat of Japan in the 1950s, he had a vision of a strong, industrial, urban nation exporting manufactured goods rather than agricultural products. More than Jefferson the inventor or Franklin the scientist, Hamilton saw the potential of technology to change society as profoundly as politics. Virtually alone among the Founding Fathers, Hamilton saw the Golden Age in the future and not in the past.

Hamilton, having been a good military bureaucrat and as much of a civil bureaucrat as the times allowed, had the bureaucratic spirit. He had goals beyond political domination or (once he had married well) private wealth, but these goals were for the country and not for himself or his party. He had a bureaucrat's faith in knowledge, structure, and regulation and little sympathy for the democratic idea that the sum total of the voters' ignorance was truth or for the laissez-faire idea that the sum total of merchants' greed was progress.

It was a political era, however, and, although some of Hamilton's ideas were adopted, party conflict and the eternal quest for domination remained the name of the game. Henry Clay's American System—

Hamiltonian economics with just a touch of Jeffersonian politics—after a promising start, failed to take hold. The bureaucrats, except for a few in the nominally private Bank of the United States and on the Supreme Court, were reduced to clerks. The private sector, though vigorous, had neither the prestige nor the power of the politicians.

Although Andrew Jackson, like most politicians, was willing to adopt any stand necessary to get elected, he did have two basic principles or prejudices. These were freedom and domination. He correctly saw that private monopoly and inherited privilege were threats to the individual that could best be fought through vigorous laissez-faire economics. He correctly saw that a strong and effective bureaucracy, such as was implicit in the programs of Hamilton and Clay, could also be a threat to the individual. At the same time, he saw domination as both a pleasure and a duty. Englishmen, Indians, and frontier gentlemen who slighted his honor were best dominated by bullets. Separatist states, rival parties, and opposing politicians would get no mercy. The high bureaucracy would be destroyed and the low bureaucracy turned into a gravy train for the party loyal.

It is probably best that in this period the ideas of Jackson won out over those of Hamilton. The economy of the United States of Jackson's time, though perhaps not that of the thirteen colonies of Hamilton's era, was too large to be guided. Subsidies, tariffs, "internal improvements," and national banks were more likely to contribute to private wealth than to national progress. A strong government, dedicated to preventing the rise of an aristocracy of wealth and to keeping the playing field level in good Smithian fashion, was probably the best that could be hoped for. But, let there be no doubt, under General Jackson the politicians dominated the triad.

THE RADICAL REPUBLICANS[3]

The Radical Republicans—an amalgam of northeastern abolitionists, northwestern racists, and amoral businessmen from all parts of the North —created a revolution more profound than that of 1776. Before the Civil War, the politicians ruled the triad. Wealth and bureaucratic achievement (essentially in the military bureaucracy) were valued largely as entrées to the political class. Merchants and generals longed to be congressmen and governors. Idealists saw politics as a way to "get things done." After the Civil War, the businessmen ruled the triad. Politicians were scorned as the errand boys of big business, the "only native American criminal class" in the words of Mark Twain, social pariahs who could be bought and sold, con men who couldn't make an honest living. Politics was, at best, seen as a way to steal enough money to enter the business class. And only the private tycoon had the power to "get things done."

Abraham Lincoln, the first Republican president and the last American president to rule the triad, was not a Radical and by and large did not sympathize with their ideas. Lincoln was a run-of-the-mill politician, not a saint like Washington or Cárdenas and not a world-shaker like Napoleon or Bismarck or Lenin. He had no particular goal except to be president and, after becoming president, he had no particular goal except to prevent a "no-fault divorce" between North and South. Although he had some genuine dislike for slavery as an institution, he seemed to dislike the abolitionists almost as much. He repeatedly stated that he was willing to accept slavery in order to preserve the Union and even pushed for a constitutional amendment guaranteeing slavery's preservation. What he could not tolerate—and here he was very true to the ethos of the cave—was that the South should be lost on his watch.

The Radical Republicans, unlike Lincoln, had goals. The abolitionists, true to their Puritan heritage, were not so much worried about slavery's existence as about its contamination. Thus, many of them pushed for the peaceful breakup of the Union. Let the South go its own way with its peculiar institution, and let the United States remain a smaller but more virtuous city upon a hill. It was only after the Civil War had started that most came to favor preservation of the Union and total abolition. The business interests were also willing to let the South go its way. Their major concern was to get rid of the Southern votes that were blocking the subsidies and protective tariffs and other probusiness legislation that they needed. It was only later that they came to see the potential of a totally defeated South as a political and economic colony.

Lincoln was not the patsy the Radicals had hoped for at the time of his nomination; he continued to dominate the triad. He fought off the Radicals in his cabinet who wished to make him a figurehead, and he did not hesitate to trample the Bill of Rights in order to control the private sector. To a degree unmatched by earlier or later presidents, Lincoln micromanaged the military bureaucracy. Like most nonmilitary leaders, he favored action over caution and often tried to push his generals into bloody battles that they had little chance of winning. In Grant, he found a general of his own kidney, whose meat-grinder approach took advantage of what the North had—men and matériel—to overcome what it lacked—military skill.

Lee's surrender and Lincoln's assassination gave the Radicals a double victory. Not only the defeated South but the victorious federal government was colonized. The same interests that looted the South looted the Federal Treasury. The same interests that wrote laws for pliant politicians in Montgomery or Tallahassee wrote laws for equally pliant politicians in Washington. The old ruling class—the heirs of Adams and Hamilton as well as of Washington and Jefferson—had been defeated and a new, rougher, ruling class installed.

At its most important level, the Civil War was a battle between a debased Jeffersonian democracy (with its support of agriculture, low tariffs, states' rights, limited government, the individual—and slavery) and a debased Hamiltonian aristocracy (with its support of industry, protectionism, centralization, strong government, the corporation—and wage slavery). While the Jeffersonian idea had many virtues, it was essentially backward looking. If the nation was to progress, it would have to be along Hamiltonian lines. Hamilton, however, had expected the politicians to guide the private sector; what happened was that the private sector ended up dominating the government. In the final analysis, Hamilton might have been no happier than Jefferson with the Civil War's outcome.

Having defeated the old ruling class, North and South, the plutocrats, robber barons, entrepreneurs, and speculators who made up the new elite turned their attention to the West. Their vision of the new America— narrow and squint-eyed in each individual but splendid in its totality— demanded that the West be settled and incorporated into the new capitalist nation. General Sheridan's remark that the only good Indian he ever saw was a dead Indian may not have been intended as an invitation to genocide—or again it may—but it worked out that way. We sometimes forget that the ethnocide, if not the actual genocide, of the American Indian did not take place in the 250 years between Jamestown and Appomattox but in the 25 years between 1865 and 1890.

The new elite, to the extent that it had a common vision, saw the West inhabited by Scandinavians and Germans, cattle and corn. The Sioux and the buffalo would have to give way to railroads and telegraph lines and commercial farms. Progress meant tying the world together, extracting the resources, putting the untamed prairie to the plow, dominating the land.

Organization on this scale required bureaucracy. The lords of the private sector not only made ample use of the government bureaucracy, especially the military, for their own purposes, they also created an immense private bureaucracy to build and coordinate their vast new system of railroads and telegraph lines. Organization and management tasks that in Europe would have fallen to the government bureaucracy were taken over by private bureaucrats in the United States.

Essentially, the United States had created a new pattern. Whereas up until this time the world's most successful governments had combined a strong political sector with a subservient bureaucracy to dominate the private sector, the American paradigm combined a strong private sector with its own bureaucracy—and the use of that of the government—to dominate the political sector. (This pattern of bureaucratic/private sector domination, though now in its Japanese form with the bureaucracy on top, is coming to the fore throughout the first world of the late twentieth century.)

And it worked. By capturing the government, neutralizing all other sectors of society, and using methods of extreme brutality, the new ruling class was able to cram centuries of evolution into a couple of decades. The nation was consolidated, populated, urbanized, and industrialized. By 1890 the industrial sector created a larger portion of GNP than did agriculture. Not too long thereafter the United States became the richest nation in the world in both absolute and per capita terms. Moreover, because of the chaotic nature of the process, the existence of the frontier, the relative shortage of labor, and the perceived need for consumers, income distribution slowly became more equitable.

To make the transition from agriculture to industry, any nation must go through a period of reorganization in which injustices are magnified and losers outnumber winners. The industrialization of the United States under the Radical Republicans was almost as rapid and almost as brutal as that of the USSR under Stalin but far more successful; it was more rapid, considerably more successful, and perhaps ultimately less brutal than that of the England of the enclosures and the dark satanic mills.

The costs were high, the results were magnificent, and it probably could not have been done any other way. The laissez-faire capitalism of Jackson's America would not have done the job. (We must remember that the robber barons were not laissez-faire capitalists; they were monopolists, the men that Adam Smith warned us against.) The industrializers of America did not want a level playing field; they wanted the total cooperation of government with all its resources. Similarly, the neomercantilist bureaucratic capitalism of Alexander Hamilton would not have worked. Mid-nineteenth-century America had little in common with mid-twentieth-century Japan, and even the wisest bureaucrats would not have been able to direct such an unwieldy, balky, undisciplined nation. Moreover, it would take a religious or ideological despot, the very antithesis of the Weberian bureaucrat, to coldly make the decisions—to wage the nation's bloodiest war, to exterminate the Indians—that just happened under the Radical Republicans.

THE ROAD TO THE NEW DEAL

If the dispossession of the political class by big business was a deliberate act—a coup d'état, if you will—the dispossession of the private sector by the bureaucracy was a slow culmination, unplanned, undesired, and largely unrecognized. The growth, the greed, the brutality, and the progress of the Gilded Age had spent itself by the turn of the century. First, there was a change of generation. The children of the tycoons—all lesser men than their fathers—turned from ostentation and creation to philanthropy and idleness. Second, there was a democratic reaction against the evils of business concentration. The politicians saw a chance to ride this reaction back into relevance.

This was the era of the muckrakers and the Progressives, of writers like Henry George and Edward Bellamy and Lincoln Steffens and Upton Sinclair and Frank Norris, of politicians like Theodore Roosevelt and William Howard Taft and William Jennings Bryan and Woodrow Wilson and Robert La Follette and Eugene Debs. This was the time when the average American, though well aware that his prosperity and opportunity were the envy of the world, began to wonder if that prosperity and opportunity remained safe. He wondered if the little man still had a chance, if the railroads would strangle the farms, if the factories were safe places to work, and what really was in those sausages that Sinclair wrote about.

The average man did not want a return to laissez-faire. He did not want to kill the goose that laid the golden egg, but he did want somebody to do something about those other goose droppings. The average man wanted somebody who would regulate but not destroy big business. Politicians, however, could no more regulate an industry than they could fight a war; they lacked both the expertise and the independence. At best they could write laws—usually bad laws unless there was a substantial expert input—but only a professional bureaucracy could make those laws work. The politicians rose to the occasion by creating a bureaucracy and then: (1) pretending it wasn't there; (2) maintaining it was under their control; or (3) claiming it was out of control. The operating idea was to take all credit for success and deflect all blame for failure.

The bureaucracy did have many failures—some were due to the intractability of the problems it was called upon to solve, some were due to political interference and inconstancy, and some were due to its own incompetence—but it continued to grow. This was not because bureaucrats were seeking to expand their turf—indeed, bureaucrats have always been notably reluctant to take on new challenges—but because the twentieth century brought a range of problems that neither the political sector nor the private sector could solve.

In World War I, the military bureaucracy did a good job. American recruitment, training, and fighting were generally good. The private sector, that magnificent American industrial machine, was not up to the task, however. Due to the lack of bureaucratic control in the United States—and this is obvious when we compare the U.S. record with that of the more bureaucratized European nations—American soldiers were forced to fight using French and British aircraft and artillery.

Greater challenges lay ahead. The Depression exposed the limits of both the political and the private sectors. Herbert Hoover, who despite his frequent denunciations of bureaucracy had been a superb bureaucrat himself in administering food relief to Europe and later as Warren Harding's secretary of commerce, saw clearly that the government had to take responsibility for the health of the economy. In fact, Walter Lippmann in his book *The New Imperative*[4] claimed that Hoover was the "radical innovator" and that Roosevelt's recovery program was largely an evolution of that of Hoover.

Be that as it may, the real growth in the size and power of the bureaucracy came under Roosevelt. FDR, a generally amiable and good-hearted man of no great intellect and few fixed principles, was a bureaucrat's dream. Within the bounds of the politically possible—and he was willing to stretch those bounds to a remarkable extent—Roosevelt gave the bureaucrats both freedom and shelter. He was willing to try anything once, or even twice, and to take the blame if it didn't work (and, of course, the credit if it did). Excitement and ideas abounded, plan followed plan, and agency followed agency. The government had its nose into everything—and, by and large, the people approved.

The new and raw American bureaucracy was nowhere near as competent as the mature bureaucracies of Europe, both totalitarian and democratic, and it was considerably less successful in fighting the Depression. Indeed, if the Roosevelt administration had ended after two terms, it might well have been considered a failure. But the American bureaucracy was learning fast; when World War II came, it was ready. A command economy was established, and, in sharp contrast to World War I, the great power and energy of the private sector were channeled into the war effort. The performance of American society and industry under bureaucratic control was far superior to that of Europe (including the Axis powers) with the possible exception of the Soviet Union.

The politicians retained the limelight, but that was all. The war was not won by Roosevelt, Churchill, and Stalin, nor was it lost by Hitler and Tojo. It was won and lost by the respective civil and military bureaucracies. At best, the "leaders" played an important but secondary public relations role; at worst, they forced their mistakes on the specialists who were doing the real work. (This is not to imply that the specialists were not capable of making their own mistakes, only that they were far less likely to do so than the amateurs who nominally ran their governments.)

AFTER THE NEW DEAL

The second half of the twentieth century has been no place for amateurs. The Cold War, atomic energy, the conquest of space, AIDS, global warming, the internationalization of production, the population explosion, repeated energy crises, the decline of economic certainty (be it Keynesian or monetarist), the stagnation of education, the intractable ghetto, and a thousand other problems and opportunities have underlined the importance of the specialist.

The bureaucrat remains an object of scorn second only to the politician, however, and the businessman—though certainly not the nineteenth-century robber baron—remains the national ideal. Yet, the businessman himself as he looks at the economic successes of a unifying Europe and a dynamic Pacific Rim wonders if he has been caught and preserved in some kind of national myth that has outlived its usefulness. He wonders if a truly bureaucratic society like that of Japan may not be the wave of the future.

CHAPTER 7

The Triad in Japan

The evolution of the triad in Japan has been far different from its evolution in the United States. The Japanese national ethos, with its emphasis on cooperation, modesty, duty, and the avoidance of shame, has made each citizen a potential Weberian bureaucrat. Indeed, Japanese governments have long had pronounced bureaucratic elements—the fortunate but by no means inevitable result of the mixing of imported Chinese Confucianism with homegrown feudalism—and, after the forced opening of the country to the West in 1853, these elements became dominant. Without a Westernizing leader on the order of Peter the Great, the bureaucrats Westernized the country; without a fascist government like that of Nazi Germany, the bureaucrats waged a fascist war; without a single truly important democrat or capitalist, the bureaucrats made Japan one of the two most powerful democratic capitalist nations that the world has known.

Civilization has at least two origins and at least two histories. The cradles and incubators of Western civilization—Mesopotamia, Egypt, the Aegean, Asia Minor, Persia, and even the Indus Valley —were interconnected. To a greater or less extent, they shared inventions and gods, forms of government, and ways of thought. They produced individualistic, heroic societies centered on religion and religion's secular child, ideology. Zeus, Thor, Yahweh, Allah, and the gods of Hindu India are heroically anthropomorphic. These gods are leaders, fresh out of the cave, thumping their chests, demanding to get their way, bringing not peace but the sword. And the heroes—men like Leonardo and Edison, Plato and Marx, Caesar and Napoleon, Muhammad and Luther—are god-like, self-confident to the point of arrogance, with a will to change the world. In the West, change, even change to the point of chaos—with individual humans and individual gods tearing things apart, having their way with history, nature, and each other—is seen as the norm.

East Asia is different. Largely cut off from Western centers of civilization, the Far East remained much closer to the shamanism and animism that was the common heritage of the Paleolithic. God-centered religion, in the Western or even the South Asian sense, never arose in East Asia. Although Buddhism, Christianity, and Islam were later imported, they were Sinicized—that is to say, secularized—at their cores, leaving only an outer shell of familiar terms and personalities.

At a still later date, the Far East was equally successful in defanging ideology. Without the millenniums of religious experience that formed the Western mind, the East Asians find it difficult to conceive of—much less adopt—ideology in the Western sense. Nothing is seen in hard-edged black and white. An East Asian may be reluctant to give up traditions or to give in to enemies, but compromise over ideas is not only possible but expected. Japanese fascism was not the fascism of Mussolini or Hitler, Chinese Communism is not the Communism of Marx or Lenin, and Vietnamese nationalism is not the nationalism of Garibaldi or Bismarck.

East Asia worshiped the past even before it had a past worthy of mention. Confucius, arguably the area's only great sage, saw himself as a restorer, a collector, a preserver of the old, not as the innovator that he was. Unlike almost all Western philosophers and most Western religious leaders, who pretend to be more revolutionary than they are, East Asian thinkers hide their innovations under layers of tradition. On occasion, they may even create spurious traditions solely as a means of hiding their novelties.

Given this mind-set, boredom is the ideal, and the greatest curse is to "live in interesting times." The hero is out of place, a threat to order and tranquillity. The Golden Ages are those in which nothing happened. War and chaos, the very factors that would make the reputation of a Lincoln or a Churchill in the West, are seen in the East, much more logically, as signs of criminal incompetence at high levels, as omens that the Mandate of Heaven is about to be lifted. The great emperors were those who did nothing, because nothing was required. To quote once again from Max Weber:

For the heavenly powers of China, however, the ancient social order was the one and only one. Heaven reigned as guardian of its permanence and undisturbed sanctity, and as the seat of tranquility guaranteed by the rule of reasonable norms—not as the fountainhead of irrational, feared, or hoped for peripeties of fate. Such peripeties implied unrest and disorder, and were specifically regarded as demonic in origin. Tranquility and internal order could best be guaranteed by a power which, impersonal in nature, was specifically above mundane affairs. Such a power had to steer clear of passion, above all, "wrath"—the most important attribute of Yahwe.[1]

THE TRIAD IN CHINA

The special position of the secular bureaucrat in the Far East, which dates from the dawn of Chinese civilization, is almost certainly related to the evolution of East Asian shamanism. The shaman was a magician, not a proto-priest. He was a fortune-teller, an earthly advisor, not an intermediary between man and God. In the West at the end of the Paleolithic, the shaman was driven underground by a new group of specialists—the priestly bureaucrats who invented and controlled writing and mathematics —and emerged only much later as the witch, the alchemist, the heretic, and the scientist.

In the East, it was the shamans themselves—not any nascent priesthood —who invented and controlled writing. Unlike in the West, where the earliest writings were priestly inventories of provisions and records of tribute, in the East the earliest writings were inscribed "oracle bones"—the shells of turtles and the shoulder blades of cattle—used by shamans to communicate with the spirits of ancestors and foretell the future. Although the shamans invented the written language for the purposes of magic, they soon used it to write history, which they probably saw as a different type of magic—the account of what had been done in the past and therefore what should be done in the present.

Thus the shamans, by now scholar-bureaucrats, through their knowledge of writing controlled both the past and the future, the histories and the oracle bones, and had an advantage over the political leadership that the priesthoods of the West were never to obtain. They alone had the magic and the models of the past, they alone knew what the ancestors wanted, they alone knew the rituals, they alone could predict the future. Unlike the prophets who ranted against evil Hebrew kings (with virtually no effect), the scholar-bureaucrats were in a position to quietly, respect-fully, almost "scientifically" warn the emperor that the Mandate of Heaven was in jeopardy. Be they ever so humble and "faceless," they had enor-mous influence with the leadership.

The nature of the Chinese written language gave the scholar another advantage over the political leader; it devalued oratory in favor of litera-ture. Much of the beauty, dignity, authority, and persuasiveness of the Chinese language lies in the calligraphy. By comparison with the written language, the spoken language is a poor, debased thing, shorn of most of its evocative power, fit only for the most mundane use. There could be no Chinese Demosthenes. And any development that undermines oratory and supports literature automatically favors the bureaucrat over the politician, reason over emotion, and civilization over the cave.

Whereas in the West the priests created caveman gods modeled on the violent and irrational kings whom they served, in the East the scholar-bureaucrats had little use for gods and created a passionless, impersonal cosmos modeled on their own self-control and reflecting their belief in ritualistic cause and effect. Good government was the highest good and bureaucracy was the highest calling. Confucius, toward the end of the Eastern Chou,[2] only codified what everyone had known a thousand years earlier at the beginning of the Shang.

The political leadership was, of course, frustrated by the bureaucratic dominance of the triad. Shih Huang-ti, literally the "First Emperor," a vigorous leader of caveman mind-set, the founder of the Ch'in dynasty and the first builder of the Great Wall, could not stand being under the control of the self-effacing scholars who fenced him in with their histories and their precedents. With an antibureaucratic fury that would have done credit to Reagan or Mao, he ordered the burning of all books (except some "useful texts" on such matters as agriculture and medicine) and the execu-tion or banishment of all scholars. Several hundred were buried alive.

Other emperors tried other ways to undercut bureaucratic secular dom-inance. Some supported Buddhism or created rival bureaucracies based on the eunuchs of the palace. Mongol and Manchu conquerors, barbarian horsemen and hunters from the north accustomed to having their way, tried the brutal methods that served them so well in Russia, the Middle East, and Eastern Europe. Much later, Mao Zedong unleashed the Cul-tural Revolution against a party bureaucracy—in some ways, more Con-fucian than Communist—that threatened to dominate his political leader-ship. All such attempts failed miserably; within a generation at most, the scholar-bureaucrats were back in control.

The third leg of the triad, the private sector, did little better in China than in the West. The Confucians, like their counterparts in the West, praised farmers and despised merchants. While they encouraged wealth—wealth was necessary in order to have leisure to devote to the classics—they feared that great differences in wealth could undermine tranquillity and good government. In the words of Max Weber: "Above all, there was the typical aversion against too sharp a social differentiation as determined in a purely economic manner by free exchange in markets. This aversion, of course, goes without saying in every bureaucracy." He adds: "There was no self-conscious bourgeois stratum which could not be politically ignored by the government. . . ."[3]

On the other hand, unlike in much of the West, including the Islamic West, material wealth was not considered a source of sin, supply and demand were understood and largely accepted, and the taking of interest was considered normal. The Confucian bureaucracy undermined the private sector not so much by its rules as by its prestige. Just as in the West wealthy merchants and prosperous artisans wasted their capital and talent buying their way into the aristocracy, so in the Far East their counterparts wasted their capital and talent buying their way into the bureaucracy. Reverse Social Darwinism was alive and well in both East and West.

THE SUCCESS AND FAILURE OF CHINESE BUREAUCRACY

Overall, the Chinese bureaucracy, along with the priestly bureaucracy of ancient Egypt, must be considered one of the greatest success stories of all time. In both cases, the bureaucracies created civilizations that were influential far beyond their boundaries and that were able to maintain themselves for well over three thousand years. Indeed, Chinese civilization continues to this day in a form that Confucius would have no trouble recognizing. In comparison with the Chinese and the Egyptian, all other civilizations, with the possible exception of the Mesoamerican from the Olmec to the Aztec, are puny and short-winded.

The Chinese bureaucracy had the typical bureaucratic virtues of rationalism and pacifism. It had a low tolerance for religion, ideology, or any other thing that was likely to inflame men's passions and disturb the orderly workings of the state. Unlike the ideologues and missionaries of the West, who were—and are—often driven by doubts of their own cause to wage furious battle against other ideologies and religions, the Chinese bureaucrats were supremely self-confident that the Middle Kingdom was the center of the world and that the ancient classics contained all wisdom worthy of the name. They could afford to be patient. Thus, they were able to absorb their conquerors and turn Mongols and Manchus and even Jesuits into good Confucians within a generation or two.

The Chinese bureaucracy, despite occasional backsliding, worked against hereditary class and caste distinctions. It was, in theory and to a large extent in practice, open to all who could pass the examinations or buy their way in. It considered virtue to be its own reward and took seriously service to the state. On occasion, it dared to remind the emperor that virtue and service were qualities greatly to be desired even at the highest level. And it did a reasonably good job of running a large and complex nation in good times and bad.

Yet the Chinese scholarly elite was far from being a modern Weberian bureaucracy. Indeed, the Confucian bureaucrat probably resembled most closely the nineteenth-century English "gentleman." Both the scholar and the gentleman valued a classical education and scorned most practical knowledge in favor of the dubious general wisdom of long-dead sages. Neither doubted his own competence to settle all questions and solve all problems, even in areas far removed from his experience. Both had a hearty contempt for the "lesser breeds without the law" and considered foreign knowledge to be an oxymoron. Both found it extremely difficult to learn from—or even to recognize—their own mistakes. Both were profoundly conservative.

For all his rationality and secularism, the Confucian was extremely superstitious, and his ideas of cause and effect were essentially magical. Because of his education, he had little feeling and respect for science, and the scientific method was alien to his way of thought. He generally failed to make use of the scientific discoveries of his fellow Chinese or to appreciate those of foreigners. Moreover, for all his bureaucratic pacificism and lust for good government, he was no humanitarian. He condoned torture and even massacre when he was convinced that it was demanded for the safety of the nation or for that of his class.

The Chinese bureaucrat differed most sharply from the Weberian ideal when it came to universal rules. In theory, the Confucian bureaucrat put his trust in universal (or quasi-universal) principles which, when properly internalized, gave him the "wisdom" to decide individual cases according to the situation. In practice, this allowed for a great deal of arbitrary judgment and capricious regulation. The Confucian adjusted the rule to the situation, having one law for family and another for outsiders, one law for Chinese and another for barbarians. (As has often been pointed out, the Confucian elite had great problems with the "morality" of a Golden

Rule that implied that one should treat a stranger or even an evildoer the same as one would treat an honored parent.) Nepotism was a duty, not a vice. Because of this emphasis on the particular rather than the universal, the average Chinese, and especially the average Chinese businessman, never knew exactly where he stood. This more than any other single factor accounts for the political and economic failure of modern China when compared with Japan.

FEUDAL JAPAN

Like the barbaric island across the Channel from Roman Gaul with which it is often compared, Japan was a latecomer to civilization. But, unlike Britain, which had Roman civilization thrust upon it by conquest, Japan was never conquered by China. It was, rather, overawed by the splendor of Chinese civilization and accepted it eagerly while molding it in its own image. Fifth-century Japanese adopted and adapted China's written language, its bureaucracy, its Confucianism, and its Buddhism in much the same way that twentieth-century Japanese adopted and adapted European imperialism or American technology.

Japan's Paleolithic shamans, while probably responsible for the beginnings of Shintoism, emperor worship, and other currents that continue to be important, did not invent a usable system of writing and thus never attained the prestige and power of their counterparts in China. They remained adjuncts to the local warrior leaders who fought among themselves and against the racially different Ainu. Without the civilizing influence of either a shamanistic or a priestly bureaucracy, the warrior chiefs created a proto-feudalistic society in their own image that emphasized the military virtues of loyalty, courage, and willingness to die.

This was the plant upon which Chinese civilization was grafted. Because, in the beginning at least, the warriors were convinced of the superiority of things Chinese and wished to see their successful adoption, Chinese culture made rapid strides and at times looked as if it might re-create the islands in the image of the mainland. By the end of the ninth century, the Fujiwara court, despite its very un-Chinese treatment of the Japanese emperor, seemed to have successfully put aside martial concerns and to be more Chinese than Japanese.

Fujiwara centralization did not last, however, and the warlords and their retainers, the samurai, reasserted themselves. Still retaining a profound respect for Chinese culture, the warlords perfected a system that was much like that of medieval Europe. In the words of Edwin Reischauer:

> Both Japanese and Western feudalism seem to have resulted from a mixture of two basic ingredients: administrative and legal institutions surviving from a more centralized state and a system of personal bonds of loyalty. In Japan these two were derived respectively from the Chinese type of organization of the Nara period and the earlier familial pattern of *uji* society; in the West from Roman law and the German tribal war bands. The two basic ingredients have frequently been present together in human history, but apparently only rarely in the proper proportions to produce a fully feudal system."[4]

Japanese feudalism, however, was in some respects very different from its European counterpart. The Japanese samurai, unlike the European knight, was literate and, indeed, came to value his skill with the pen as highly as his skill with the sword. (On the other hand, the Buddhist monks were rather less literate than their European counterparts, and Buddhism did not come close to playing the role in Japan that Christianity did in medieval Europe.) Moreover, the samurai's reverence for the Confucian classics made him quieter, more self-effacing, and less bombastic. The knight, raised on the ideas, if not the words, of the *Iliad,* lived and died a chest-thumper and a braggart.

The Japanese emperor, from almost the beginning, had been a symbol or a god rather than a force. He had never been an Augustus or a Shih Huang-ti; he would never be reincarnated as a Charlemagne or a Mao. He was a source of legitimacy but not of authority. A series of great families ruled—very discreetly—in his name. Later the power would slip from the great families surrounding the emperor to the shoguns and then to the great families surrounding the shoguns. The real holders of power were self-effacing, always scheming to maintain their power but quite content to appear to be serving someone else.

Political unity and a general reduction of internal warfare under the Tokugawa shoguns led to the conversion of the samurai into proto-bureaucrats. As Reischauer writes: "To rule a land at peace, the Tokugawa needed educated administrators more than rough soldiers. The writing brush replaced the sword as the chief implement of the samurai, as they rapidly evolved from a body of fighting men into an urbanized class of well educated bureaucrats and petty government functionaries."[5]

Thus, by the middle of the nineteenth century, the ruling strata of Japan had something of a Weberian bureaucratic ethos and had established something of a rational bureaucracy, even though it differed as much from the Weberian ideal as it did from the Chinese model. The men of the ruling strata were hierarchical, patriotic, modest, given to duty, results-oriented, literate, and driven by fear of shame rather than by personal ambition. All they needed was a transcendent goal to turn them into model bureaucrats.

BUREAUCRATIC JAPAN

The opening of Japan, like the opening of China, was traumatic, but the reasons were different. China's self-image as the center of the universe, the only civilization, the home of all wisdom, knowledge, and virtue worthy of the name, was shattered by the pushy gentlemen from the West who would not take no for an answer. Japan, having borrowed much of its civilization from China, had no grand illusions about its position in the world; it was simply a tribal society and, as such, didn't much like the intrusion of foreigners. China reacted like an offended prima donna and retired to sulk in her dressing room. Japan reacted like a small boy beaten up by bullies and went behind the barn to build up his biceps.

The arrival of Commodore Matthew Perry in 1853 and the humiliating ease with which he opened the country destroyed feudalism and created bureaucratic Japan. It ushered in a decade and a half of chaos, civil war, and revolution. After it was over, the shogunate was destroyed and the emperor was "restored." The samurai who orchestrated the Meiji Restoration pretended that they were restoring the authority of the emperor, and did restore his prestige. They probably thought that they were re-creating a system of court control as in Fujiwara times, but they ended up establishing bureaucratic rule.

The time was ripe for bureaucracy, because much of thinking Japan now had a goal: to make itself respected in the West and thereby regain control of its destiny. Everything—the rivalries of the political class and the profits of the business class—had to be subordinated to this goal. Everything had to be judged according to its efficiency. This was no time for sentimentality, for old loyalties, for clinging to tradition. Unlike China, burdened with its Middle Kingdom conceit, Japan was quite willing to recognize the superiority of the West. It was not, however, willing to accept that superiority as a permanent condition.

The results were amazing: an "economic miracle" far greater than that of the second half of the twentieth century. The orderly Japanese with

their self-effacing patriotism and their sense of shame proved more efficient in developing a powerful state-of-the-art economy than the sons of
Puritans who created the Industrial Revolution in England or the robber
barons who organized industry in America. The Japanese of this period
were not original, but they did not need to be original. Europe and America were great storehouses of technologies and ideas. They had only to
choose. And they generally chose the best.

They remodeled their society as thoroughly as they did their economy.
They abolished feudalism and, through financial settlements, turned old
feudal daimyo into new capitalists with money to invest. In what Reischauer calls the most revolutionary step in the modernization of Japan,
the samurai who led the Restoration also established universal military
conscription and thereby destroyed the basis both of the Japanese class
system and of their own prestige. They centralized government and created a bureaucracy modeled on that of Prussia. Along with ironclads and
factories, European-style titles of nobility and muttonchop whiskers, they
borrowed the pieces from which to make central banks and constitutions,
tax systems and political parties.

All this was done in the space of a few decades, without outside pressure and without a unique source of internal direction. For the modernization of Japan was, from the very beginning, the work of bureaucrats and
proto-bureaucrats. Political leaders in the Western sense had little input.
As Chalmers Johnson notes: "It is important to recall that, in the wake of
the Meiji Restoration of 1868, Japan's system of ministries and agencies
came into being well before its political parties, constitution, or parliament."[6] The shoguns and daimyo were discredited, and the emperor was
never intended to hold power. The samurai and court leaders of the Restoration—men such as Iwakura, Kido, Okubo, and Saigo—were more like
senior bureaucrats than political leaders in that they sought national goals
rather than personal power. And these goals existed outside of their minds
and wills; one or all of these leaders could be killed (like Okubo) or turn
apostate (like Saigo) without jeopardizing the bureaucratic momentum.
There was no room—and no need—for a Japanese Atatürk or Peter the
Great.

The third element of the triad, the private sector, also had an important
role to play. Under the shogunate, the private sector had been limited by
the Chinese model. As in China and medieval Europe, merchants could
become wealthy but not respected. And even their wealth was not safe;
forced loans to the various levels of political leaders—with little prospect
of return—were as common in Japan as in Europe. The Meiji leaders,
however, saw a strong, Western-style private sector as essential for mod-

ernization, and they were as willing to break with centuries of tradition in this area as in others.

The modernizing Meiji bureaucrats, unlike the Confucian bureaucrats of China, built a favorable environment for business by establishing universal rules, as well as by removing feudal restrictions on trade and industry, creating a sound currency, and doing all those other things that progressive nineteenth-century governments did for their private sectors. Yet, from its beginnings, modern Japanese economic policy was neomercantilistic, and the government provided the once-scorned private sector with benefits and direction that would have won the approval of Colbert or Hamilton.

The business class, which was characterized by the patriotic and bureaucratic virtues of the rest of Japan rather than by the individualistic and entrepreneurial virtues of its counterparts in the West, responded splendidly. In business as in government, men of samurai background played a major role and, as might be expected, put the development of the nation ahead of profits. In less than four decades and starting from scratch, they built an industrial economy superior to that of most of Europe.

"FASCIST" JAPAN

When the Japanese took up Western fashions in clothing, they were always a few years behind Paris and London—and the same was true of political fashions. They created a European-style titled aristocracy just as Europe was getting rid of its nobility. They established the so-called Taisho Democracy just as Europe was beginning to flirt with totalitarianism. And they became ardent imperialists just as Europe was having second thoughts about imperialism. It was this last miscued effort to flatter through imitation that most annoyed the "civilized world"; Caucasian imperialists found it profoundly disturbing to see a yellow man pick up the White Man's Burden.

For the Japanese at the end of the nineteenth century, the taking of colonies seemed both a necessity for their overpopulated, resource-starved nation and a means of showing that they were worthy members of the community of great powers. They had learned from Europe and America that it was a glorious mark of civilization for one "developed" nation to fight another and, if victorious, to seize any "undeveloped" nations that happened to be lying around. Moreover, the Japanese saw expansion into Korea and Taiwan and later Manchuria as "natural," akin to the Russian drive across Siberia or the U.S. conquest of its western hinterland and not to, say, Leopold's rape of the Congo.

The Japanese of this period—though not those of later periods—were better-than-average colonial masters. Japan created at least as much as it exploited, and much of the present economic success of South Korea and Taiwan lies in the infrastructure built and discipline instilled during the Japanese period—a fact that the Taiwanese are more willing to admit than the Koreans. Compared with the record of the British on the Indian sub-continent, the French in Indochina, the Dutch in Indonesia, the Americans in the Philippines, or anyone in Africa, the Japanese record looks very good indeed.

Even as the Japanese aped and often improved upon European indus-trialization and imperialism, they also aped European democracy. Parlia-ments and parties proliferated, and elections were hard fought. But, as in Europe, the reality was less democratic than the appearance. Despite the sound and fury of elective politics, despite a growing interest in imported extremisms, despite occasional riots, strikes, and assassinations, decision-making was largely insulated from popular pressure.

Behind the façade of public conflict, Japan was ruled, as usual, by pri-vate compromise. Although the Diet and the various ministers and ex-ministers of the Imperial Court had some influence, most power was held by the military, civil, and private bureaucracies. There was, however, little agreement among the bureaucrats. The navy wanted one thing, the army another, the economic ministries another, and the zaibatsu still another. Nor were the individual elites united. "Rather, within each elite there existed rival cliques: coteries competing within the Peers, bureaucratic factions within the ministries, a Choshu clique versus non-Choshu officers within the army, a Satsuma clique versus opposing cliques in the navy, parties within the Diet, Mitsui versus Mitsubishi among the zaibatsu, and Ito and Saionji versus Yamagata and Katsura among the oligarchs."[7]

Yet, in stark contrast to similar situations in the West, the object of these contests was not to win, but to achieve a consensus. Since these were bureaucrats intent upon accomplishing a goal rather than leaders intent upon dominating other leaders, they recognized that too complete a vic-tory for one side might alienate other elements whose cooperation would be necessary for successful policy implementation. A policy that could be associated with the name of a particular person was well on its way to failure.

Thus, the "fascist" Japan that went to war with the United States and much of the rest of the world in the 1940s was no different in structure from the "democratic" Japan of the 1920s. There was no organization that in any way resembled the Nazi Party, and there was no person who in any way resembled Hitler. (A proto-fascist group of young officers who carried out a series of assassinations in the 1930s was effectively destroyed by the older officers who eventually led Japan to war.) What happened was that those elements of the elite favoring war outargued those elements favoring peace over a period of time, and in true democratic fashion the losers (many in the navy, the zaibatsu, the Diet, and the Foreign Ministry) swallowed their doubts and threw their full weight behind the war effort.

Japan lost, but, because it was a bureaucratic society fighting a bureaucratic rather than a political war, it had no mechanism for surrender. Unlike Italy and Germany, Japan had no "democrats" eager to claim that they had been against the government all along and willing to cut a deal to end the fighting. The Japanese bureaucrats, military and civil, had a single rigid ethic: to achieve their goal or die trying. And to die trying was a perfectly acceptable outcome in the Japanese context. With a bureaucratic government and a bureaucratic population fatalistically waiting for their destruction, it fell to the emperor to make the political decision to surrender. Hirohito, god and powerless figurehead, was the only person who had the "power" to do so.

Although Nazi Germany went to war under the leadership of a charismatic politician, while Showa Japan went to war under the guidance of a group of largely faceless bureaucrats, the results for both victims and aggressors were much the same. In both cases, it was allowed to happen because the private sector had become a part of the bureaucracy. Businessmen, although most were skeptical and many were completely opposed to war, put duty above profits and supported the will of the *Volk* and the wish of the emperor—as fictitious as both might be. The close public/private cooperation, which even today is the basis of Japanese and German economic success, negated one of the major benefits of an independent private sector: the separation of the citizen from the state.

VICTORIOUS JAPAN

Japan, however, was about to have separation thrust upon it by the American military administration. And, as in the fifth century, Japan was to prove itself able to absorb a dominating culture and to transform it to its own advantage.

CHAPTER 8

Postwar Japan and the United States

The end of World War II forced both Japan and the United States to become less insular and more outward looking. Victory compelled the United States, that quintessential business culture, to subordinate economics to international politics, while defeat forced Japan to renounce politics for business. Both countries, unexpectedly, became very good at their new roles. By the 1980s, however, both countries had largely achieved their postwar goals and struck out in new, much less promising directions.

Japan, although it had suffered reverses such as Perry's Open Door, had never before been defeated. It had never before had its islands invaded and occupied. It had never before been dependent on the benevolence of a foreign power. It had never before delivered up its life and its culture to the whim of an inscrutable alien conqueror. It didn't know what to expect.

Japan, true to its history, was prepared to change, to learn from events, and to accept outside wisdom. The Japanese people, whether or not they had approved of the war, realized that collectively they had lost and that collectively they had dishonored themselves. That shame—which was much closer to accepted responsibility than to felt guilt—could only be wiped away by something akin to a symbolic national suicide, the deliberate renunciation of much, though certainly not all, that had made prewar

Japan what it had been. The Japanese turned their backs on militarism and embraced democracy, land reform, labor unions, a new educational system, whatever the bureaucrats of the military occupation wanted. They delivered up their leaders to be hung and their zaibatsu to be disassembled. They watched endless reruns of *Gone with the Wind* to learn how to behave in defeat. And they regarded Douglas MacArthur as second only to the emperor. Ambassador Reischauer gives a good description of the period:

> MacArthur was an extremely self-willed, dynamic, and charismatic leader, who brooked only general guidance from Washington and none at all from the Allied nations. His messianic cast of mind and phrase appealed to the Japanese, who in their desperation looked for inspiring guidance. The Japanese, to their surprise, also found the American troops to be not vindictive but essentially well intentioned and benevolent. Since the United States had apparently proved its superiority by defeating Japan, the disillusioned, demoralized Japanese, instead of reacting to the army of occupation and its leader with the normal sullen resentment of a defeated people, regarded the Americans as guides to a new and better day.[1]

But they could not transform themselves completely. They could, in the words of the emperor, "endure the unendurable," but they could not remake themselves in the image of America. Unlike the genial Americans, the Japanese could not depend upon luck, gumption, know-how, two oceans, and a continent to drop success in their collective lap; to become democratic and prosperous they would have to plan well and work hard. To become more like Americans, they would have to reinforce the traditional Japanese virtues.

THE JAPANESE MIRACLE

The Japanese miracle was no miracle. To a large extent, it was predictable. In the first place, Japan was no third-world parvenu; it had achieved economic transformation before and had been a major industrial power before the war. In the second place, the MacArthur reforms made Japanese society more efficient by clearing away much that was no longer functional. The land reform strengthened the rural economy, increased production, and established a more favorable resource base for reindustrialization. Other U.S.-demanded changes in labor relations, education, and government—even when they didn't work as intended—helped to break down traditional practices that had limited economic mobility. And, of course, U.S.-inspired restrictions on the Japanese armed forces combined with U.S. military protection to allow Japan to avoid the expense of a military establishment commensurate with its size and position.

In the third place, the world economic climate was exceptionally benign for Japanese economic growth. The United States, operating under Cold War imperatives (and perhaps a small bit of residual guilt about Hiroshima and Nagasaki), supplied large amounts of food and other aid, and occupation spending was a major factor in restarting the Japanese economy. By 1950 the Japanese were in a position to profit from large orders placed by the U.S. military to support the Korean conflict. Moreover, world trade was rapidly expanding, protectionism was low, money was cheap, and advanced technology was available from U.S. companies virtually for the asking.

These were probably necessary but certainly not sufficient conditions for Japan's spectacular postwar growth. The more basic reasons lay in the skill and dedication of the public and private bureaucracy, the governmental system that protected that bureaucracy, and the culture that accepted that government.

THE POSTWAR BUREAUCRACY

Any country under military occupation is a bureaucratic, not a political, state. It is "administered," not "governed." As in a private corporation or a government bureau—and not as in the political state, whether tyranny or democracy, where public opinion must be listened to in order to be suppressed or to be heeded—the occupying power gives orders and promulgates rules and expects them to be obeyed. And at some point the bureaucracy of the occupiers must mesh with that of the occupied. The Japanese bureaucracy—"cleansed," of course—was the only possible mechanism with which the Americans could democratize and revive the nation.

This allowed the bureaucrats, already dominant in prewar Japan, to increase their domination. It is no exaggeration to say, with Bill Emmott, that "in Japan, bureaucrats matter more than politicians. Since the end of the American occupation in 1952, ministries rather than parties have run the country, initiating as well as executing policy."[2] Moreover, this domination was achieved with the full knowledge and cooperation of the politicians and the people. All recognized that the rebuilding and redirection of Japan was a job for the experts.

Given the power and the prestige of the bureaucracy, it is not surprising that the ministries attracted the best minds in postwar Japan, just as business attracted the best minds in the United States. The relationship among the bureaucracy, the political leadership, and the private sector was more "both/and" than "either/or," however, as bureaucrats often entered politics or business after retiring. Even outside the formal bureaucracy, however, they remained the elite, and their thinking dominated the triad.

As is well known, the bureaucracy rebuilt the Japanese economy on a neomercantilist basis. Its strategy, as it was eventually worked out, had the following elements:

• Government guidance of the economy through the product cycle, including a willingness to cede some low-technology industries to other nations, using credit allocation and like measures to influence the private sector

• A general eagerness to import foreign technology while largely spurning foreign loans and direct investment

• Encouragement of high domestic savings positively through tax incentives and negatively through the lack of an adequate pension system

• A combination of import substitution and export promotion, using import regulations, tariffs, and subsidies

• Encouragement of an economic ethic based on teamwork, company loyalty, and seniority at the expense of individual initiative and flexibility

• A willingness to hold down domestic living standards in the interest of production and exports

• Tolerance of a dual economy in which an underdeveloped domestic distribution sector provided a low-paying safety net for much of the Japanese population at the cost of inefficiency and high prices

In general, it worked. Per capita GNP rose from about $200 in the early 1950s to $2,300 in the early 1970s, when Japan's total product became the third largest in the world after those of the United States and the Soviet Union.

The Japanese bureaucrats, brilliant though they were, were not infallible. They made mistakes, they took wrong turns, they fought among themselves, and they learned on the job. Occasionally they overrode the desires of the private sector when they would have done better to have listened. Occasionally they listened when they shouldn't have. But they rarely, if ever, had to tailor their recommendations to the demands of politicians or the whim of the people.

THE POSTWAR POLITY

The occupation reinforced an ancient characteristic of Japanese government—hidden rule. Just as the emperor and eventually the shogun had become figureheads, "reigning" while the real rulers modestly went about their collective work elsewhere, so too the elected politicians and parties contented themselves with democratic sound and fury, signifying nothing, while the faceless bureaucrats, first under American tutelage and later alone, ran the country.[3]

Of course, the politicians—at least those of the ruling Liberal Democratic Party—were consulted. (In consensus-minded Japan, virtually everyone is consulted in order to give policy the collective patina that makes it work.) Occasionally they even changed bills to make them more acceptable to politically important groups such as farmers and small businessmen. But, by and large, they took what the bureaucracy gave them. Their rubber stamp was what made bureaucratic rule "democratic" and acceptable to the world at large.

There was an air of unreality about postwar Japanese politics—almost like a theme park in which "leaders" emerged from the cave to harmlessly beat their chests and give a frisson to the assembled spectators. Elections were hard fought (though they were until recently always won by the LDP), great sums of money were spent, ideological slogans were shouted, intrigue was common, corruption was pandemic, back-stabbing was not unknown, and factionalism was rife, especially within the governing party. On the street, students rioted, laborers struck, and terrorists exploded bombs. It was better than a soap opera.

And hardly more real. To at least one longtime foreign observer, the politicians—government and opposition, legal and illegal—resembled actors playing parts. Each was his own director, saying to himself, "This is how a powerful faction leader is supposed to act, this is how an opposition firebrand is supposed to act, this is how a corrupt operator is supposed to act, this is how a sociopathic terrorist is supposed to act." Like the ritual suicides of an earlier generation, it was real, but it was also theater. They could explode their bombs, verbal or physical, knowing that behind the scenes responsible people were running the country.

Nevertheless, for all its sham, the political system served its function.

The bureaucracy was insulated, and under its guidance the postwar aims of Japanese society were achieved.

THE UNITED STATES IN THE POSTWAR ERA

The United States was as ill prepared for victory as Japan was for defeat. True to its Puritan heritage and to the admonitions of George Washington, the United States had traditionally feared the contamination of Europe and its sinful, pragmatic ways. It would rather sit behind its oceans, smugly superior in its prosperity and its democracy, and be a city upon a hill, a beacon for lesser peoples everywhere. It would cheer on foreign revolutions, at least until 1917, but rarely get involved. Occasionally, like some comic-book hero, it would selflessly sally forth to right some wrong or smite some villain and then—after defeating the Barbary pirates or Kaiser Bill—return home, asking for nothing more than to be let alone.

Americans could, and did, wield the big stick in the hemisphere and mess in the internal affairs of countries from Canada to Argentina, but they scorned European-style imperialism. They felt that Manifest Destiny at the expense of Mexico and the Native Americans, and later the Polynesians, was all right, but they couldn't bring themselves to hang on to Cuba and the Philippines and they felt guilty about Puerto Rico and the Canal Zone. Although they shared Wilson's idealism, they scorned the League of Nations as one of those entangling alliances that Washington had warned them about.

After World War II, however, America had no choice. It would have to get its hands—and its conscience—dirty. With the exception of the United States and the Soviet Union, the war had destroyed the winners as well as the losers. No longer could the unseemly task of running the world be left to England and France. If democracy and capitalism were to prevail against the rapidly expanding USSR, the United States would have to become a world power.

THE COMMAND ECONOMY

The United States had won World War II (and incidentally pulled itself out of the Depression) by turning its back on Smithian capitalism. Between

1941 and 1945, America responded to bureaucrats, not to market signals. The United States was able to arm, feed, and clothe not only itself but much of the free world, even as it diverted much of its workforce to the military. Moreover, the standard of living for most Americans was probably higher in 1946 than it had been in 1940.

The bureaucrats who made it happen were (for the most part, at least) not ideologues. Although they believed in free enterprise and the market, they had a job to do and that came first. They were paid to get results, not to be pure. And they got them. Once the war was over, they had no doubt that the economy would return to normal capitalistic practice and that they would help it get there. They were horrified to see themselves compared with the men who had collectivized Russia or who were bringing socialism to much of Western Europe.

To some extent, normal capitalistic practice did return. Rationing disappeared, wage and price controls were lifted, labor was released from government service, and thousands of other details were taken out of the hands of the bureaucrats. This return to the market was all to the good. It allowed the economy to prosper in peace as it had in war. Freedom and individual choice—always the first casualties of war even in a democracy— were reestablished. Wages and profits soared, and most Americans agreed that they had never had it so good.

Much of the demobilization of the command economy, however, was temporary. The country found that laissez-faire was incompatible with being a world power. Europe and Asia had to be fed whether they could pay for it or not. Otherwise, they might fall to Communism. The police action in Korea underlined the continuing need for a draft and for a huge and expensive defense industry. And the Soviets' rapid duplication of U.S. achievements in nuclear arms and jet aircraft showed that research and development could not be left to the vagaries of the market.

Moreover, the American public was demanding things from government that it had never demanded before. Capitalism had given Americans cars, but only the government could give them roads to drive on. A highway system that was the envy of the world was completed. Hearing often exaggerated stories of what the U.S. government was doing for the poor overseas, Americans demanded more for the poor at home. And the veterans certainly had earned the right to education, housing, medical care, and jobs, even if they had to be subsidized by the government.

Internationally, while there was a great demand for U.S. goods and for U.S. dollars to pay for them, a great power could not afford to let the market operate untrammeled. U.S. businesses were restricted from exporting certain items to certain countries and subsidized to export other items to other countries—all in the name of the higher good of the nation and the world. U.S. economic interests were defended, but only where they did not conflict with U.S. political interests. (An elected government was overthrown in Guatemala not, as some neo-Marxists appear to think, because it seized lands belonging to United Fruit, but because it was perceived as a potential outpost of Communism.) Very few, however, recognized the new reality that the business of America was no longer business; it was defeating Communism. Even fewer recognized that this battle was being fought, first and foremost, by the bureaucracy.

THE POLITICAL DIMENSION

Paradoxically the overriding importance of international political goals that came with great power status did not return power to the politicians. At best, they were able to maintain the illusion of power. Truman could fire MacArthur, but he couldn't fire the military. Eisenhower could inveigh against the military-industrial complex, but he couldn't wage the war against Communism without it. Kennedy could set the goal of putting a man on the moon, but he couldn't put one there. The civilian, the military, and the party bureaucrats—all with their conflicting agendas—would push and pull until an implicit agreement was worked out. Then the president would change a few things to show who was boss and "decide" to implement it. He really had no other choice. Never had it been more true that knowledge was power.

In an effort to recoup some vestige of their old power, politicians created new bureaucracies to fight the old. Presidents became secretive and hid their goals from the experts, who might give convincing reasons why they couldn't be accomplished. They collected informal groups of "can do" types who might not be too bright but were at least their own men. Watergate and Iran-Contra were the result. Congress, for its part, created its own massive bureaucracy to keep tabs on that of the executive branch.

The congressional bureaucracy, parts of which were quite competent, and the informal presidential bureaucracy were very different from the formal government bureaucracy in that the former were more concerned with status and the appearance of power than with goals. The new bureaucrats, true to the ideas of 1776, fought each other—to the point of gridlock if necessary—to preserve the division of powers and maintain the prerogatives of their bosses. The old bureaucrats were left to try to achieve the goals of the nation.

THE GOALS OF THE NATION

And what were the goals of the nation? During the two decades after the end of World War II, the nation was in remarkable agreement that Communism should be stopped, that democracy should be spread around the world, and that the good life should be fostered at home and abroad. Different Americans, however, had different ideas as to how these generous but arrogant goals should be accomplished. The mainstream political parties reflected both the general agreement and the differences.

The Democrats, by and large, preferred to fight Communism overseas and poverty at home. They were willing to pay any price, bear any burden, meet any hardship, support any friend, oppose any foe, to assure the survival and success of liberty. That was the spirit that led to U.S. intervention in Korea and Vietnam and to the naval blockade of Cuba. The Democrats also made a genuine, if less than successful, effort to rid the United States of poverty and racism.

The Republicans, by contrast, generally preferred to fight Communism at home and leave poverty to take care of itself (which, for much of this period, it appeared to be doing). They got the United States out of the wars in Korea and Vietnam and avoided a possible war in Hungary in 1956 (and, to their everlasting credit, they rolled back the British-French-Israeli attack on Egypt during the same year). But, if their isolationist inclinations saved American and other lives abroad, their Puritanical fear of the Communist virus at home put domestic freedoms in jeopardy. Firmly believing that extremism was no vice when it came to protecting the American Way, they trampled the Bill of Rights with Lincolnesque abandon.

Protecting their flanks from an ever-more-fickle electorate, both parties lied. The Democrats talked peace while making war and managed to convince themselves and most of the world that they were the party of peace. The Republicans talked war while avoiding it at all cost and convinced themselves and most of the world that they were the only party willing to stand up to the Communists. And the two parties' words and actions on domestic issues were equally confused and confusing.

Party actions and attitudes reflected almost slavishly those of the American population. Americans and their congressional mouthpieces were eager to go to war with Truman and Kennedy/Johnson, and they were equally eager to bug out with Eisenhower and Nixon. They and their mouthpieces agreed with Johnson that something should be done about racism and poverty, and they agreed with Nixon that something should be done about street crime and welfare abuse. They and their mouthpieces were sure that there was a Commie under every rock, and eventually they were equally sure that McCarthyism was un-American.

In general, the goals of the nation were met. One can point to sins of omission and commission at home and abroad. One can argue that the country should have gone into Hungary and not into Vietnam, or vice versa. One can deplore that solemn government promises to foreign nations and groups were ignored when they became unpopular or praise the responsiveness of U.S. foreign policy to the people's will. One can see the War on Poverty as a great beginning or as wrongheaded from the start. But, in general, the postwar goals had been met.

JAPAN AND THE UNITED STATES IN THE 1980S

By the beginning of the 1980s, Communism was clearly a spent force (though this was to become even more apparent during the course of the decade), more countries than ever before were calling themselves democratic with some justification, the United States and its allies were prospering, and Japan was respected as a major democratic and capitalist power. Yet, despite the fact that the two countries had largely achieved their postwar goals, both the United States and Japan were seized with what Jimmy Carter accurately described as a "malaise." In both countries, people were asking themselves, "If we won, why don't we feel like we won?"

The United States, having been beaten by a small country in Southeast Asia, was now being kicked around by a small country in the Middle East. The economy was gripped by stagflation. Heroes were hard to come by. The elected Democratic president was giving virtue a bad name, while the Democratic pretender to the throne was doing the same for vice. One of the most competent Republican presidents in this century had had to state that he was not a crook—and he was probably lying. Crime was raging in the streets, the bureaucracy was on people's backs, and the status of minorities was being steadily eroded.

Japan, the world's most dynamic economy, was being threatened on all sides. In many parts of the world, democratic Japan was hated as Imperial Japan had never been. The United States and Europe were turning protectionist, and Taiwan and Korea were stealing Japanese markets. The old egalitarian Japan was being split between rich and poor as never before.

Real estate was so expensive that only the rich could afford to own their own homes. The well-to-do were eking out third-world lives on first-world incomes. Japanese electronics and optical goods could be bought in London or New York for half their price in Tokyo. Work hours were long, pay was low, and the commutes were horrendous. Political scandal was mushrooming, and pollution was endemic.

Americans and Japanese responded to this malaise in much the same way: by turning away from the postwar goals and the bureaucracies that had achieved them. Technocratic national progress was out; democratic personal selfishness was in. Sacrifice was replaced by a kind of joyless hedonism. The people were tired of experts telling them to eat their spinach and flocked to the politicians who would not only give them candy but tell them it was health food.

The American case is well known. The American people overwhelmingly elected and reelected Ronald Reagan, and he gave them just what they wanted. Taxes were cut and spending was increased, and Americans (except for the poor) lived it up. When the United States spent all its own money, it borrowed from foreigners—no one, except the economic bureaucracy, saw any need to stop the party. Little wars were fought against little countries. This was known as "standing tall," and it made everyone, except the military and foreign policy bureaucracy, feel good. Like Stalin's Lysenkoists, Reagan's engineers defied the scorn of their scientific and military peers to design a fantastical Maginot Line in the sky. Hey, it's only money!

The Reagan administration and the era that it introduced bore a strong resemblance to the Grant administration and the Gilded Age. In both cases, a popular but limited president reigned over an exaggeratedly probusiness regime that gutted governmental independence and integrity. In both cases, economic criminals had the ear of high officials, and honest regulators were told to stand down. In both cases, the president was always out of the loop. In both cases, the corruption engulfed both parties. In both cases, compassion was "scientifically" proven to be counterproductive. The big difference is that the crooks surrounding Grant were building railroads and steel mills, while the crooks of the Reagan era were dealing in junk bonds and leveraged buyouts. The robber barons, for all their brutal ways, built America; the business Mafia of the Reagan years tore it down.

Japan's shift in the 1980s is not so well known. Most foreigners assume that the Japanese continued much as before, busy little ants working, saving, and planning with threatening efficiency. And, in truth, the shift away from national goals toward individual selfishness had not progressed as far in Japan as it had in the United States. But the fact that it had happened at all was startling.

Japan in the 1980s turned away from both the American model and the goal-oriented work ethic. Much of this was, of course, to the good. There is no reason why the Japanese should have continued to imperfectly ape a foreign culture that was in some ways inferior to their own. And certainly the Japanese deserved and perhaps even needed to slow down and enjoy some of the fruits of their spectacular labor. Yet, in so doing, they turned away from much of what was best in their own tradition.

Like Americans of the Gilded Age, the Japanese adopted conspicuous consumption with enthusiasm. Utility was out of style, and all classes stood in line to buy whatever was most expensive, from old masters to imported candy. Real estate and stock market speculation replaced hard work as the road to security. Savings decreased along with the workday. The once slavishly loyal Japanese discovered job-hopping, and the once xenophobic Japanese discovered foreign travel and imported luxuries.

Right-wing nationalists argued that the American road should never have been taken. Racism popped up in store windows and in public statements. The minister of education asked that more patriotic textbooks be written because the Japanese did "nothing to be ashamed of" during World War II. Responsibility, always a strong Japanese trait, was eroded; now everything was the foreigners' fault. And the Japanese told each other that they should learn to say no.

Bill Emmott's book *The Sun Also Sets* gives the best description of Japan in the 1980s. He sums it up by writing:

> Suns do not just rise. They also set. That is the new era in Japan, the era of the setting sun. It was already under way in the mid-1980s, even as Japan's exports of capital were prompting speculation and concern about the emergence of Japanese power. The factors that characterized Japan's rise have changed, under the influence of the rise itself: that is, of affluence, international exposure, the capital surplus, and the now-strong yen. Japan is becoming a nation of consumers, of pleasure seekers, of importers, of investors and of speculators. Abundant money and free financial markets risk turning this new nation of speculators into one of boom and bust."[4]

Most important, from our viewpoint, the primacy of the bureaucracy began to be eroded. Both the steadily internationalizing business class and the politicians became more assertive. The rubber stamp was left in the drawer. Political interests began to supersede national interests, and reelection became more important than disinterested policy. Bribery in various guises became even more common. A few timid political "superstars" began to raise their heads above the consensus. The theme park was slowly becoming reality, the bureaucrats were no longer as insulated from selfish political pressures, and knowledge was now only one among many sources of power.

The Japan of the 1980s was converging with the America of the 1980s. In turning away from the American road, Japan had moved even closer to the United States, because Reagan's America had also turned away from the American road. In neither case was this done behind the backs of the people. Indeed, the Japanese and the Americans welcomed the change. Democracy had arrived with a terrible vengeance.

CHAPTER 9

Democracy in the Developed World

Regimes, like individuals, face two radically different categories of problems: those that have objective answers and those that do not. The question, for example, of whether a particular aircraft can perform a particular function is a technical one that can only be answered by the specialists of the bureaucracy. The question of whether that aircraft should be produced is a political one, a suitable subject for the vote. The question of whether the theory of evolution is "true"—that is, in accord with the latest thinking of modern science—is a technical one, while the question of whether the theory of evolution should be taught in the schools is a political one. Yet, the technical answers drive the political answers. In effect, one is given the choice of deliberately voting to build an inferior aircraft or to teach a scientific absurdity or not. Once one gets beyond the largely trivial, truly optional questions, there is little middle ground between the rubber stamp and the irrational. Those regimes that habitually choose the irrational have little future.

Democracy can be, and has been, defined in a number of different ways. Totalitarians, whether Jacobins or Communists or militant Christians, tend to define democracy as "doing what the people would want if the people were smart enough to know what's good for them." This manner of thinking is not limited to totalitarians, however. Some U.S. liberals have complained that certain elections in Guatemala were "undemocratic," not because the process was tainted, but because the people had the nerve to vote for an "undemocratic" candidate.

Others, usually self-appointed spokesmen for racial majorities such as some elements of the Sinhalese establishment in Sri Lanka or of the Pan-Africanist Congress in South Africa, see democracy as majority rule, pure and simple. Human rights become dependent on the vote. You lose the election and you may well lose your property or even your life. This manner of thinking also finds at least temporary advocates in developed countries. That is how the United States got Prohibition and how many local communities became saddled with laws against Sunday shopping, the practice of homosexuality, or the sale of *Playboy*.

Still others move away from politics to adopt a social or economic definition of democracy. The criteria become freedom from want, relative equality of income, social and economic mobility, and the absence of marked class distinctions. By such criteria, Taiwan under the KMT (for many years at least) was probably the most democratic country on earth, and Kuwait—for its citizens, if not for all its residents—may have a better claim to democracy than the United States or Great Britain.

Despite their differences and inconsistencies, most people in the developed world would probably define democracy in a way that would be recognizable to the men of 1776. Such a definition would be based on the election of representatives, under broad suffrage, to make laws and carry out policy. It would also include some guarantee of "natural rights" (essentially beyond the reach of the democratic process) to protect unpopular individuals and groups. It might or might not be a "one man, one vote" system; special treatment for U.S. states and Swiss cantons is not considered undemocratic. It might or might not have an elected judiciary. It might or might not have the formal goal of guaranteeing social and economic equality or opportunity.

In my discussion of democracy in the developed world, I will use this last definition, and, because I am using this definition, my discussion will center on the United States. The United States, for better or for worse, still comes closest to reflecting the "government as enemy" ideas of 1776. Given that politics is the enemy of orderly government, though occasionally the friend of liberty, and that bureaucracy is its ally, the nations of the developed world can be ranked from the "political" United States to the "bureaucratic" Japan, with the United Kingdom and Australia leaning toward the U.S. side and France and Germany closer to Japan. All of these countries meet the basic Western definition of democracy, and all face, to a greater or lesser degree, the same challenges, but their capacity for effective government differs.

THE PREHISTORY OF DEMOCRACY

In the "state of nature," human life was solitary, poor, nasty, brutish, short —and democratic. It was democratic in the sense that the prize ring is democratic: any pug can challenge the champ and, if he is the better boxer, become the new champion. It was democratic in the sense the world of popular music is democratic: the rock star depends entirely on his or her audience and may be thrust down for any reason or for no reason at all. It was democratic in the sense that the leader was always being judged —and judged severely—by those who saw themselves as his potential peers and by the mass of the tribe.

History is essentially the story of mankind's efforts to overcome this primitive democracy in the interest of tranquillity, prosperity, and security. This well-grounded fear of unstable Darwinian democracy is the origin of the "social contract" that brought about the authoritarian state.[1] Paradoxically but correctly, the mass of the tribe saw greater danger to its interests in the unbridled competition for leadership than in the establishment of despotic rule, and it was more than willing to sacrifice democracy to stability.

Those tribes that were able to achieve stable rule prospered, and those that were not able to do so did not. On the one hand lay wealth, civilization, and empire, Sumer and Egypt; on the other, the fear and freedom of the cave. Even the meanest slave in the great empires lived a better and longer life than his counterpart who remained outside the reach of the authoritarian state. The palace and the temple, constructed by men, enmeshed mankind into the hierarchical machine of civilized society; the cave, unconstructed, left man alone and paranoid, free but vulnerable.

It was inevitable that a certain *nostalgie de la tribu* would remain. After all, most of humanity's short life had been spent in the cave and old habits die hard. Once civilization had progressed enough to fill bellies and calm fears on a fairly regular basis, men (but not women, who generally lost less and gained more in the transition from democratic barbarism to despotic civilization) began to realize what they were missing. Even if they could no longer remember the violent democracy of the tribe, they chafed under the hierarchical rule of the autocrats. Some primal instinct told them that men had not always had to bow to other men.

Those who were fully integrated into one or another of the great civilizations quickly banished such thoughts as impractical, dangerous, and ultimately retrogressive. (Although the empires had their share of revolts, a desire for individual freedom and self-rule was not their cause.) The tale was somewhat different for those not so well integrated, for the barbarians who hung around the edges of civilization absorbing what they could of the higher material (and especially martial) culture. The Indo-European and Ural-Altaic hordes who lurked on the northern borders of the great empires understood nothing of the core ideas of civilization but were fascinated with its trappings and its technology. Bringing civilization to Scythians or Greeks was like giving Uzis to apes.

Although all of these semicivilized tribal peoples tried to combine the material and cultural virtues of civilization with the individualistic and egalitarian virtues of the tribe, it is only the Greeks who are idolized in the West as inventors of democracy. But what does Greek history show us? Only that something called democracy is compatible with revolution and counterrevolution, slavery and racism, censorship and judicial murder, treason and imperialism, plutocracy and mobocracy, war and civil war, piracy and corruption, religious obscurantism and xenophobia. In short, all the evils of the cave combined with all the evils of the palace.

There is another side, however, to the Greek example. Although only a Eurocentric chauvinist would claim that the culture of Greece was superior to the civilization of Egypt or Persia, the Greeks did prove that civilization and individualism were at least somewhat compatible, that there was room for the private sector, that a human being could be more than just a subject. After Greece, it was no longer quite as self-evident that one had to choose between security and liberty, hunger and freedom. Although Greek democracy had many warts (which Plato was more than willing to point out) and, for that reason and others, did not become the preferred governmental form, it did constitute a new model. The ancient Greeks had proven, once and for all, that a form of democracy could exist outside the cave.

The Greek (and Roman Republican) example was never far from the minds of the men of 1776 and 1789. As we have seen, they came to two radically different answers to the same question. The men of 1776 said essentially that humanity could exist, and indeed prosper, outside both the cave and the palace, while the men of 1789 said essentially that humanity could leave the cave and storm the palace. These two concepts of democracy have been in competition ever since. The men of 1776 have not yet been proven correct, but the men of 1789 have repeatedly been proven wrong. The collapse of the Communist bloc is only the most recent example.

THE (VERY TEMPORARY) END OF TOTALITARIANISM

Although individual democracies can be destroyed or replaced by totalitarian states, Democracy itself is never really threatened. Fascism and Communism have collapsed, and Islamic fundamentalism is rapidly losing its purity (and therefore eventually its power). The remaining external threats to Democracy (with a capital *D*) are not competitive, totalitarian ideologies, but aggressive, authoritarian states. This is due not to the nature of Democracy, but to the nature of totalitarianism.

In truth, totalitarianism, like chastity, is a doctrine so extreme that it must be diluted if its practitioners are to survive. But, with the first hint of pragmatism, totalitarianism ceases to be totalitarianism. The diluted totalitarian state becomes just another run-of-the-mill dictatorship concerned with survival rather than principle. And the genie cannot be put back into the bottle. Soviet totalitarianism ended with the New Economic Policy and Chinese totalitarianism ended with the Hundred Flowers—and neither gulags nor Cultural Revolutions could bring them back.

Of course, no one would argue that Stalin's nuclear superpower of the postwar period was a lesser threat than Lenin's weak and divided totalitarian state of 1918. Indeed, the immediate effect of pragmatism on the recently totalitarian state—Stalin's Soviet Union, Napoleon's France—is to strengthen the government. The new authoritarian state retains much of the popular basis and ideological force of the old totalitarian state but is no longer hampered by rigid adherence to principle. This surge of strength is temporary, however; just as surely as principle evolves into pragmatism, pragmatism evolves into sloth and tolerance. Détente ceases to be a subterfuge and becomes real peace.

Nevertheless, while Democracy wins all the battles, it never quite wins the war. Old ideologies are revived and new ones devised. Fifty or a hundred years from now, some charismatic leader will slouch out of the cave to claim that Communism (or National Socialism or Christianity or Islam) "didn't fail; it was never tried!" If he is a "principled" enough leader, he may be able to convince others, and in time a critical mass may be reached and the state may fall. And idealism, once armed, becomes totalitarianism. The new totalitarian state may make everybody—especially its own citizens—miserable for a while, but it will not last.

Thus, in the last decade of the twentieth century, the individual democratic states of the developed world face little external threat from totalitarianism. The internal threat, though much less predictable, is also probably slight. Chauvinist groups in Japan, racist groups in Western Europe, and the Christian right in the United States, even if they were to mushroom in a period of prolonged economic distress, seem unlikely to achieve the critical mass necessary to take over the state.

The threat from militant authoritarian states, despite continued tension in the Middle East and simmering conflicts elsewhere, also appears to be declining. In the age of economics, even the most retrograde cave dwellers are finding war an anachronism. The states of Western Europe, warmongers par excellence of modern history, are no longer a danger to each other or to the world, while the states of Eastern Europe are only a danger to each other. And much of the third world is now either too poor or too sophisticated to see external war as a solution for anything.

THE JURY AS MICROCOSM

What, then, is the threat to Democracy? To get some insight into this, we should examine a typical American jury as an example of democratic government writ small.

The jury, drawn by lot from a roll of eligible citizens, much as magistrates were selected in some periods and places of ancient Greece, is certainly democratic. Indeed, it is arguably the most democratic and certainly the least corrupt institution in the U.S. political system. Jurors need not worry about PACs or polls, the National Rifle Association or the Israel lobby, fund-raising or reelection. Occasionally they may be bought, occasionally they may be intimidated, and occasionally they may be biased by race or class hatred, but not nearly so often as their counterparts in elected office.

The first act of the jury, after it is sworn, is to elect a foreman. This is a task well suited to democracy. The jurors vote, the votes are counted, and the winner *is* the foreman. The other votes that the jury may take are not so well suited to the democratic process. The jury may vote that X is guilty of murdering Y, but the vote does not make X guilty in the same sense that the vote for foreman makes a certain juror the foreman. Nor would a vote for X's innocence make him innocent.

Most juries take their responsibility very seriously and are only too aware of their fallibility. Indeed, the almost simpleminded seriousness and humility of the typical juror are in marked contrast to the laid-back amiability and narcissism of the typical politician. How does the typical juror cope with this combination of responsibility and fallibility? He looks to the expert.

The typical juror is almost visibly relieved when the duly sworn expert explains that the fatal bullet was fired from X's revolver, that Y's blood group is consistent with the stains found on X's sleeve. The juror may have felt sorry for X, thought he had an honest face, liked his family sitting in the front row of the courtroom, but he is eager to take the expert's word and vote for conviction (or for innocence, if the expert testimony so indicates). He doesn't want to make a mistake. (And he can always allow his pity for X to surface when it comes to the sentencing—another suitable task for the democratic vote.)

Sometimes, of course, the jury is mistaken or misled. The experts may be incompetent or biased or have their own agenda. But by voting with the experts, the jury increases the probability that justice will be served. Any juror who persists in voting against the evidence is subject to intense peer pressure to change his or her vote. When no expert testimony is available, the juror is, of course, forced to make his or her own judgments. But even here, the juror has an advantage over the elected politician in that the juror is only limited by his or her intelligence and by the inadequacies of the prosecution and defense, while the politician has built-in conflicts of interest that almost assure biased judgment.

The elected politician in the United States and most other parts of the developed world is as dependent as the juror on outside expertise to determine the most appropriate course of action. There is one major difference, however. The juror, not being a professional, can afford to adopt the most appropriate course of action, whereas the professional politician cannot.

THE DEBASED LEGISLATURE

Politicians, unlike jurors, are professionals. Politics is their job and very likely their calling. They depend upon elected office to keep food on their tables and to supply their children with shoes. And perhaps most important, they depend upon elected office for their identity. A defeated politician, like an actor unable to get a part, is a failure. He knows it, his family knows it, his party knows it, and the world at large knows it. Defeat is not something to be risked lightly.

Yet, both the politicians and the people who elect them pretend that this is not the case. Although both sides know better, both sides maintain the pretense that the politician is driven by idealism and public spirit, a disinterested desire for good government, a lust to serve the people. Normal human selfishness that we readily accept in businessmen and plumbers, even in doctors and artists, we find scandalous in politicians. The politicians know this, but they find it impossible to live up to our, and their own, illusions. They still need food, shoes, and self-esteem. So they are forced to lie to themselves and to the voters.

Politics is probably the only profession—except that of the gigolo—that has dishonesty at its very heart. This is not optional. Although many honest men and women become politicians, there is no way for them to remain honest and remain in office. While the actor, like the politician, has to please the crowd to keep his job, the actor, unlike the politician, can admit what he is doing. The politician has to claim he is serving some higher cause.

There is no way the politician can say, "The F-XXX is a lousy plane but, because it is built in my district, I have to vote for it or lose my job." He has to convince himself, the people of his district, and, if possible, the people of the nation that the F-XXX is the greatest thing since Kitty Hawk. Both the politician and the people of his district may suspect the truth about the F-XXX, but both want to believe that they are doing something for their country rather than to it. The willful self-deception on both sides is mutually reinforcing.

In theory, the built-in dishonesty of the representative supporting the F-XXX should be counterbalanced by the built-in dishonesty of other representatives supporting the F-YYY and the F-ZZZ manufactured in their districts, with the final choice being made on more rational grounds. In practice (except in time of war), this is rarely the case. The politicians, who are as adept at serving each other as at serving their districts, do the generous thing, and the nation ends up with three lousy airplanes rather than one.

The obligatory dishonesty of the elected politician is not limited to affairs of pork. The brilliant Rhodes Scholar from Arkansas (long before Bill Clinton) enters politics and finds that there is a lot to be said for racial segregation. The Phi Beta Kappa economist from Yale embraces voodoo economics when his political future hangs in the balance. The refreshing third-party candidate guts his courageous but unpopular stands as soon as it appears that he has a chance of winning. Otherwise intelligent and honorable people are quick to convince themselves that abortion is murder, that homosexuality should be a crime, that the North American Free Trade Agreement would destroy the economy, that "politically incorrect" speech and writing should be banned, or anything else necessary to assure their election and reelection by the voters of their districts.

Although all politicians try to give the appearance of courage, it is nothing more than show. As Senator Charles Percy of Illinois found out, a truly courageous politician is an unemployed politician. It is only possible to be "courageous" about issues that are largely unimportant to one's constituents and financial supporters. While a Boston politician of the 1950s might "courageously" support desegregation and an Atlanta politician of the 1990s might "courageously" support a tax on fuel oil, they do not have the option of switching positions. In politics courage is just another name for foolhardiness.

As Hedrick Smith points out in his good-naturedly chilling study of Washington, *The Power Game*,[2] the elected representative has two other masters in addition to the voter of his district: the media expert and the lobbyist. Whereas, in the not-too-distant past, party discipline and personal philosophy largely determined political stands, positions are now determined by how they play and how they pay. When confronted with a conflict between the media experts and lobbyists on one side and the voters of his district on the other (an event that—happily—is relatively rare), the politician will almost always go against the voters. In the more common case in which the lobbyists, the media experts, *and* the voters of his district line up together against the national interest, the politician has no hesitation whatsoever.

The lobbyists (with a few honorable exceptions such as the American Civil Liberties Union and Common Cause) serve narrow interests which, because they are narrow, are generally antagonistic to the broader interests of the nation. While General Motors, the AFL-CIO, South Korea, the black community, wheat farmers, and hunters may all be worthy groups, a single-minded devotion to the interests of any one, to the extent it is successful, distorts the society (and especially the economy) of the nation as a whole. While the rights of minorities (including the rich, the criminal, and the unpopular) should be safeguarded, to work for the few (even if the few constitute the majority in one's district) entails working against the many. Thomas Jefferson or Adam Smith would have regarded this as self-evident.

If lobbyists undermine good government, media experts on political staffs trivialize the democratic process. Certainly since the advent of television—and probably going back to Roosevelt's fireside chats and Hitler's radio rantings—the medium has eclipsed the message and style has become more important than content. It's not what you say, but how you say it—and maybe how you comb your hair or tie your tie. Politics in the developed countries was taken over by actors long before Ronald Reagan ambled onto the scene.

THE WILLFUL EXECUTIVE

Executives—presidents and prime ministers—having reached the "highest office in the land," often think that they should do something. Some, like Reagan and Thatcher, come ready equipped with an ideology and plan of action; others, like Lincoln, Roosevelt, and Churchill, find themselves faced with a crisis and are forced to create a plan of action (and often an ideology) as they go along; still others, like Cárdenas and Johnson, see the opportunity to right a few specific wrongs; but most do not have even the foggiest idea of what they want to do.

By nature and training, they are fighters, not doers. Having achieved their lifelong ambition by *winning* the presidency, they find that actually *being* the president is a tedious letdown. Compared with the campaign, it is no fun at all! Now the problems of the nation, which they solved so easily on the campaign trail by the magic of the promise, are all in their laps. They find that the incantations that worked so well against their rivals in the election have no power in the real world of government.

Soon it occurs to them that what they really want—indeed, need—is an enemy. The instinct of the cave, which they have in abundance or they would never have risen so high, tells them that aggression and domination are what leadership is all about. The enemies may be domestic—malefactors of great wealth, abortionists, welfare queens, drug lords, racists, illegal migrants, the courts, Congress, the oil companies, Wall Street, Washington, gun nuts, tobacco pushers, the bureaucracy. Or they may be foreign—Japanese, Serbs, South Africans, human rights abusers, trade cheats, Noriega, Ortega, Castro, Qadhafi, Colombian drug cartels, Arabs, would-be nuclear powers, a united Germany.

Some or all of these targets of executive wrath may be worthy of condemnation, but rarely do they constitute a clear and present danger to the national interest. Even in those cases where they do—the Communist bloc in former times, imperialist Iraq more recently—it is usually counterproductive to adopt the mind-set of the cave in opposing them. But, while it is far more effective to think in terms of problems rather than enemies, such a course does not meet the psychological needs of the leader. David before Goliath, Horatio at the bridge, Gary Cooper alone on a sun-drenched street at high noon—we have no other model of leadership.

The supreme leader, be he prime minister or president, is far too often a national catastrophe waiting to happen. While activism in the defense of freedom may be a virtue, most activism is only atavism.

THE ABSENT ELECTORATE

The voter—a species rapidly becoming endangered—votes either for continuity or for change. Despite his heartfelt statements to the contrary, he is not really interested in personalities or platforms. If things are going well, he finds great wisdom in the platform of the incumbent and high moral fiber in his person; if things are going ill, he likes the platform and person of the challenger. Yet, even as he votes, he is beginning to doubt that his vote has any connection with either the continuation or the restoration of good times.

Thus, it is no surprise that the private citizen, without admitting it and probably without realizing it, is losing faith in representative democracy. Around the world, except where required by harshly enforced law, people are avoiding the vote. This is true even in the recently emerged democracies of Eastern Europe and the third world, where the novelty of free elections appears to have worn off very quickly. In recent years, only slightly more than half of the eligible voters have bothered to vote in U.S. presidential elections. (The 1992 presidential election is something of an exception, in part because of the energizing effect of a viable third candidate.) Even fewer take part in lesser contests. And the situation is not much different in Japan and Western Europe.

There are a number of reasons for this state of affairs. First, because the manner in which candidates are selected by the parties is much less democratic than the way they are elected, the average voter is faced with a very limited choice. He or she can vote for the Republican or the Democrat offered, but not for another Republican or Democrat of his or her own choosing. The voter may have a greater choice of party in Italy or France, but no greater say in the selection of the candidate. The apologist may object that the voter can play a part in selecting the candidates if he or she cares enough to become a dedicated, long-term party worker. That is true, but that was also true in Stalin's Russia and Hitler's Germany.

Second, because the developed world does not look kindly upon extremists, the parties and their candidates tend to move toward the center, blurring rather than emphasizing differences. The leftist party in a two-party system assumes that it already has a lock on the leftist vote and moves right to capture any loose votes in the center; the rightist party moves left for the same reason.[3] As the parties try to be all things to all people, the reasons for party loyalty disappear. The average voter has more loyalty to his football team than to his party—if he even admits to having a party.

Third, because there are better ways of securing one's political interests, the relevance of the vote has declined. After all, it's not whom you vote for but whom you pay for. As the Keating Five have proven, liberal Democratic senators can be quite accommodating to conservative Republican businessmen who pay the fee. Moreover, even if the voter is lucky enough to find a candidate whom he or she agrees with on gun control, or abortion, or war, or taxes, or Israel, he or she knows that any politician's views are subject to a 180-degree shift if his job appears to be in jeopardy.

The average voter knows that it is more effective to put his or her faith in the National Rifle Association or the American Medical Association or the National Organization for Women or Amnesty International or the Chamber of Commerce or the Knights of the Ku Klux Klan than in the hack who solicits his or her vote. He or she knows that it is more effective to ignore the democratic process and march on Washington to wave signs, spill fake blood, and raise a row in front of the TV cameras. It is easier to intimidate than to elect. Direct action. Isn't that what democracy is all about?

The average voter, though he or she may vote, no longer believes that his or her vote has much relevance. The average voter, though he or she may belong to a political party, no longer believes that the party is more important than the candidate. The average voter, though he or she may favor a particular candidate to the point of fanaticism, no longer believes that the candidate can be trusted to maintain either his general philosophical orientation or his specific promises. The average voter, though he or she may decry the corruption of the lobbyists or the pressure of the demonstrators, does not object when they are applied to favored causes. The average voter is well on the way to becoming a nonvoter.

THE DECLINE OF GOVERNABILITY

Adam Smith, satirizing the protective tariff, suggested that the same effect could be obtained by dumping rocks in a nation's harbors. The political system of the United States, and to a lesser extent those of the other nations of the developed world, consists of rocks dumped as a matter of policy in the harbors of effective government. The men of 1776 did this with their eyes wide open, well aware of the disadvantages of weak government but fearing the possible tyranny of strong government.

Yet, despite the hopes of 1776, the trade-off has rarely worked; modern government in the West is too often both tyrannical and weak, inefficient yet meddling. The legislature (and this tends to be true even in parliamentary systems) spends much of its time trying to sabotage the executive even when it is of the same party—witness the Carter administration—and the executive spends much of his time trying to emasculate the legislature. Like street dudes willing to kill for "respect," the trigger-happy politicians of both branches of government don't care who gets caught in the cross fire.

Government has become intrusive without being effective. The two branches and the two parties—each seeking to be seen as dominant in the pale light of the TV screens—contest each other by taking "forceful" action, whether or not it makes sense. The politicians love to wage "war" on domestic problems. This is how the United States has been able to combine the world's largest per capita prison population with the developed world's highest crime rate. This explains why the limited government of the men of 1776 has injected itself into the bedroom, the schoolroom, the doctor's office, the bookstore, the library, the museum, and the pressroom. True to the leadership ethic, the blackjack and the bribe, depending upon whether one is conservative or liberal, are the politician's only solutions to whatever problems the nation faces.

THE PLACE OF THE BUREAUCRACY

When the street dudes fire at each other, the national interest is often shot down by mistake; when they aim at the bureaucracy, the national interest is shot down by intent. Government works, and can only work, through the medium of the bureaucracy. If the bureaucracy fails, government fails. No president, senator, congressman, governor, or mayor ever pays a welfare check, builds a dam, collects a tax, tests a drug, drops a bomb, fights a fire, explores space, or rescues a child. What is not quite so obvious is that no politician ever creates an economic program, a military strategy, or a war on poverty, drugs, or disease. All of these things are the work of bureaucrats in one of the branches of government or employed by private think tanks and lobbying organizations.

Yet, precisely because of its importance to good government, the bureaucracy is a favorite target for politicians in both branches.[4] After all, the voters elected the politicians to take control, didn't they? Bureaucracy is too important to be left in the hands of the bureaucrats! There is, of course, no way that the elected politician can understand more than a small part of what the various bureaucracies do or should do. Most politicians recognize this and rubber-stamp most of what the bureaucracy does while giving the occasional speech lambasting whatever mistakes the bureaucrats make.

Those politicians who happen to have a program (or who have been given a program by the lobbyists and media experts) are not so accommodating. A president may not relish being told that Star Wars cannot work or that taxes must be raised. A senator may not like being told that his pet law against pornography is probably unconstitutional or that the F-XXX is not the plane the Air Force needs. A congressman may object when he learns that a wealthy supporter is being investigated for criminal activity or that the Israeli version of an event is being questioned by the "Arabists" of the State Department.

In these cases, the politician may call for an investigation of the offending bureaucracy or may only issue a statement implying that the bureaucrats in question are ignorant, lazy, unpatriotic, out of touch with mainstream America, and, most important of all, "unelected." These are only holding actions, however, while he brings up a counterforce of other bureaucrats. The Heritage Foundation can always supply an economist to prove that raising taxes would be bad, and Inadequate Aviation, Ltd., will be glad to furnish a team of engineers to support the F-XXX. One must fight fire with fire, bureaucracy with bureaucracy.

The opposition bureaucrats of the lobbies, the think tanks, and the staffs of the president and the individual legislators may be every bit as competent as those of the formal bureaucracy of the executive branch. They have a built-in conflict of interest, however. Their goals are to reelect a congressman, land a contract, or influence legislation to favor a particular interest or ideology. Their paychecks (food, shoes, and self-esteem) depend upon how well they achieve these goals, not upon how well they advance the national interest.

Pressures from the other branches of government have the additional unfortunate effect of politicizing the formal bureaucracy. In order to survive and earn *their* paychecks, bureaucrats are forced to play the political game. (Modern political dynamics not only undermine the ideas of 1776, they also undermine the Weberian bureaucratic ideal.) The bureaucrat's goal may no longer be to get the best plane for the Air Force but to get any plane through Congress. It may no longer be to devise a narcotics or energy or welfare plan that works but to devise one that steps on as few important political toes as possible. It may no longer be to give unbiased advice to policymakers but to avoid being hounded out of government for being "soft on Communism" or a "stooge of the oil companies."

Fortunately, however, the politicization of the bureaucrat does not go deep. The bureaucrat, unlike the politician, does not want to play politics. He would much rather use his expertise to conquer inflation or predict the course of a hurricane. She would much rather use her expertise to cure AIDS or design a space station. They have no affinity for the cave; they get no pleasure from the "give-and-take of politics," from the constant need to dominate. They are politicians out of necessity only.

In time of crisis, when the constraints of political necessity are loosened, they come into their own. When it becomes more important to win a war—or to avoid one—than to make political points with the electorate; when it becomes more important to restore the economy than to kowtow to this ideology or that; when the danger of poverty, crime, or ignorance becomes so threatening that even elected politicians are forced to swallow hard and put the national interest first; then the bureaucrats have their finest hour.

This is true around the world. The Japanese gave their bureaucrats free rein in international economic policy and created a trading superpower; they politicized economic decision-making in matters of agriculture and small business and condemned the average citizen to near-third-world standards of living. The Soviets gave their bureaucrats free rein in military-scientific matters and created a world-class military-industrial complex capable of amazing scientific and engineering achievements; they let politics and ideology overrule bureaucracy in "less important" areas and created an economic disaster. The British, always a nation that valued amateurs more than professionals, gave their very un-Weberian bureaucrats as little rope as possible, while their politicians careened between ideological extremes; they created a second-class nation.

In all nations of the developed world, the bureaucrats try to pilot a safe course through the deliberately rock-strewn harbors of good government. Rarely are they fully successful. Sometimes they are overcome by the elements (their goals are objectively unachievable); sometimes their ship founders (the bureaucrats themselves are incompetent); but most often they hit the rocks deliberately put there to endanger navigation. They are then derided by the pampered politicians along the shore, who, even as they prepare another load of rocks for dumping, wonder when those incompetents will ever be able to deliver a cargo.

THE FUTURE OF DEMOCRACY IN THE DEVELOPED WORLD

At the present time, bureaucracy is the greatest enemy of democracy. Democracy rests on the idea that when all is said and done, one person's opinion is as good as another's. Bureaucracy rests on the idea that the expert's opinion is worth more than the nonexpert's. To the extent that bureaucracy surges, democracy ebbs, and vice versa. Each is a danger to the other.

To the degree that democracy limits bureaucracy, governmental goals will be jeopardized, and people will (in general) be poorer and less safe. To the degree that bureaucracy overrules democracy, people will be less sovereign and run the danger of being less free. Yet, the bureaucrats are not power-seekers. Indeed, they think of themselves as democrats, and some, in their private lives, may be passionate supporters of one or another political cause.

No, the bureaucrats will not take power by coup. Any power they obtain will be the gift of the people through their elected representatives. This is what has happened in the past in time of war or other crisis. On such occasions, government became too important to be left to those who were elected to govern. The experts took over, and the politicians got out the rubber stamp.

In the world of the twenty-first century, crises may well be more frequent and more complicated than ever before. There will be a great temptation to turn over all matters of more than trivial importance to the bureaucracy, while the politicians maintain the forms (and the option) of being in control. Some nations will, of course, resist that temptation better than others. Those that resist it the best are unlikely to survive.

PART TWO

NICs and Police States

The Importance of the Second World

The meteoric rise and sudden fall of the Communist bloc, and of Communism as an ideology, is the most important story of the twentieth century. Yet the Communist states were not the only members of the second world. In the long run, they may not even be the most important.

CHAPTER 10

The Nature of the Second World

The second world consists of those countries that, despite having achieved a high degree of political control—indeed, even the illusion of political stability—lack either the desire or the capability to be part of the democratic, capitalistic "first world." These states base their control more on ideology and coercion and less on perceived benefits and consent than is generally the case in the developed West. Second-world governments, however, are far from identical. At one extreme, we have revolutionary political regimes—the Nazis, for example—that divert first-world states onto alternative paths for ideological reasons. At the other extreme, we have modernizing elites, such as took power in South Korea and Taiwan, that downplay ideology but use authoritarian methods in a calculated effort to catch up with the first world. Somewhere in between, we have besieged, ethnically based democratic regimes, as in Israel and South Africa, that use ideology to justify police-state measures against racially distinct internal enemies.

Sometime after the end of World War II, journalists and scholars arbitrarily split the earth into three parts. And, as an indication of the seemingly unbridgeable gulfs that separated the three segments, they designated each group of countries a "world" in itself.

The boundaries of the three worlds were fluid and definitions differed. For most people, the first world consisted of the NATO countries, the industrialized countries, the "white" countries with the eventual addition of Japan, the countries where the plumbing could be depended upon. Some argued for dropping Portugal or Greece or Ireland; others wished to include Israel or South Africa; but the general outline was clear. The second world consisted of those countries that claimed to be Marxist, though some argued to exclude Cuba, Angola, Ethiopia, or even China. The third world (often capitalized) embraced everything that was left.

I will try to be more precise. For our purposes, the first world consists of those countries that are: (1) politically stable; (2) not dependent for that stability upon police-state methods or foreign support; (3) economically advanced in terms of per capita income, levels of industrialization, price stability, and other generally accepted measures of economic modernity; and (4) socially developed in terms of education, life expectancy, public health, and other generally accepted indicators of social well-being.

When I say that the first-world states are politically stable, I mean that they are in stable equilibrium. I do not mean to suggest that first-world countries cannot have crises. They can and do—economies collapse, administrations are ousted in disgrace, minorities riot, blood runs in the streets—but these crises, however severe, tend to be self-correcting, largely because of the weakness of the political sector(s) relative to the other sectors. Indeed, in terms of the triad, the first world is characterized by the increasing but generally unnoticed dominance of the bureaucratic sector and the bureaucratized private sector, which tend to favor order, over the political sector, which tends to favor conflict. In a phrase, the first world consists of those nations that have advanced furthest from the cave.

The second world consists of those countries that are in disequilibrium —because their regimes have powerful and relentless internal enemies— but have devised effective methods to control that disequilibrium over an extended period. By this definition, the second world expands to include not only the former Communist bloc countries but also the newly industrialized countries, or NICs (Taiwan, South Korea, Hong Kong, Singapore, Mexico, and—until recently, at least—Brazil) and an arguable list of other countries such as Iran, Iraq, Syria, Israel, South Africa, and Indonesia. The second world is characterized by the dominance of the political and bureaucratic sectors over the private sector.

The third world consists of those countries that are in unstable equilibrium. Such regimes generally lack legitimacy and governmental authority and are chronically unable to enforce their will throughout their national territories. Although many differences exist among the countries of the third world—more than among those of the other two "worlds"—the group clearly includes much of Africa, much of Latin America, the Indian subcontinent, and a number of non-European Marxist states. In the third world, a weak private sector combines with a weaker political sector to dominate a still weaker bureaucracy.[1]

In a sense, the first-world state is like a cruising sailboat with a deep and heavy keel. The more the boat is heeled, the more gravity works to bring it back into equilibrium. The second-world state is like a sailboard being maneuvered by a strong man in a fierce wind. If the man tires before the wind abates, the board goes over. The third-world state is like a broad and heavy raft. Although its initial stability is great and depends little upon the strength and skill of the skipper, once it is heeled beyond a certain point, it is more likely to capsize than to return to equilibrium.

These designations are not permanent. Countries can move from world to world, though usually there is a delay in recognizing the change. Japan, a first-world "Great Power" during the 1920s (though often not recognized as such for racial reasons), slid slowly into second-world police-state authoritarianism in the 1930s, was defeated in war and became briefly a member of the third world in the 1940s, worked itself into second-world NIC status in the 1950s and 1960s, and became again a first-world power in the 1970s. Argentina fell from first-world, or near-first-world, status in 1930 and has tottered between the second and third worlds ever since. Greece and Thailand also totter between second-world authoritarianism and third-world chaos. India, Pakistan, and Sri Lanka—all third-world countries—once appeared firmly entrenched in the second world.

HISTORY

Although the term "second world" dates only from the end of World War II, the political-bureaucratic state form can be traced to Sumer and Egypt. For most of history—indeed, through the early years of the nineteenth century—all of the "Great Powers" and most of the would-be powers were political-bureaucratic states with relatively weak private sectors. In most areas of the "civilized" world, democracy was seen as an invitation to riot and capitalism was considered synonymous with greed and corruption.

The earliest empires were essentially police states with autocratic political sectors—limited only by the dictates of religious ideology—supported by powerful military and religious bureaucracies.[2] And, like more recent religious and totalitarian governments, these empires were seen by many as promising alternatives to the constant strife of the more democratic tribes and city-states. They were seen as the wave of the future, and indeed they were.

With the decay of Rome in the fourth century, the West tumbled into what today would be called the third world. As the Dark Ages descended, the organized police state gave way to random tyranny. Barbarian mercenaries rampaged through the heart of a dissolving empire, while corrupt and short-lived emperors showed that egotism was no substitute for strength. The private sector—peasants, sturdy beggars, merchants, moneylenders, and bandits—slowly gained in freedom and power what it lost in safety and prosperity. Bureaucracy disappeared (except in the Church), and civilization guttered.

As we have shown in an earlier chapter, the slow strengthening of national governments that characterized the waning of the Middle Ages was accompanied by the rebirth of civil and military bureaucracy. Slowly the police state—in this case, the state with a standing army that could be used internally as well as against foreign forces—was re-created, justified at first by religious ideology (Lutheran, Calvinist, Catholic, or Muslim), later by nationalism, and finally by prosperity, habit, and fear of chaos. The private sector, though losing power relative to the politicians and the bureaucrats, gained power absolutely—in part by infiltrating the other two sectors.

The first modern police state and, in many respects, still the most popular model was France's Republic of Virtue. Like its mid-twentieth-century counterparts, it combined nationalism with internationalism, democracy with state terrorism, idealism with slaughter, selflessness with megalomania. It saw itself, and was seen by others, as a true alternative to corrupt and hidebound governments everywhere. And, after the ebbing of Jacobin totalitarianism and the consolidation of authoritarianism under Napoleon, it created the most efficient bureaucracy that the West had known.

The defeat of Napoleon, the essential failure of European revolutions in 1830, 1848, and 1871, the Union victory in the American Civil War, and especially the new imperialistic thrust into Africa and Asia created the state of consciousness that would later be called the first world. Indeed, during the nineteenth century, a part of the world appeared to be pulling away from the rest. A few European countries plus the United States became "who" (to use Lenin's term); everyone else was "whom." The "who" was fairly elastic. Influenced by the rising private sector, it favored democracy (within strict limits, of course) but was willing to put up with czars, kaisers, and even another Napoleon.

The "civilized world" or the "Great Powers," as the first world came to call itself, wanted no part of the Republic of Virtue. It scorned ideology, except for muscular Christianity, antislavery, the White Man's Burden, and eventually Social Darwinism. It thought that the police should be unobtrusive (though certainly public order should be maintained) and that the bureaucrats should remain in their bureaus (though it increasingly depended upon their specialized services). It was earnest, religious, "scientific," hardworking, orderly, and arrogant. It was convinced that it represented the acme of progress and that lesser countries—with discipline and perhaps a change of skin color—could eventually reach its level.

Yet, even as the first world was patting itself on the back, hundreds of madmen, utopians, reformers, revolutionists, and crackpots were dreaming of alternatives, creating second worlds of the mind, designing new and improved Republics of Virtue. Some of these dreams came to fruition in the twentieth century.

THE IMPORTANCE OF IDEOLOGY

Most second-world governments, with the partial exception of the NICs, have an ideological foundation that allows them to wield enough police power to maintain internal control in the absence of broadly accepted legitimacy. It is this totalitarian lack of doubt that distinguishes much of the second world from the third world. In the third world, insecure leaders, ruled by greed and fear, are as nervous and as little driven by ideology as Wall Street speculators. Would-be tyrants, too weak to establish police states, live in fear and trembling, more concerned with surviving than with ruling, beset by the generals, the tribes, the urban mob, the peasants, the landowners, the foreign powers, and the International Monetary Fund. The most skillful of them, men like Zaire's Mobutu, may have a wily genius that can keep them on top for years or decades, but none represent an idea sufficiently strong to induce part of the country to subjugate the rest as a matter of moral duty.

Ideology, the certainty that one is doing the right thing, makes weak nations strong. Men, women, and governments are willing to run physical and moral risks—that is, to trample over other men and women—to further the Revolution, to make Europe *Judenrein*, to reestablish a united Ireland, to save the Afrikaner people, to support the line of the imam, or to unite the Arab Nation. They would never be willing to run those same risks merely to satisfy greed or lust for power. Ideology transforms crime into heroism.

It is no accident that most second-world governments have their origins in conspiratorial, revolutionary, "coupist," or terrorist movements. The initial leaders—the Lenins and the Trotskys—are hard men, firm in their belief that their causes are not only important enough to die for but also important enough to kill for. They are as ready to sacrifice others as they are to sacrifice themselves. And once their causes are victorious, they are equally ruthless in their efforts to make those victories irreversible. The police state, often little more than a legitimization of the revolutionary terrorist group, comes naturally to these men and women.

These men and women, even when they don't take power in their own right, give their stamp to the state. They are the honored heroes, the stuff of legend. They are the ones without whose daring the state would not exist. A Dzerzhinsky, a Himmler, or a Borge may be content to remain in the shadows, to play second fiddle, to let others—the "politicians"—have the limelight. But no one doubts that they and their successors were necessary in the past, are necessary in the present, and will be necessary in the future. They are the bloody-handed but obedient Calibans who, more than the noble but squeamish Ariels, enable Prospero to work his magic.

Ideology also creates external support for the second-world state both before and after its consolidation. Ivory-tower intellectuals and artists troop to Leningrad to declare that they have seen the future and it works. Pious Catholics say novenas for Franco's soldiers, and pious Jews save their pennies to buy guns for the Stern Gang or Irgun. American racists flock to Rhodesia to defend "civilization." Third-world students rally to defend Nasser's Egypt or Castro's Cuba, and first-world politicians learn to pander to those of their constituents who have a romantic infatuation with this or that second-world ideology.

BUREAUCRACY

The half-life of an ideology is quite short. It has at most a couple of generations either to create enough material benefits to allow the police state to be dispensed with or to cow the population sufficiently to establish the police state on a firm and lasting basis. If it does the former, like Spain, it gives the nation a chance to enter the first world. If it does the latter, like Syria, it allows the nation to maintain second-world status. If it does neither, like Nasser's Egypt, the nation falls back into the third world. The first two outcomes require the creation of a strong and relatively independent bureaucracy.

Most second-world states face—or at one time faced—substantial internal and external threats. Thus, their security bureaucracies—the army and the secret police—have first claim on resources and personnel. Some second-world states never get beyond this point; they have excellent armies, top-notch police forces, and perhaps even efficient arms industries, but their economic and social bureaucracies, often hobbled by ideology, may lack even the most rudimentary competence.

The NICs are a major exception. Here, the economic bureaucracies reign supreme and the main function of the security forces is to protect the economists from political pressures. It is not a coincidence that many NICs were established and initially ruled by the military. These leaders, unlike those bedazzled civilian politicians who credit their militaries with virtues that they themselves lack, know the limitations of their own organizations. They know that the goal they have for their nations—eventual first-world status—depends more on exports than on arms, more on economics than on ideology. Indeed, the history of the NICs is that of generals in power—Cárdenas, Chiang, Park, Castello Branco, and their successors—slowly deemphasizing the military and the police in favor of the economic specialists. The police state evolves into the developmentalist state.

In general, the second-world political leadership respects the bureaucracy, civil or military. It sees bureaucracy not as an enemy, as is so often true in the first world, nor as a resource to be milked, as is so often true in the third world, but as a tool to be used to achieve ideological goals or economic development. It is only when an ideology—such as Marxism—seeks to specify means as well as ends that the political leadership and the bureaucracy come into conflict. In such cases, the leadership usually wins, professionalism suffers, and the second-world state runs the risk of sliding into the third world.

THE DECLINE OF THE SECOND WORLD

Second-world states decline when the ideologies that sustained them become shopworn and threadbare, when both leaders and led lose their pride in being different and long to join the first-world mainstream. Russians wonder why, if Marx was right, capitalism should prosper and socialism falter. Koreans wonder why, if their country is such an economic miracle, their paychecks aren't growing faster. Afrikaners wonder why, if they are the last bulwark of civilization in Africa, the civilized nations regard them as barbarians.

Both leaders and led wonder if it is not time to make the leap. But, to enter the first world, these states must abandon the authoritarian structures and practices upon which their fragile stability is based. Political leaders, secret police, and economic planners must be willing to risk not only their own power but the very future of their nations. Like blind aerialists, they let go their trapezes, do their breathtaking flips as the world gasps in admiration, and hope that there will be other trapezes to catch. A few states are successful, others abort the attempt, and still others fail and fall back into the third world. It is an act without a net.

CHAPTER 11

The Newly Industrialized Countries

The newly industrialized countries, or NICs, differ from the rest of the second world in that their goals are more economic than political. They value pragmatism over ideology, what works over what is correct. Unlike the Communists, they have no grandiose schemes to save humanity, and, unlike the Nazis, they have no interest in imposing themselves upon others. Nor do they see themselves cornered and vulnerable, fighting for their lives and national identities, like the Israelis and the Afrikaners. They do not present themselves as an alternate model of society. Yet, for much of the third world, they constitute just such a model.

A small number of developing countries have records of economic growth so exceptional that journalists and scholars have termed them "economic miracles."[1] Beginning in the mid-1930s with Mexico and Brazil and continuing after World War II with Taiwan, South Korea, Hong Kong, and Singapore, the growth of these economies has been faster than that of all others in both the developing and developed worlds.

Mexico was the first and, in some respects, is still the most impressive of the NICs. As Gary Gereffi points out:

Mexico has the longest record of sustained economic progress. From the mid-1930s until the late 1970s, while experiencing uninterrupted political stability under its dominant party, the Partido Revolucionario Institucional (PRI), the Mexican economy grew at an average annual rate in excess of 6 percent, and manufacturing output rose approximately 8 percent a year. Mexico's real GDP increased most rapidly (about 9 percent per annum) from the mid-1950s until 1970. . . .[2]

Growth in the other five states, though over a shorter period of time, was even more rapid.

These economic statistics—and what they imply about the achievement of modernity—are the NICs' entire raison d'être, their claim to special status, their reason to be included in the second world. Economic growth is for these states what Marxism was for the Soviet Union, what Afrikaner survival was for white South Africa, what Zionism is for Israel. But, whereas Marxism, apartheid, and Zionism are now seen as dead ends by many in the third world (and in much of the first world), the economic success of the NICs appears to hold a key to first-world status. Unlike the pure police states, the NICs appear to be weakening, not just containing, the forces of disequilibrium. The NICs are the success stories of the second world.

ECONOMIC STRATEGIES

Success has a thousand fathers, and claims of parenthood have been made for even the most impotent of economic theories. Journalists, scholars, and axe-grinders—armed with invincible ignorance and the ability to make even the most awkward facts fit into preconceived belief—have been ever ready to point to the NICs with paternal pride. On the right, they see the validation of laissez-faire and the bankruptcy of socialism. On the left, they see justification for near-total state control of the economy and for substantial state ownership. On the extreme left, they see no miracle at all—just another case of the hoodwinking of the masses.

In truth, all industrialized countries were once newly industrialized countries. And they all followed one of two basic strategies to become industrialized. Small countries with small resource bases and relatively stagnant domestic markets, such as England in the nineteenth century, sought to become "workshops of the world," exporting manufactured goods and importing food and raw materials. Large countries with large resource bases and rapidly expanding domestic markets, such as the United States in the nineteenth century, saw little need for extensive foreign trade in industrial products.

In the second half of the twentieth century, most of the nations of the third world tried to industrialize and most failed. Those that were successful were those that followed one of the two patterns already established in the previous century. Mexico and Brazil, with large land areas and ample natural resources, followed the U.S. pattern. The East Asian NICs, relatively small countries with limited resources, followed the British pattern.

It is misleading, however, to speak of strategies, as if each of these countries had a well-worked-out "master plan" (though many NICs did—and still do—publish Soviet-style Five Year Plans). Like England and the United States before them, the rising LDCs (less developed countries) tried to seize opportunities and avoid disasters with little regard to theory or even consistency. Most began as exporters of commodities and importers of manufactured goods. At some point, however, external events such as depression or war sharply reduced their exports, their imports, or both. At this point, they adopted import-substituting industrialization (ISI) in order to provide themselves with the manufactures that had once been imported and/or to absorb the labor released from the declining commodity export sector.

The Latin American NICs, with stronger resource bases, were generally able to pay for the first stage of industrialization with their commodity exports. With their large domestic markets, they were also attractive to foreign direct investment. The East Asian NICs, whose main resources were cheap labor and a strategic location in the Cold War, financed the first stage of ISI with massive foreign aid. At that time, Western firms did not see countries such as Taiwan or South Korea as potential sources of profit, but Western governments, and the U.S. government in particular, did see them as bulwarks against Communism. Both sets of NICs spurred the development of their industries through heavy government intervention and high protective barriers.[3]

The first stage of ISI eventually played itself out in both Latin America and East Asia. In both areas, domestic markets became saturated with textiles, shoes, cement, beverages, and similar first-stage products. If the economies were to continue to expand, new strategies would have to be adopted. It was at this point that the Latin Americans and the East Asians parted company. Mexico and Brazil went into a second stage of ISI, producing automobiles, petrochemicals, and the like for their domestic markets, financed as before by commodity exports and foreign direct investment. The East Asians, by contrast, began to export the manufactured goods that they had originally developed for their domestic markets, as well as some purely export goods of a similar technology level, and to pay for the second stage of ISI out of these earnings.

Once again, both the Latin American and the East Asian strategies played themselves out. The Latin Americans, faced with erratic demand for their commodities, skittish foreign investors, and massive foreign debt, began to export ever-increasing amounts of both first- and second-stage manufactured goods. The East Asians, faced with rising competition from other East Asian exporters of first-stage manufactures as well as rising costs at home, followed much the same course. In general, the East Asians have been more successful than the Latin American NICs in creating viable economies based on second-stage exports, though not to the extent that many in the first world believe.

As the twenty-first century approaches, it has become obvious that industrialization for domestic markets alone is no longer a viable strategy even in the largest countries. The two historical models of national industrialization have merged. Just as the United States has had to adopt much of the export orientation associated with nineteenth-century England, so Mexico and Brazil are eagerly adopting important aspects of the East Asian model.

THE POLITICAL CONDITIONS FOR ECONOMIC SUCCESS

It is not so much economic policy as political conditions that differentiate the NICs from the LDCs and make possible the NICs' economic success. Third-world states that attempt to follow the economic strategies of the NICs often fail, not because they apply the wrong economic policy, but because they lack the brutal authority to make any economic policy stick. As one development economist noted, "The existence of an effective economic policy is prima facie evidence that we are not dealing with a democracy."

The NICs—although very much a part of the second world in that they are authoritarian states with strong political and bureaucratic sectors— differ from other second-world states in that they do not usually let ideology get in the way of sound economic policy. The leaders of the NICs have no religious reverence for the Marxist scriptures, no antieconomic desire to "make the desert bloom" at any cost, no a priori racial ideas as to who is qualified for what job. Unlike the pure police states, the NICs are not trying to create alternatives to the first world; they are trying to join it.

Rather than using ideology to justify police-state methods, the NICs justify their often heavy-handed authoritarianism by economic results.

Their leaders look forward to a time when economic success will satisfy their populations and authoritarianism can be abandoned (or at least moderated), thereby transforming second-world controlled disequilibrium into first-world stable equilibrium.

The NICs, like many of the other second-world states, were created out of numbing political chaos that left their populations disposed to accept any authority that plausibly promised the illusion of stability. Just as the Soviet Union and Nazi Germany were forged in the aftermath of World War I and South Africa and Israel were in part responses to British and Nazi concentration camps, modern Mexico was the result of the bloody, decades-long Revolution of 1910 and the four East Asian NICs were born out of war, civil war, and revolution. Only Brazil, though no stranger to violence, did not re-create itself out of the shambles of a nation-shaking breakdown.

If, however, violence, political chaos, and a certain numbness on the part of the population were enough to create stable authority, a good part of the third world would be candidates for the second. Structure is also needed. This structure was provided by the military in Brazil and South Korea, by monopoly political parties in Mexico, Taiwan, and Singapore, and by the colonial government in Hong Kong. In all of these cases, except possibly Hong Kong, which is something of a case by itself, preexisting bureaucracies were revitalized by strong political leaders in the face of extreme challenges.

These bureaucracies were not all-wise—they made mistakes and took wrong turns—but they were protected from political fallout by the government leadership. They had only to convince a small group of generals or party leaders—sometimes only a single person—and not the population at large. This gave them the luxury of taking one approach and, if that failed, of substituting another. Moreover, they knew that they could enforce their will on business, labor, and the general public. They could, directly or indirectly, force saving and investment, hold down wages, and postpone consumption. All that was required of them was eventual success. It was a perfect task and perfect conditions for Weberian bureaucrats.

The necessary (though certainly not sufficient) condition for rapid industrialization is apparently the ability and inclination on the part of the political leadership to insulate economic policymaking from popular pressures. This is not only true of the modern NICs but was also true of the present first-world states that industrialized during the nineteenth century. The United States and Western Europe industrialized under conditions of limited suffrage, massive political corruption, miserable working conditions, widespread police-state tactics against labor, and systematic destruction of the environment. It should not surprise us that the NICs are only able to industrialize under authoritarian regimes; it instead *should* surprise us that they are often able to do it more humanely—and even more democratically—than their first-world predecessors.

DOMINANT-PARTY STATES: MEXICO AND TAIWAN

Although it makes sense to separate Latin America from East Asia when speaking of economic strategy, this division makes less sense when it comes to political structure and dynamics. Politically, Mexico and Taiwan belong together as ideological states that have only been able to progress when they downplayed ideology.

Mexico in 1910 and China in 1911 underwent the first of the great social revolutions of the twentieth century. The leaders of Mexico's Partido Revolucionario Institucional (PRI) and Taiwan's Kuomintang (KMT) see themselves as—and, in most respects, truly are—the political heirs of Francisco Madero and Sun Yat-sen. However, between the initial reformist steps of Madero and Sun and the present-day, second-world controlled disequilibrium of Mexico and Taiwan, there was a long and bloody period of revolution.

This was not revolution in the sense of reformation or rebirth; it was revolution in the sense of chaos, massacre, starvation, vandalism, and pillage. In both countries, it was a time of opportunism, changing alliances, foreign intervention, hollow idealism, and innocent death. Rival warlords, without fixed principle, rampaged across both countries, melding, separating, attacking, retreating, killing. In Mexico, something like 1.5 million died out of a population in 1910 of 15 million, while in China the absolute number, though not the proportion, was much greater. In the end, both countries were exhausted, ideologically numb, and eager for stability.

Mexico was the first to achieve some semblance of stability under the "Maximato" of General Plutarco Elías Calles, who came to power in 1924 and controlled the government directly or through puppets for the next ten years. This was by no means a period of reform, but, except for the bloody conflict with the Catholic Church, it was a period of increasing peace and relative stability. That was all the country asked for. The economy—no more equitable than before 1910 but now under the vigorous new leadership of Calles and his Revolutionary cronies and business partners—revived and expanded.

Calles established the PRI (then called the PNR, or Partido Nacional Revolucionario) as a means of controlling and defanging the various and violent members of the "Revolutionary Family"—the generals, the *caciques* (local bosses), the labor and peasant leaders, the bureaucrats. General Lázaro Cárdenas, as we noted in chapter 4, was appointed president by Calles, refused to be a puppet, and exiled his mentor. Cárdenas put the capstone on the Mexican system of controlled disequilibrium by instituting a form of serial dictatorship with regular and complete changes of government that continues to serve the country well. To complete the institutionalization of control, it only remained for the next president, General Manuel Ávila Camacho, to remove the army from politics by appointing a civilian to the presidency in 1946.

China was not to achieve political stability until Chiang Kai-shek was driven from the mainland by the Communists in 1949. At that time, although both sides refused to recognize the fact, China split into two second-world states: the police state under Mao and the future NIC under Chiang. At this point, Chiang made a strategic decision. Recognizing (but not accepting) the completeness of his defeat on the mainland, he opted to create a new state on Taiwan rather than to waste resources in fruitless attempts to regain what he had lost. The reconquest of the Chinese mainland, like the fulfillment of the social promises of the Mexican Revolution, would have to wait.

Achieving control on Taiwan was very different from the task that had eluded Chiang on the mainland. It was a question not of defeating or buying off Communists and warlords, but of uniting the majority Taiwanese with the very different ruling refugees from across the Formosa Strait. Starting with a thorough and very successful land reform, Chiang (and later his son, Chiang Ching-kuo) wooed the Taiwanese with economic progress at the same time he strengthened the economic base of the island for possible conflict with the Communists.

Although the ruling party, which has been described as "Leninist but not Marxist," was always willing to use police-state methods when it believed them to be necessary, such tactics became less frequent as the economy soared and the results of that growth were distributed with unparalleled equity. By the early 1970s, native Taiwanese made up the overwhelming majority of the KMT, had won many elected posts, and had become prominent in the Japanese-style, merit-based bureaucracy and in the private sector. Through integrated education and increasing intermarriage, the two peoples were becoming one. By the time Chiang Ching-kuo died in 1988, a control had been achieved that, while authoritarian, depended very little upon coercion.

Both Mexico and Taiwan carried out their rational and largely successful economic policies while giving lip service to ideologies that demanded very different courses of action. Any serious attempt to achieve the goals of the Mexican Revolution, like any serious attempt to reconquer mainland China, would have risked destroying the prosperity and illusion of stability upon which NIC status depended. Indeed, as we will see later, when oil wealth made Mexico rich enough to attempt to live up to its principles, the results were disastrous.

NATIONAL SECURITY STATES: BRAZIL AND SOUTH KOREA

If Mexico and Taiwan fall naturally together as dominant-party states that ignored their ideological principles, Brazil and South Korea may be seen as national-security states that maintained their military orientation. Whereas the generals who led Mexico and Taiwan thought of the military in terms of divisive and threatening rival revolutionary armies, the generals who led Brazil and South Korea thought of the military in terms of a unified, disciplined national bureaucracy. What was seen as a threat by the former was seen as salvation by the latter. The dominant-party regimes based their initial legitimacy on revolutionary ideology, which, like Nazism or Communism, demanded a civilian party in control of the armed forces, while the national-security governments based their legitimacy on "verticality," institutional discipline, and "stewardship," which demanded that the military be in a position to protect the nation from corrupt and unpatriotic civilians.

In South Korea, the corrupt civilian government of Syngman Rhee, which lasted from 1948 to 1960, had given democracy a bad name with both the military and the general population. The military in particular asked itself why honest but poorly paid soldiers should daily risk their lives in the often "hot" war with North Korea, while their "democratic" government—well away from the front lines—squandered lavish U.S. aid to buy votes and enrich civilian officials and their business allies. The generals genuinely feared that the economic failures and reactionary policies of the Rhee government could so alienate the South Korean population as to make North Korean conquest inevitable. National security demanded a military takeover.

The Brazilian generals who led the "Revolution of 1964," like those of South Korea, saw it as their duty to protect the country from the chaos, corruption, and possible treason of the democratic civilian government. Forced industrialization under the government of Juscelino Kubitschek combined with declining exports, to say nothing of the construction of Brasília, had led to large public deficits and massive inflation. Real wages had plummeted and unemployment soared as economic growth came to a halt. Moreover, the quirky government of Jânio Quadros had ended with the resignation of the president, leaving not-to-be-trusted Vice President João Goulart in tenuous charge. The populist alliance, which had brought stability and elements of progress to the country in the past, had come apart, and a leftist revolution—perhaps winked at by Goulart—seemed just around the corner. As in South Korea, national security demanded intervention.

The Brazilian military—much more than that of South Korea, which was troubled by rivalries and by the curse of hormonal leadership—was a true bureaucracy. In contrast to the stereotype of South American militaries, the Brazilian generals distrusted charisma and would not have tolerated the creation of a cult of personality around a president from the barracks. They saw themselves not as individual prima donnas, but as a *group* of patriots willing to make the hard political and economic decisions needed to put the nation back on track, after which they would retire. Although differences existed between the hard- and soft-liners within the military government, the presidency was regularly rotated during the more than two decades of military rule with remarkably little friction.

The national-security governments of South Korea and Brazil, in contrast to the dominant-party governments of Mexico and Taiwan, were neither limited nor aided by ideology. Indeed, the generals saw themselves as essentially above ideology. This stance, although it protected them from the occasional self-defeating, ideologically motivated action of a Mexico or a Taiwan, left them with no "defense" against democracy. When they had brought their countries back "on track," the generals had no justification for retaining power. Either they must—reluctantly and with well-justified misgivings—make way for democracy, or they must base their continued rule on naked force. Both South Korea and Brazil chose the democratic option.

NICS AND POLICE STATES

Despite the fragility of many NICs, especially Brazil, and the dangers inherent in the rapid growth of the NIC middle class with its penchant for ideology, the NICs remain the success stories of the second world. Indeed, Spain, one of the few second-world nations that have clearly evolved into first-world states, did so by first evolving from a police state into an NIC. Moreover, all of the other candidates for possible first-world status are also NICs. (The case of Japan, which was briefly a NIC—and, indeed, the model for the other East Asian NICs—before reentering the first world, is atypical because of the influence of the U.S. occupation. Nazi Germany is also atypical because it did not evolve into a first-world state; rather it was destroyed as a second-world state and re-created as a first-world state.)

CHAPTER 12

A Gallery of
Police States, I

A police state exists when a government is only able to rule because it controls a loyal and effective police force. A police state may be of the left or the right, democratic or dictatorial, brutal or benign, traditional or revolutionary. It may be warlike or peace-loving. It may worship the jackboot as a symbol of disciplined superiority, or it may regret it as a distasteful necessity—but it cannot survive without it.

By definition, the police state rules over a divided nation in which a majority or a large minority of its residents do not recognize its legitimacy. The division may be racial or tribal—that is to say, between the fully human and the less than human—or it may be philosophical— between the true believers and those who are slow to get with the program.

The only way for a police state to cease to be a police state is for the nation it rules to cease to be divided.

Once humanity had progressed beyond the Darwinian democracy of the tribe, the police state became the ideal if not the norm. From the beginnings of complex society until quite recently, it was axiomatic that political stability depended upon the credible threat of force. The emphasis is on the word "credible." Those city-states and empires that could credibly threaten force—without having to use it—prospered in domestic peace, while those that could not exhausted themselves in riot, revolution, and dynastic rivalry. Only slowly did other factors, such as consent and material advantage, that worked to eliminate social divisions come to outweigh coercion as a guarantor of stability.

Ideology made the threat of force legitimate and therefore credible. The divine right of kings and the secular ideologies that followed justified the division between rulers and ruled, who and whom, actors and acted-upon. Ideology gave prophets and emperors, commissars and dictators, the authority to give orders. It gave soldiers, spies, and policemen the justification to enforce those orders. It gave the average person reason to obey those orders. And, finally, it gave potential dissidents, nascent democrats, gripers, unbelievers, and individualists—Prometheus and Hester Prynne— the feeling that to protest those orders was perhaps hopeless (or even against the will of God) but heroically necessary. Ideology was a means of uniting the leadership and the bureaucracy to control the private sector, a means of protecting the community from the individual.

Of course, every state is to some extent divided, and every viable state is a police state to some segment of its population. Criminals from murderers and rapists to tax evaders and jaywalkers, by their very actions, show that they do not accept the authority of the state in one or more areas. They must be coerced into abiding by the laws that others willingly obey, and the majority of the population, even in a tyranny, probably regards such coercion as just and necessary. In other cases there may be less agreement. Some democratic countries make criminals out of barkeeps, prostitutes, abortionists, adulterers, contraceptive users, homosexuals, writers of dirty books, and conscientious objectors to military service, while other democratic countries do not. In these cases, many citizens who have no intention of breaking the law may still wonder if such activity is a proper concern of government.

Such states are not true police states, however, because their "criminal" element, however defined, is not large enough to threaten the continued existence and authority of the government. A prolonged police strike might (or might not) lead to a sharp increase in the incidence of murder, rape, tax evasion, and jaywalking, but—in the undivided state—it would not seriously undermine the government. The true police state requires the juxtaposition of two factors: (1) a powerful racial or intellectual minority (or majority) in direct opposition to the ideology of the regime and (2) a regime with the political will and bureaucratic muscle to enforce its ideology by suppressing that minority (or majority).

THE SOVIET-NAZI PARADIGM

All twentieth-century police states owe something to the similar but opposing models of Lenin's Russia and Hitler's Germany. The Communist state has become the archetypical example of the totalitarianism of ideas, while the Nazi state has come to represent the totalitarianism of race: the Master Plan against the Master Race, Mind against Blood, Marx against Wagner, Ideal against Will, Jacobin against Puritan, the Church Militant against the Tribe. The left objects to your thoughts; the right despises your genes.

Marxism was the religion of the twentieth century. No other religion, not even seventh-century Islam, had ever expanded so rapidly over so broad an area. Like the other great missionary religions, Marxism was open to all who were willing to accept its dogmas and its discipline. Like the others, it filled a spiritual vacuum. Like the others, it was based on faith rather than reason and was ultimately antiscientific. Like the others, it has had its share of schisms and intrafaith wars.

Russia's defeat in World War I gave Marxism the opportunity to incorporate itself into a political body. The czarist autocracy—and the certainties that it represented—had been discredited. The elites wanted a way out—the *trahison des clercs* was well under way—while the masses demanded land, food, and peace. Thousands of officerless soldiers roamed the countryside. Alexander Kerensky, a decent man without a strong ideology, shrank from imposing his rule with blood and duplicity; Lenin had no such qualms.

Although by no means the largest or most popular or even the most extreme of the parties contending for power, Lenin's Bolsheviks were the best prepared and probably the least given to self-doubt. Whereas others saw the support of the masses as a justification for seizing power, Lenin's Marxist ideology required no such justification and Lenin correctly saw that the seizure of power could itself be a means of gaining the support of the masses. A few machine guns and the willingness to use them were worth far more than a mob of cheering enthusiasts.

Nazism, like Communism, had its origins in World War I defeat. The kaiser, like the czar, and all he stood for had been discredited. The Weimar Republic, like the Kerensky government, was decent and moderate and was hated by all sides for its very decency and moderation. Individual Germans looked east and saw the future in Communism or looked south and saw it in fascism; few if any saw a future in democratic moderation. Democracy and liberal capitalism had clearly had their day.

Hitler was more charismatic and less intelligent than Lenin. Failed artist, defeated soldier, inept conspirator, vegetarian, avuncular friend to children and animals, scorner of everything that was foreign to the German lower middle class, Hitler reflected a sentimental and ruthless Germany that was fed up with the Weimar Republic. Hitler, unlike Lenin, made up his ideology as he went along. In its essence, his ideology was that he—and Germany—could do no wrong and that nothing was ever Germany's fault, though much could be laid at the door of individual German "traitors." It made no sense, but it made people proud to be Germans. The German masses—and their betters—embraced Hitler and his ideas.

There is a certain irony in the conflicting Nazi and Soviet attitudes toward democracy. Hitler, who became the choice of the great mass of Germans, scorned democracy as decadent and foreign to the heroic German tradition. Lenin, who was never really popular with the masses before his death and deification and who would probably have been defeated in a free election, claimed that Communism represented a higher democracy. The Nazis, with no ideology except pure leadership, could not afford to believe that the *Führer* depended upon the *Volk*. The *Führer*, like God, was creator, not created. The Communists, by contrast, saddled with an ideology that gave the masses a starring role, had to believe that their system was somehow democratic.

Both Soviet Russia and Nazi Germany were police states and owed their existence to a loyal and efficient security bureaucracy (including the military). But, even here, there were differences. The Soviets, being the more rational, rarely let ideology get in the way of security. Whether it came to using czarist personnel in the Cheka or letting suspect scientists develop weapon systems, Moscow, at least before the days of Stalin, generally knew better than to micromanage the security bureaucracy. The economic bureaucracy, not being as important to state survival, was subjected to strict Marxist ideology with eventual disastrous results.

The Nazis, although equally dependent upon their security bureaucracy, allowed it to be undermined by ideology—that is to say, by Hitler's whim. In the early days of his rule, Hitler often seemed to prefer the bludgeon to the stiletto, the mob to the Gestapo, the people to the bureaucrats. Many of the mistakes that cost Germany the war—the attack on Stalingrad, the priority given to the Final Solution—were recognized by some in the security bureaucracy, but their complaints were stifled. Toward the end, at a time when the average German still fanatically supported Hitler, large parts of the military bureaucracy were plotting against him.

When it comes to continuity and orderly change of leadership, we have no good basis for comparison. Regimes of the totalitarian right rarely outlive their leaders, and Nazi Germany was no exception. Nazi Germany was born, lived, and died in ideological purity. Like Jim Jones and his followers at Jonestown, much of the Nazi hierarchy found it easier to die in purity than to live in the real world.

The Russian Communists did not allow themselves the luxury of thanatotic fanaticism. Lenin, who had never been a mindless slave to Marxist orthodoxy, did not shrink from adjusting ideology to assure regime survival. This had the unwanted effect, however, of diluting ideology. After the New Economic Policy and especially after Lenin's death, Soviet Russia essentially ceased to be a totalitarian state striving for Utopia and became an authoritarian state striving for national survival and expansion—a dictatorship like any other.

Soviet leaders from Stalin on, moving ever closer to czarist traditionalism and ever further from Marx and Lenin, tried to keep up pretenses, pretending that their "Internationalist Duty" was something different from the old Russian imperialism, pretending that they were competing with ideas as well as throw weight. They had no trouble convincing their knee-jerk friends and enemies in the developed West. They were less successful in the third world, where increasingly sophisticated leaders admired the USSR as an effective police state but not as a workers' Utopia. They were least successful of all in convincing themselves and the Russian people.

Thus, we have two models of the police state: the emotional, people-oriented, right-wing model and the cerebral, leadership-oriented, left-wing model. Both stem from France's Republic of Virtue, and both are reflected in varying proportions in the police states of the second half of the twentieth century.

COMMUNIST CHINA: CHARISMA VERSUS BUREAUCRACY

The Communist victory over the Kuomintang in 1949 was the making of Chiang Kai-shek and the undoing of Mao Zedong. Defeat allowed Chiang to stop trying to be a leader—a task for which he had few talents except an occasional flair for duplicity—and start being a manager. Mao, whose genius for leadership made victory over Japan and the KMT inevitable, had no talent—or even toleration—for the orderly administration of a peacetime government. Chiang protected his economic bureaucracy, while Mao made war on his. Taiwan's relative democracy and economic success are Chiang's monument. China's political oppression and economic chaos are Mao's legacy.

If charismatic leadership can be likened to the reptile brain deep beneath the human cortex, Chairman Mao was all lizard. He could cope with enemies but not with problems, and he found enemies on all sides. For reasons that probably had more to do with his relationship with his father than with China or Communism, Mao hated authority, expertise, bureaucracy, and even to a large extent Chinese culture. Anything that was old and traditional was bad, and anything that was new but might in time become old and traditional was also bad.

Undereducated and far from naturally brilliant, Mao appears to have suffered from gross feelings of inferiority which he attempted to smother under barrages of self-aggrandizing bombast. As early as 1940, he was claiming equality with Sun Yat-sen, Marx, Engels, Lenin, and Stalin. He was jealous of his abler colleagues and ended up by betraying most of them, including his comrades of the Long March. He chose and discarded wives and aides largely on the basis of their ability to flatter. He elevated even his most trivial writings to the status of infallible scripture. Red Guards did not so much study his thought as chant his words like Buddhist mantras and wave their Little Red Books like so many Tibetan prayer flags. The cult of personality came naturally to Chairman Mao.[1]

Mao was in many respects very un-Chinese. The Chinese traditionally have respected authority, bureaucracy, age, parents, learning, the right to make a buck and, if possible, to live well. But, most of all, the Chinese have traditionally valued tranquillity, the boon of not having to live in "interesting" times. Mao induced a large minority of Chinese youth to trample all of this underfoot in a decade-long *Kristallnacht*. No life, reputation, position, or policy was safe during the Cultural Revolution. Education was a high crime, even minimal competence was suspect, and any success in alleviating the poverty of the nation branded one as a "capitalist-roader."

If Mao was un-Chinese, he was also un-Communist. Communism has goals and views the class struggle only as a means of achieving those goals. On the road to the ultimate goal of "true Communism," the socialist state recognizes such subordinate goals as creating a strong government, achieving economic growth, and raising living standards. Mao would have none of this. He valued only struggle, never goals: antithesis, not synthesis;

victory, not achievement. His ideology of Continuous Revolution, decidedly un-Marxist, had a Wagnerian ring of heroes in Valhalla endlessly battling for no reason at all except an atavistic love of combat.

The Cultural Revolution came about because Mao, being the epitome of the leader, could not solve problems—he had earlier proven that trait by virtually destroying the economy with his Great Leap Forward—but could only defeat enemies. With both the Japanese and the KMT vanquished and with "class enemies" eliminated by the socialization of the means of production, Mao had to create new enemies within the party hierarchy and among his onetime allies in the USSR and Eastern Europe. "Revolutionary values," the willingness to be stirred by Mao and to strike out blindly in all directions—against both left and right, depending upon the state of the Chairman's paranoia—became more important than the security and success of the Revolution or the material progress of the masses.

The Chinese Communist police state was established in spite of Mao, who put his trust in the mob rather than in the security bureaucracy. It was the work of the rest of the Communist leaders of both left and right, who were more willing to put ideology (and practicality) before ego. The old men who slaughtered the students in Tiananmen Square in 1989 were not Mao's heirs. They were Mao's betrayed comrades who had suffered it all before, who now looked out at the masses of young enthusiasts defying authority and saw a new Cultural Revolution beginning. Mao's heirs are rather the Khmer Rouge and the Sendero Luminoso on the killing fields of Cambodia and Peru—men and women who regard the police state as entirely too civilized.

IRAN: FROM AUTOCRACY TO THEOCRACY

It is Persia's misfortune to be ruled by men who think they are God or the darlings of God. From the days of Cyrus, Cambyses, Xerxes, and Darius to the period of the recent shah, Persian rulers have thought themselves favored of Heaven, men who did not have to take the ordinary precautions of second-world politics, men who could issue commands into the air and then turn away, blindly assuming that those commands would actually be carried out. After the Islamic Revolution brought him to supreme (though unofficial) power, the Ayatollah Khomeini had much the same attitude.

Reza Shah Pahlavi, the father of the recent shah, had started out differently. A hardheaded, undereducated soldier from a poor family, Reza

Khan and his military allies overthrew the barely reigning Qajar dynasty in 1921 and set about to organize a modern police state on the model of Atatürk's Turkey. In contrast to the Qajars, Reza Khan intended to establish central control over all the peoples of Iran—Kurds, Arabs, Lur, Qashqai, Azeri, and Baluch—over the dozens of semi-independent Persian tribes and clans, and over the legion of untamed landlords and petty religious despots. He also intended to bring Iran into the twentieth century. For a while, it appeared that he would be successful on all counts.

Reza Shah—he crowned himself in 1926—had no illusions that he was doing the will of the people. He knew that in the absence of an effective security bureaucracy, non-Persians would choose to go their separate ways and Persians would choose to remain firmly in the Middle Ages. While he believed that social reform and secularism—that was his ideology, to the extent that he had one—were necessary to strengthen the state, he knew that they would not be popular even with those who benefited. Both lion and fox, Reza Shah destroyed enemies, co-opted neutrals, and created alliances. His abdication and exile in 1941 were forced by the British, not by internal opposition.

His son, Muhammad Reza, born to the purple, shared most of his father's goals but lacked his father's skills and attitudes. Initially shy and dependent—the result of seeing his father deposed, his country invaded by two powerful opposing nations, and himself almost overthrown by his own prime minister—the new shah slowly gained confidence and then overconfidence. With the advent of oil wealth, massive U.S. assistance, and fulsome Western praise, and having "miraculously" survived several attempts on his life or rule, the "modernizing monarch" came to believe that he had a divine mission to free Iran from its reactionary, obscurantist, feudal past. His inability to see the inherent contradiction between having a divine mission and being a modernizing ruler was a reason for his ultimate failure.[2]

As time went on, the *shahanshah* ("king of kings") came to associate himself less with the great Shi'ite shahs and more with the near divine kings of the pre-Islamic past, when Persia was truly the center of the world. In 1971 he celebrated the twenty-five hundredth anniversary of the founding of the Persian Empire with a lavish, expensive pageant in the ruins of Persepolis. What if such pagan goings-on did not endear the shah to his firmly Islamic subjects? Was it not beneath the dignity of a near-god to make decisions on the basis of grimy politics?

The shah's official ideology of modernization—the "White Revolution" or the "Shah and People Revolution"—churned on in a godlike political vacuum. A genuine and far-reaching land reform was undertaken, but, whereas his father had used land reform to destroy existing enemies, the shah created new enemies without destroying them. Moreover, he made no effort to mobilize support among the peasant beneficiaries of the reform to offset the enemies he had made among the dispossessed landlords and religious officials. Similarly, his efforts to roll back inflation in basic goods with drastic penalties (including death) against price gougers earned him the hatred of the powerful bazaari merchants without gaining him the gratitude of the common people.

In sum, the shah took a divided country and divided it even more. Reform became possible only when backed up by SAVAK, the deadly efficient secret police. The road to the twentieth century passed through the torture chamber. Modernization, which had already essentially failed because of the emphasis on leadership rather than bureaucratic competence, became a dirty word. The once-derided "turbans" became heroes of a greatly expanded middle class.[3] Ph.D. engineers from MIT let their beards grow. Emancipated women took up the veil. A cramped and iron-willed mullah from the Middle Ages became a rallying point for all elements of the nation.

In the end, the shah's will broke first. The near-god who thought he had seen the Hidden Imam crumbled before the old man whom many thought *was* the Hidden Imam. In the terms of our analysis, it was a victory of the right over the left, of ignorant emotion over spurious intellect.

Ignorance and emotion carried the Iranian Revolution far. Despite having destroyed most of what was efficient in the shah's generally inefficient bureaucracy—namely, much of the security, oil, and financial establishments—the Revolution was able to rule, to suppress revolt, and to fight a decade-long war with Iraq. A fundamentalist Republic of Virtue was established, and religion turned Iran upside down. The last became first, the meek inherited the earth and bared their teeth, and those who were persecuted took over the torture chambers.

The Islamic Republic of Iran only evolved into a true police state after the death of Khomeini. While the ayatollah was alive, Iran was ruled through a kind of semidirected chaotic fury with little or no bureaucratic backup. With great stores of patriotism, as well as the huge arsenal of American arms that the shah had left behind, masses of death-seeking Iranian youths (thoughtfully supplied with "passports to Heaven") dealt Iraq defeat after defeat despite generally incompetent leadership and micromanagement from Tehran. At home, civilians rejoiced even as material hardship increased and freedom, which had been rather extensive under the shah, disappeared.

But emotions sag and enthusiasm cannot last forever. Slowly the ruthless bureaucrats of Baghdad turned the tables on the fevered theocrats of Tehran. After winning a thousand impossible battles, the God-intoxicated Iranian patriots lost the war to a much smaller and less enthusiastic force of Iraqi conscripts. The bazaaris looked at their empty shelves and looted bank accounts and thought that perhaps they had judged the shah too harshly. Western-educated technocrats shouted against the Great Satan and then sneaked home to share a hidden bottle of Scotch. Young women let strands of tempting hair escape from under their chadors. In the slums, people thought more about food and less about God.

Ali Akhbar Hashemi Rafsanjani, Hojjat al-Islam and general all-around opportunist, worked his way to the fore, co-opting emerging social forces and isolating enemies, downplaying xenophobia, speaking words of sweet reason, slowly rejuvenating the economy, and establishing control over the forces of coercion. Competence and loyalty to Rafsanjani became as important as religious correctness. Chaotic totalitarianism was slowly replaced by more orderly police-state authoritarianism. The Revolution was dead, and the Iranian Thermidor had begun. As Iran entered the 1990s, it was once more a state that even the shah would recognize.

CHAPTER 13

A Gallery of
Police States, II

SOUTH AFRICA: THE DEMOCRACY
OF THE WHITE TRIBE

C alvinism, because of its doctrine of the Elect, has always been
tribal. The true Calvinist, if any still exist, sees a fundamental
difference between himself and his coreligionists, who have at
least the possibility of salvation, and the rest of the world's population, who
have been damned since the beginning of time. The outsider is suspect—a
source of contamination at best and a tool of Satan at worst—and should
be avoided or destroyed. Humanity begins and ends with the tribe.

But, even in the heyday of Calvinism, not all Calvinists were equally
serious about their religion. The Dutch and the French Huguenots and
the Germans who went to do the Dutch East India Company's bidding at
the Cape of Good Hope in the middle of the seventeenth century were far
different from the East Anglians who settled New England slightly earlier.
Mostly poor and undereducated with little future in dynamic Holland,
they were interested in earning a living rather than in building the New
Jerusalem. Their tribalism resembled more the rough-and-ready egalitarian racism of the Scotch-Irish Presbyterians of the American frontier than
the more sophisticated intolerance of the New England Puritans. While
they lacked the intellectual hardiness and the Protestant ethic to evolve
into good entrepreneurial capitalists, they also lacked the theological assur-

ance to hang witches. Leonard M. Thompson gives us a good description of these early migrants:

> The South African fragment . . . was not a microcosm of seventeenth-century Dutch society. It was an inferior, partial selection from it. The cultural attainments and interests of Dutch society—the art, the literature, the spirit of scientific enquiry—were almost completely absent from the fragment. What were present were the toughness of the peasant and the unsuccessful townsman, their capacity to endure adverse circumstances, and their receptivity to a simplified version of the gloomy doctrines of primitive Calvinism.[1]

Unlike the New Englanders, who left Europe as something of a tribe and steadily detribalized under the influence of New World wealth, the Afrikaners began as a motley group of different nationalities and languages bound loosely by religion and steadily tribalized under the influence of African poverty. Cut off from Europe in a way that the New England colonists never were, both exploited and ignored—first by the Dutch East India Company and, after 1795, by the British—living in a land of poor soil and sparse rainfall, many Afrikaners deliberately turned away from the sea and Europe and inward toward Africa. They became seminomadic farmers, a mixture of the pioneer and the Okie. Surrounded by real and imagined enemies, both European and Bantu, they also turned in upon themselves and created a *broederbond* of the spirit long before they established the political secret society with the capital *B*.

They became the "poor white trash" of the African continent, living under conditions often as bad as and in some cases worse than those of the native population, continually losing, abandoning, or being driven off their lands; nearly destroyed by a brutal (indeed, near genocidal) war waged largely against women and children; diseased, undernourished, and undereducated; considered lazy and stupid by the British, who often preferred blacks to Boers in matters of employment. More than a few Afrikaners entered the twentieth century as beggars on the streets of the British-built cities if male or as servants to "Coloreds" and Asians if female.[2]

But their tribalism had been hardened and their luck was about to change. The British government, ashamed of its motivations and conduct in the Boer War and not at all eager to fight more battles against such formidable guerrillas, had begun a policy of rapprochement with the Afrikaners in the early 1900s. The Boers, for their part, hard and bitter, were ready to seize the proffered British hand and to make use of British democratic institutions as a means of gaining political control. After a series of partial victories—and conflicts among various tendencies within the Boer community, some of which favored genuine cooperation with the British—hard-line Afrikanerdom came to full power with the election of D. F. Malan's Nationalist Party in 1948.

Malan, acting legally, wasted no time in setting up a police state. To quote Thompson once more:

> Since 1948 a revolution has taken place in South Africa: a reactionary revolution, designed to ensure the survival of the Afrikaner nation, pure and unsullied; and a creeping revolution, which advanced step by step, in due constitutional form, by the enactment of laws, by placing loyal men in key positions, and the silencing of opponents. Its relentless advance toward authoritarianism was marked by changes of leadership, from the ponderous Malan, to the shallow Strijdom, to the inflexible Verwoerd.[3]

The rights of blacks and Coloreds, including the latter's right to vote, were abolished; humiliating pass and residence laws that discriminated against nonwhites were enacted; British officials were forced out of the police and military; existing regulations and new laws were used to harass but not completely silence white opposition; and, in a final revenge for the Boer War, South Africa was withdrawn from the British Commonwealth. A grossly inefficient civil bureaucracy was created as a home for otherwise unemployable members of the Afrikaner tribe, while a chillingly efficient security bureaucracy drew upon the best and brightest of the Boer nation. Spies were infiltrated into even the most secret black organizations, and dazzling commando raids were conducted far from South African borders.

Yet South Africa remained a kind of democracy. Within the white minority, meaningful elections were held, argument was vigorous, power shifted, new faces and ideas came to the fore, parties split, formed, and re-formed. An independent judiciary of Afrikaner judges sometimes ruled against white policemen in favor of black defendants, and an independent white press noted the mistakes and sins of the government. Liberal novelists and journalists, both Afrikaner and British, demanded justice for blacks, and liberal organizations such as the Black Sash aided the black community in matters both practical and political. The security forces, especially the police and the navy, integrated blacks at low and mid-levels. Democracy, even democracy used to protect (though clearly not to empower) blacks, existed within the Afrikaner tribe and the broader white community; it did not exist within the country as a whole.

The Afrikaner police state was at the top of its strength and self-confidence during the three decades that followed the 1948 election. During much of this period, a large minority of Afrikaners—the *verkrampte* nationalists, paranoid and fearful of attack, as all tribal peoples tend to be— probably favored doing away with even the limited democracy of the white community and establishing a totalitarian state devoted to Afrikaner supremacy and security. Most Afrikaners and virtually all of the large British and Jewish communities, however, continued to cling to the ideal and forms of democracy.

Democracy was a tie to Europe, to Western civilization. And, in the final analysis, most South African whites did not want to cut that tie; they wanted to be Europeans. During the 1980s, the *verligte* majority—still conservative, still racist, but increasingly troubled—began to take control and to drive out the most hard-line of the *verkramptes*. The emphasis came to be placed on how to soften rather than how to strengthen apartheid, on how to reach some kind of agreement with the black majority, on how to remain "Western," even if it meant dismantling the police state and detribalizing the Afrikaner people.

It can be argued—and, indeed, it is argued by the fascist right of Afrikanerdom—that the small, hard group of well-armed racists who openly scorn the West and have chosen to fight it out with Africans on Africa's own terms is more in tune with the situation than is the *verligte* white majority. The fascists are not the majority, however, and their eventual defeat is near certain. The South African police state is dying, but this by no means assures the success of the *verligtes*, their black allies and competitors, or the nation as a whole. Apartheid is near dead as an ideology, but nontribal democracy remains a distant dream.

ISRAEL: *HERRENVOLK* DEMOCRACY

Zionism is not a particularly old current in Jewish culture and religion. Indeed, it hardly existed before the 1880s. It came about not because many Jews longed for a homeland in the Middle East—indeed, most displaced Jews then as now preferred the United States over Palestine, and those Jews who were already living in Palestine correctly saw attempts to establish a Jewish state as a threat to their generally good relations with the Arab majority—but because a small but growing minority of European Jews despaired of finding a home in Europe. The Russian pogrom of 1881, following after and followed by many other similar incidents, reminded

Jews that their lives were in constant danger in the East, while the Dreyfus trial of 1894, following after and followed by many other similar incidents, underlined that assimilation was close to impossible in the West.

The early Zionists, even more than the early Afrikaners, who at least had the same religion, had little in common with each other. They were capitalist cronies of the Rothschilds and socialist followers of Marx. They spoke dozens of different languages. They were orthodox and atheist, pacific and pugnacious, Russians with no concept of democracy and Englishmen with no concept of anything else, Ashkenazim and Sephardim. Some demanded their own state; others only wanted a bit of living space in the Ottoman Empire. Some saw Jew and Arab living side by side in socialist harmony; others forecast a war of extermination. Some demanded Jerusalem and dreamed of Eretz Yisrael; others were ready to transform Uganda or Tripoli into the Jewish homeland.

Indeed, about the only thing all the early Zionists had in common was the belief that the Jews needed and deserved a land (not necessarily an independent country) of their own. These early Zionists were under no illusion that Palestine was a "land without people" awaiting a "people without land." Some were brutally realistic in recognizing that the "natives" would have to be driven out. Theodor Herzl, the most important figure in early Zionism, stated: "We shall try to spirit the penniless population across the border by procuring employment for it in transit countries, while denying it any employment in our own country. . . . Both the process of expropriation and the removal of the poor must be carried out discreetly and circumspectly."[4]

The ideology—and the justification for the police state—came slowly as part of the struggle that brought Israel into being. In the 1920s the struggle was, in part, between the largely secular socialist Zionism of the Histadrut and the quasi-fascism of the followers of Vladimir Jabotinsky (whom Ben-Gurion called "Vladimir Hitler") and, in part, between the Jewish settlers and the aroused Palestinian population. In the 1930s and 1940s the struggle was transformed into an effort to save European Jewry and to create an independent state in which Jews would be forever safe, even if it had to be built on the dead bodies of British administrators and Arab peasants.

In the process of building and freeing the state, the Zionists stripped away much of the dreamy idealism of their ideology and gave it a sharper, more brutal edge. The Haganah, the underground Zionist army, was formed, and out of the Haganah came the terrorist Irgun and out of the Irgun came the Lehi or Stern Gang. As millions of Jews were being killed in Europe and as England and the United States refused either to accept large numbers of refugees or to allow them to go to Palestine, Zion's terrorist right wing struck and it continued to lash out even after the war was over. Lord Moyne and Count Bernadotte were assassinated, the King David Hotel was blown up, killing ninety-one people, British railroads and ships were destroyed, some two hundred Arab civilians were slaughtered at Dir Yassin, and so forth. After partition, terror was used as a deliberate mechanism to drive—or scare—much of the Arab population out of all areas seized by the Jews.

Few Zionists or other Jews completely approved of these actions, but most realized that they were necessary if a Jewish state was to be established in an area where Jews were a minority. While mainstream Labor Zionists, now Israelis with their own country, might refuse to shake the hand of a Menachem Begin or a Yitzhak Shamir, they made no demand that the terrorists and their henchmen be brought to trial. Like liberal planters of the antebellum South who despised but still employed brutal overseers, mainstream Zionists knew upon what hard rock their state was built.

Thus came to be established what Meron Benvenisti, the onetime deputy mayor of Jerusalem, has called a *"Herrenvolk* Democracy."* He notes that "in such a system the minority (sometimes even the majority) is disfranchised and deprived of basic civil rights; in contrast, the ruling group enjoys all the attributes of democracy. Such a system should not be confused with a dictatorship. On the contrary, the dominant ethnic group plays by all the rules of democratic freedom, but only that group can benefit from them."[5] Or, as another Israeli official put it, the Palestinians "had never had democracy before. Since they never had it, they never missed it. The separation made it possible to maintain a democratic regime within the Jewish population alone."[6]

Other Zionist thinkers and Israeli patriots were equally clear-sighted as to the nature of the Israeli state. Jacobo Timerman, certainly no stranger to the police state, quotes Jacob Talmon's description of Israel as a "totalitarian democracy." Timerman at one point compares Israel with Great Britain between the wars, which was a democracy at home but a harsh and hated overlord in India and other colonies. At another point, he compares Begin with Juan Perón, who used the "democratic system for undemocratic ends."[7]

Yet Israeli democracy, within its tribal limitations, was real. Indeed, once the state had been secured and a large part of the Palestinian population expelled, there was a turn toward liberalism. The remaining Arabs were given the vote and certain other benefits, to the effect that Israelis could claim with a certain amount of justification that "their" Arabs were better off than those of many Arab countries. Moreover, many Israelis were willing to argue bitterly with their fellow countrymen in favor of justice for Arabs within the country and peace with Arabs outside. Politics were lively, elections were meaningful, and the press was largely free.

Nevertheless, even the most liberal Israelis recognized that they were unwelcome guests in a dangerous world and gave first priority to developing the security bureaucracy. The Haganah was transformed into one of the world's best and largest armies. Mossad and Shin Beth were built upon the old terrorist organizations—Shamir had no trouble finding a home and a career in Mossad—and a near-world-class defense industry was created.

As in South Africa and all the other second-world police states, including the Soviet Union and Nazi Germany, that part of the bureaucracy not directly linked to defense was subordinated to ideology. A rational economic course, such as was followed by the East Asian and Latin American NICs, was never seriously considered. As Bernard Avishai has suggested, Zionism, both before and after statehood, had to be protected from market forces.[8] In order to attract Jewish migrants from Europe or the United States in the absence of a new Hitler, wages and living standards had to be maintained at artificially high levels even if it meant pricing Israeli products out of the international market.

The Israeli armed forces proved themselves once again in the Six-Day War, acquiring at remarkably little cost East Jerusalem and other areas of Palestine that the state had long coveted. Even the most idealistic Israeli could not help feeling pride when, responding to crisis or perceived crisis, he donned the khaki uniform of what was probably the most admired fighting force in the world. He began to think that perhaps Begin was right to herald the "new specimen of Jew . . . the Fighting Jew. . . ." Perhaps the new Jew, who fought more and thought less, was the better man.

The stunning victory of the Six-Day War and the near defeat of the Yom Kippur War combined to put the new Jew firmly in the saddle. The country, feeling alternately omnipotent and in mortal danger, turned sharply to the right. For probably the first time in recent history, ex-terrorists came to rule a major democracy—and the old Labor idealists only shrugged their shoulders. As master of vast new areas and hundreds of thousands of defeated and demoralized Arabs, with an army that had routed all comers with elegant ease, supported ever more strongly in the domestic opinion polls, the new Jew was on a roll. He swaggered into Lebanon and winked at the slaughter in Sabra and Shatila. He spread out onto the West Bank, meting out "collective punishments," destroying villages, shutting schools, tearing up olive trees, guzzling water, expelling peasants and merchants, jailing intellectuals, destroying the economy, glorying in his orders to "break bones."

The new Jew, son of the Maccabees, spiritual heir of Sparta, Rome, and Prussia, protected a society that Jews of the Diaspora found easier to support than to recognize. The new Jew, closer to Rambo than to Spinoza, might be brutal and coarse, but he could protect his people from pogroms and holocausts. The new Jew was very much at home in the second world.

SPAIN: TRANSITION TO THE FIRST WORLD

Spain is one of the few true success stories of the second world. During the past sixty years, it has gone from police state to NIC to first-world democracy. There are reasons to believe that any second- or third-world country that wishes to attain first-world status must follow a similar trajectory—and must have an extraordinary degree of good luck as well.

Unlike the rulers of most police states (Chile's Pinochet is a similar exception), Francisco Franco was a professional soldier who gave little thought to ideology and had no political ambitions. A stolid, self-righteous, unimaginative man without charisma, Franco had nothing in common with Lenin, Hitler, Mussolini, Mao, Castro, or most of the other midwives of revolutionary regimes of the left or right. Under normal conditions, he would have served his time in skilled obscurity, retired with a few small military honors, and died unknown to the larger world. He very possibly would have preferred such a biography.

Franco was not the initial leader of the Nationalist revolt against the Spanish Republic. Rather, he was one of a cabal of conspirators and only assumed command, in true military fashion, when those generals of higher rank were killed or captured. Once victorious, however, he took complete control over all aspects of the Spanish state and, to the extent possible, over all aspects of Spanish society. He accepted no interference, not even from his military colleagues or his totalitarian supporters at home and abroad. His methods were often brutal.

Franco's ideology was nothing more exotic than the conservative Catholicism, the military discipline, and the fervor to maintain Spain's territorial unity that he had been taught in his youth. Although he unselfconsciously called his rule "totalitarian," he was more medieval Spanish than twentieth-century fascist. Indeed, his main quarrel was not with any domestic regime or foreign government, but with the twentieth century itself, which he seemed to consider unacceptably un-Spanish and un-Catholic.

Unlike most second-world leaders who either made up (Hitler) or adapted (Lenin) their ideology as they went along, Franco had no real control over his ideology. As Ramón Arango points out, "The Catholic doctrine that Franco claimed his regime was based on was determined not by Franco in Madrid but by the Pope in Rome. Moreover, according to Franco's belief, the salvation of the soul in the keeping of the church was the primary purpose of human existence, not service to the state—the basic tenet of totalitarianism."[9]

As the war began to shift against the Nazis, Franco had no trouble shifting his stance from pro-Axis neutrality to pro-Allied neutrality. Despite having sent a voluntary air unit to fight on the Russian front in the early days of the war, Franco was never particularly enamored of Hitler, his war, or his racist policies. Indeed, throughout the war, Spain remained the major escape route for Jews and other refugees from Nazi terror.

With the end of World War II and the beginning of the Cold War, Spain, although still a poverty-stricken and politically suspect pariah in Europe, was adopted by the United States. In exchange for basing rights, Washington supplied arms, much-needed funds, and support for United Nations membership. With U.S. troops and U.S. tourists, the twentieth century began to trickle in. Democracy, Protestantism, pornography, contraception, and a thousand other evils oozed out from the bases at Rota and Torrejón and from the beaches of the Costa del Sol and Mallorca. The people of Spain were not unaffected.

Luckily for Spain, Franco was a calculating realist as well as a provincial moralist. Whenever he was faced with overwhelming odds, he would retreat—slowly, carefully, without panic—to new positions already prepared well in advance. If there was no place for dictatorship in Europe in the second half of the twentieth century—and Franco recognized this well ahead of his colleagues in Portugal, Greece, and Eastern Europe—then Spain would have a constitutional king, but only one selected by Franco and only after Franco's death. If medieval Catholic corporatism was more beautiful than viable, then Spain would adopt capitalism, but only a Catholic capitalism designed and administered by the technocrats of the Opus Dei. If Catholicism itself was transformed under John XXIII into something that seemed a travesty of all he had fought for, then Franco would bow his head and accept the Church's discipline for himself and his country. He was only the *caudillo;* he had never claimed to be pope.

Although Franco was never personally sympathetic to capitalism—it was a sordidly selfish philosophy without discipline or nobility, decidedly un-Spanish and un-Catholic—he gave his economic bureaucracy the authority and protection it needed to create the "Spanish Miracle." In so doing—in subordinating ideology to economics rather than vice versa—he transformed Spain from a police state into an NIC. During the 1960s, Spain came to resemble Taiwan or South Korea (if anything, it was less dictatorial) in its authoritarian pragmatism and, for a few years at least, in its economic growth rates.

When Franco died in 1975, Spain was on the threshold of the first world; there was no guarantee, however, that it would or could cross. It could easily have reverted to police-state harshness or even to third-world chaos. (The attempted military coup of 1981 shows that such chaos was at least a possibility.) Most likely it would have remained an NIC, stressing economics and pretending democracy. That it did not reflects Franco's planning and acceptance of democracy—though not in his lifetime—and the new king's position and personality. To quote Arango:

> The complex position of Juan Carlos I serves both to maintain continuity and to break it at the same time, to change Spain fundamentally politically while leaving the centerpiece, the king, untouched. To repudiate the new democratic regime one must repudiate Juan Carlos, and hence both the legacy of Franco, whose heir he is, and the Bourbon dynasty. To accept Juan Carlos, one accepts the new democratic constitution that established him.[10]

The first world, as we have seen, is characterized by a stable equilibrium which is made possible by a partial eclipsing of the political sector, the source of most instability, by the bureaucracy and the private sector. The establishment of democracy weakens the political sector and allows this to happen. The danger for the second-world state in transition is that, without political support, the bureaucracy—economic in the case of an NIC, or security in the case of a police state—will be undermined by the private sector in league with a new political sector. (Brazil is an example that comes readily to mind.) This combination of the freedom-loving private sector with the atavistic power-seeking political sector creates the unstable equilibrium characteristic of the third world.

This did not happen in Spain. Franco did his part by reducing the strong political power he had wielded in favor of the weaker power embedded in democracy. After Franco's death, two very competent prime ministers, aided by Juan Carlos, restrained the private sector with the very real prospect of first-world status if Spain could prove to the rest of the world that such status was warranted. The private sector, ever stronger in both economic and social terms, by and large accepted the restraint. The bureaucracy, no longer Opus Dei but still expert, was allowed to continue managing the country.

It worked. In 1982 Spain was accepted in NATO, and in 1986 it was allowed to join the European Community. Spain had arrived in the first world.[11]

OTHER POLICE STATES

A number of other countries—Syria, Algeria, North Korea, Cuba, Indonesia, and Vietnam, for example—are either clearly or arguably police states, but we have little to gain from considering them at this time. Two additional cases, however, are worth a brief discussion.

Chile may—or may not—be following Spain's route into the first world. Augusto Pinochet, who appears to have many of the same character traits as Franco (and who has stated that Franco is *"mi Dios"*), first created a brutally efficient police state and then presided over its evolution into something resembling an NIC. (Chile is still overly dependent on nonmanufactured exports.) Jonathan Kandell nicely stresses both aspects of the Pinochet legacy when he writes: "Chileans seem reconciled to the reality that the most brutal dictatorship in their history presided over the creation of the soundest economy in Latin America."[12]

After saving Chilean society and government from real or imagined enemies and creating a more modern economy, Pinochet restored democracy. True, Pinochet's cession of power was grudging, partial, and hedged. It was not, however, forced. He ceded government voluntarily because he realized that, as long as he maintained military rule in its pure form, Chile would continue to be shunned by the first world of which it wished to become a part.

It remains to be seen whether Patricio Aylwin, the democratically elected president, and his successor, Eduardo Frei, will be as able in Chile as Adolfo Suárez, Felipe González, and Juan Carlos were in Spain to convince the private sector to allow the economic bureaucracy to continue to manage the country. Without the promise of NATO or E.C. membership, everything rides on the population's view of its long-term interests. This can only be determined over time.

Bureaucracy and civilization were born on territory that is now part of Saddam Hussein's Iraq, and it is fitting that the most efficient bureaucracy in the Middle East, with the possible exception of that of Israel, is that of the Ba'thist Iraqi state. This is not Saddam's doing; Saddam is merely another despotic leader, like all the others who sat on the thrones of Sumer and Babylon, who used the organization of civilization to promote barbarism.

Iraq lost the war, but Saddam (as of this writing), though discredited, is not gone. Much of the country's infrastructure has been destroyed, an embargo and other sanctions are still in effect, massive reparations are being demanded, some Iraqi territory is under what amounts to occupation, and revolt is sputtering in many areas. Iraq is very much in the position of Germany after its defeat in World War I and the signing of the Treaty of Versailles.

As Alfred Chandler has pointed out in his study of U.S., British, and German business, the Germans were able to snap back better than the British after World War I because, in many industries at least, they had the habit of bureaucratic organization.[13] Iraq is showing much the same spirit. Virtually without help or resources—and with the political sector of the government still playing the counterproductive games of leadership—the Iraqi bureaucracy, government and private, is reorganizing and solving problems. Given that Iraq has the habit of bureaucracy in the Weberian (not the third-world) sense, with a new government and some luck, it could become the Middle East's first NIC. We should not forget, however, that despite its spectacular snapback in the 1920s, Germany went on to adopt Hitler and Nazism in the 1930s.

CHAPTER 14

Democracy and the Second World, I

All second-world states—even those that hold meaningful elections—are nondemocratic in that they depend upon force rather than consent for their preservation. The NICs justify their authoritarianism by economic success; the police states, by ideology. Although the constant application of government force against societal counterforce may give the illusion of equilibrium to the second-world state, it is only an illusion.

In general, time is not on the side of the second-world state.

The private sector, eager for present gratification and skeptical of future Utopia, is the agent that undermines the second world. The businessman, the labor leader, the private citizen, the tribesman, the priest, the libertarian, the criminal, the democrat, the malcontent—all those who see their interests circumscribed by those of the government— slowly sap the strength of the regime. In the NICs, the private sector militates for consumption and against investment; in the police states, the private sector militates for democracy and against whatever ideology is used to justify its limitation.

To the extent that the private sector expands at the expense of the bureaucracy, the state risks falling into the third world, where politicians of all stripes but no fixed principles vie with each other for the illusion of power against a background of corruption and nepotism. Ideology dies, the security forces lose competence and confidence, the economy withers, and crime rises. Nothing works. Nationalism is hollowed out as the family, the tribe, and the locality become all important. Private agendas replace public goals.

Such a decline in state power is not an unmitigated disaster. The third world may be—and often is—a step upward from the second world for the average person. What the state loses in power and prestige, the citizen gains in autonomy and scope. One no longer has to fear the secret police, though the threat from the street criminal, who has also gained autonomy and scope, has probably increased. Regimented uniformity enforced by the state is out, but regimented uniformity enforced by one's neighbors, who are also no longer held in check by the state, may well be in. There are no more ideologies worth dying for, but there are a thousand scams worth living for. Connections mean more than the party line, and money will get you everywhere. Parties and politicians proliferate; regimes are unstable; the political class expands; and elections, coups, and revolts keep the elites in circulation. Freedom and inequality, opportunity and insecurity, hope and fear, circle warily.

To the extent that the private sector expands at the expense of the political sector without undermining the bureaucracy—or rather that part of the bureaucracy that conforms to the Weberian definition—the state improves its chances for first-world status. Goals replace enemies. Individuals increase both their freedom and their security. Faceless experts determine policy, while emasculated leaders bask in the glory of name recognition. Politics becomes more and more of a sideshow, whose main function is to legitimize bureaucratic management.

NICS AND THE RISE OF THE MIDDLE CLASS

The emerging middle class constitutes the greatest threat to the NIC political-bureaucratic alliance and to the continuation of the economic success upon which the illusion—and the possibility—of stability is based.

Industrialization and growing wealth seem inevitably to lead to the expansion of the middle class. Economic progress requires and can afford to pay for an increasing number of experts: skilled workers, government and private bureaucrats, merchants, bankers, engineers, educators, health professionals, lawyers, journalists, and the like. This group, which might represent 5 to 10 percent of the population of a stagnant LDC, expands to 30 to 50 percent of the population of a typical NIC. In gross terms, it includes everyone (aside from the 1 to 5 percent of the population that is clearly upper-class) whose income, education, or responsibility puts him or her above the "crowd" in his or her own eyes and in the eyes of others.

For many members of the middle class—with better education, broader horizons, and greater options than others in their society—ideology (usually but not always the ideology of democracy) may begin to take the place of fear, greed, and personal loyalty. It is no longer a question of accepting the country as it is but of trying to make it what it could be. What was good enough for a poor LDC is no longer good enough for an increasingly rich NIC. Old traditions, old methods, and old personalities become suspect. It seems only natural to the middle class that, having gained a greater share of the economic pie, it should also have a greater share of political power. Yet much of the NICs' economic success lies in their governments' ability to put managerial pragmatism ahead of middle-class ideology and to protect bureaucratic expertise from popular pressure. Continued success generally requires that the governments maintain control of the political process.

As the wealth of the middle class increases, both the carrot and the stick become less effective. The businessmen, the skilled workers, the students, and the intellectuals become simultaneously both more selfish and more idealistic. They are no longer grateful for a crust of bread or the opportunity to make a buck. They are no longer influenced by the policeman's club or the bureaucrat's suggestion. The factory owner, believing that the economic miracle was his own doing, scorns the grim general or stodgy government minister who only makes a tenth of his income. The skilled worker, feeling that he has earned higher wages and shorter hours, faces down the undereducated cop who only makes a third of his income. The student and the intellectual, sure that they are better equipped to rule, sneer at past achievement and throw firebombs for a better world.

Students riot, workers strike, businessmen stash their profits in Swiss banks. Wages soar, only to be eroded by accelerating inflation. Savings decline and foreign borrowing increases. Luxury imports play havoc with the balance of trade. Labor discipline dies, quality erodes, and "zero defects" becomes a joke out of the past. Rational management wanes, while "aggressive" leadership waxes. Executives enlarge their offices and their salaries, even as their balance sheets deteriorate. Politicians, having seen the light of democracy, renounce their authoritarian past and buy votes with massive spending projects and lavish promises. Present gratification eclipses future security, speculation undermines all markets, and corruption becomes the leading growth industry.

When the storm has passed, the middle class, impoverished now but still middle-class (there are some things that can never be taken away), looks around and finds itself becalmed on a broad and heavy raft going nowhere.[1] It wonders whatever happened to the economic miracle.

This model—or prophecy—of a prosperous state done in by its middle class is loosely based on the experience of Argentina, which ended some seventy years of lightly authoritarian political stability and rapid economic progress (which brought it to the very portals of the first world) in about 1930. The sixty or so years since then have been characterized by harsh authoritarianism alternating with near anarchy, by ideological expansion and economic decline, and by the steady growth of what was already in 1930 the third world's largest and most influential middle class.[2]

The Argentine disease has two major symptoms: protectionism and ideological discontent. The Argentine middle class expanded in size and power under protectionism, and it needed continued protectionism to maintain its standard of living. The middle class—which, in the Argentine case, includes skilled labor—was subsidized at the expense of the rest of the economy, and eventually such subsidies came close to destroying not only the economy but also middle-class standards of living. In this situation, rampant "relative deprivation" gave rise to ideological discontent. No sooner was a democratic government installed than the middle class clamored for authoritarian leadership; and no sooner was a military government in power than it screamed for democracy. The middle class, proudly independent, gave no government or policy the benefit of the doubt.

Although all of the six modern NICs show some signs of the Argentine disease, the Argentine fate is not the only possible one. (Indeed, Argentina itself, under Carlos Saúl Menem, is showing signs of a cure.)

THE FUTURE OF THE NICS

The continued progress of the NICs is by no means assured. All face political and social threats at a time when the global economic climate is much less benign than in the past. Around the world, protectionism is growing, economic growth is slowing, and competition for both markets and funds is rising. Increasingly the NICs are squeezed between first-world states intent upon monopolizing the high-technology market and ambitious, low-wage would-be NICs such as Thailand and Malaysia intent upon taking over the low- and medium-technology markets.

At home, wage rates are soaring and domestic firms are going offshore —often to future rivals such as the aforementioned Thailand and Malaysia.

Income inequality is beginning to increase even in such egalitarian paradises as Taiwan and South Korea. Unemployment is on the rise and the streets are no longer safe. The air is unbreathable and the water is undrinkable. Xenophobia and scapegoating are in vogue. Populism and demagoguery are edging into the political process. The middle class has never been more powerful and never felt itself more under siege.

Within this new, more dangerous world climate, Mexico and Taiwan stand the best chance of following Spain into the first world. These two countries have done the best job of combining continued bureaucratic authority in the economic sphere with increased regime legitimacy. Brazil and South Korea, by striving too hard for democracy, may have undermined both bureaucratic authority and regime legitimacy. Singapore and Hong Kong are each in a special position—with special dangers and, perhaps, special opportunities.

The dangers faced—and largely overcome—by Mexico and Taiwan were dangers of ideology. In the case of Mexico, the discovery of huge amounts of oil under the jungles of Tabasco and the seas of the Bay of Campeche in the early 1970s allowed Presidents Luis Echeverría and José López Portillo to begin to fulfill the collectivist promises of the Mexican Revolution. In the case of Taiwan, the death of Chiang Ching-kuo loosed the ideologues of both the "One China" mainlanders and the "Taiwan for the Taiwanese" islanders. Although government control was never threatened in either case, regime popularity declined and, especially in the case of Mexico, economy-threatening measures were undertaken in an effort to regain support.

In the late 1970s Mexico went into an economic slump that lasted for well over a decade. The PRI, which had been able to hold the allegiance of the urban and rural poor for generations through a combination of Tammany-style patronage and rapid economic growth, saw its popularity fall through the floor once it began to keep its Revolutionary promises. The real losses, however, were among the middle class, which split: political idealists flocked to a stodgy but honest old-line party of the right, while social idealists moved to a chaotic and self-contradictory conglomeration on the left. The PRI, which could do no wrong as long as the economy went from strength to strength, lost all credibility and came close to losing control when it gained a social conscience.[3]

The twelve-year lurch to the left under Echeverría and López Portillo destroyed the Mexican public's enthusiasm for statist solutions even as it brought the reputation of the PRI and that of the Mexican political system to their nadir. Although the economic course was reversed by Miguel de la Madrid in 1982, the economy and the popularity of the system continued to decline. Nevertheless, the system held together, and Carlos Salinas, de la Madrid's appointed candidate, took office with the customary dictatorial powers.

In a number of daring strokes, Salinas made full use of those powers against a range of enemies and problems. Alternating the roles of *caudillo* and chief bureaucrat, Salinas increased his power at the expense of rivals within the system even as he turned seventy years of Revolutionary rhetoric and practice on their head. Age-old problems were addressed in new and daring ways. And, even before the economy revived, the popularity of the presidency soared. The possibility of entering the first world, made more real by the North American Free Trade Agreement (which is playing much the same role that the European Community played in the Spanish case), has made the Mexican population—even the Mexican middle class —see harsh economic measures as stepping-stones to modernization rather than as impositions on the popular will.

The political evolution of Taiwan is, perhaps, not as far advanced as that of Mexico. Nevertheless, as in Mexico, an old ideology—honored but little used—is rapidly being overturned. As the government makes it ever more clear that political union with the mainland is no longer on the agenda, regime legitimacy and popularity are strengthened. The old-line mainland ideologues, though still fighting, are on the verge of extinction, and an increasingly democratic KMT is becoming the government of the island and nothing more. Conflict remains, but it is a first-world sort of conflict with little relevance to vital issues.

In terms of economics, Taiwan is far ahead of Mexico. This, however, may be a dubious benefit. Whereas the Mexican economy has plenty of room left for expansion, Taiwan's high wage rates are pricing it out of the low- and medium-technology markets at a time when it is not yet competitive in high-technology markets. Nevertheless, even more than in Mexico, the economic technocrats remain in control; while democracy has eroded the power of the bureaucracy's authoritarian political protectors, it has also shifted attention away from basic policy to lesser issues. To the extent that Taiwan's economic problems can be solved, the island's able bureaucracy should be able to do so without public interference.

The position of Brazil and South Korea is not so promising. These onetime military national-security states have not yet achieved political and economic consensus. Unlike states with dominant civilian parties such as Mexico and Taiwan and, for that matter, Japan, the military states were transitory by design. By their own "custodial" ideology, they were forced to return to democracy once they had "saved" the nation. They were lame ducks from the very beginning in that both the generals and their civilian opponents expected an eventual return to a somewhat reformed "business as usual." Thus, their opening to democracy was almost entirely at the expense of the bureaucracy and not at all at the expense of the political sector (though certainly at the expense of the formerly dominant military politicians).

Unlike first-world political conflict—sound and fury, signifying very little—the multisided political battles now being fought in Brazil and Korea are crucially important for the economic and political futures of the two nations. In a sense, the very fact that they are being fought at this late date means that, from the point of view of the good of the nation, they will probably be lost. There is no way a nation can enter the first world without general agreement as to the parameters within which political and economic policy will be made. Even the best bureaucrats can only mark time until the leaders finish their hormonal combat and slink back into the cave. Long before that time, the miracle may well be dead and the country back in the third world.

The Argentine disease, which snatches defeat from the jaws of victory, is much more advanced in Brazil than in South Korea because of the age and importance of the Brazilian middle class. The Korean middle class is largely a result of the miracle, while the Brazilian middle class preceded the miracle. Thus, the Koreans tend to think in terms of economics and are still somewhat reluctant to jeopardize economic progress—their claim to fame—as they agitate for political and social change. For most of the Brazilian middle class, however, the miracle is foreign, suspect, not of its doing, something the generals cooked up when they weren't torturing people. The Brazilians think in terms of politics, connections, individuality, agility, *jeito,* and the deal. Discipline and expertise, even in the economic area, stink of the barracks.

The future of Hong Kong and Singapore will depend upon the extent to which they control, rather than are controlled by, their hinterlands. Hong Kong, because it will revert to Communist China in 1997, is already losing some of its human capital and commercial dynamism. Singapore, having deliberately raised wages in an effort to reorient its manufacturing away from low-technology, low-value-added products, now increasingly depends upon associated factories in Malaysia and Indonesia. If everything goes right, both Hong Kong and Singapore may be able to transform themselves into leaders of subnational and transnational super-NICs. Such an outlook is made more problematic, however, by the necessity of sharing political authority with Beijing, Kuala Lumpur, and Djakarta.

The NICs remain the success stories of the second and third worlds. It seems probable that no nation can achieve first-world status and stability except by serving time as an authoritarian newly industrialized country. Most NICs, however, will not rise to the first world. Some, with wise political leaders and skilled economic bureaucrats, may be able to repeat the miracle year after year and thereby remain in the second world. Others will succumb to the Argentine disease and find themselves middle-class societies trapped in third-world economies.

CHAPTER 15

Democracy and the Second World, II

IDEOLOGY AND WORLD OPINION

I f economic success, the rock upon which the NIC is built, is vulnerable, ideology, the basis of the police state, is even more vulnerable.

An ideology, to survive as anything more than a fossil, must triumph. An ideology that is not in a position to shape world opinion will, in time, be itself shaped by world opinion. One generation or perhaps two can, with heroic idealism, hold out against the world, but as the years pass, a decent respect to the opinions of mankind comes into play. Even the most steadfast of true believers begins to doubt a cause that all the world scorns. And, once the virus of doubt is introduced, it can only be suppressed, never eliminated.

In some cases the hollow form may remain—may even be honored— long after the ideology is dead. Monarchs persist in Europe despite the almost universal rejection of kingly rule. The Congregationalist, Presbyterian, and Dutch Reformed churches continue as viable organizations, though their memberships have long ago dropped most of the Calvinist dogmas upon which they were founded. The YMCA, still thriving, is now more attuned to exercise freaks than to would-be Christians.

In other cases, organization and ideology collapse together. The Inquisition and the ideology of the Inquisition died as one. The ideology of American slavery, though not of racism, collapsed with Lee's surrender.

Nazism did not survive the death of Hitler, nor did Italian fascism outlive Mussolini. Although the hidden erosion of Marxism preceded the Marxist *Götterdämmerung,* the open rejection of Marxist truths had to await, and accompany, the dominolike fall of the Communist states.

In all of these cases, the failure is not of courage, but of certainty. Although the individual may still be willing to die for the cause, he is less eager to kill. He no longer seeks to convince the unbelievers through argument but, uncertain of the strength of his own belief, seeks to avoid argument lest he be shaken by some undeniable proof. Slowly he begins to ask himself if it is logical that only he and his comrades are right and all the rest of the world is wrong. Sometimes he tries to stop thinking entirely, hoping that his own personal Masada or Alamo will be overrun while he can still see himself as a beleaguered hero and not as a credulous dupe.

The leaders, the ideological professionals, are often the first to sense the weaknesses of their creed.[1] While the average citizen may complain of this or that politician or this or that policy, he is not likely to question the ideological basis of his system before the process of decay is well advanced. The average citizen, preoccupied with his own affairs, assumes that the leaders must have answers for the criticisms of the world. But it is the leaders, the politicians, the party members, the high bureaucrats, the people in a position to know, who are the first to suspect—and often the first to admit—that the criticisms of the world cannot be answered.

THE DECLINE AND FALL OF THE USSR

In 1968, when Samuel P. Huntington published his *Political Order in Changing Societies,* he was able to write that "Communist totalitarian states and Western liberal states both belong generally in the category of effective rather than debile political systems" and that the systems of both groups of countries embody "consensus, community, legitimacy, organization, effectiveness, stability."[2] He contrasted these effective governments of the North with the ineffective governments of the third world.

By the end of the 1980s the legitimacy and stability of the Communist countries were much less apparent. In the Soviet Union, Mikhail Gorbachev saw what Huntington could not have seen twenty years earlier: that his country was little more than an incoherent assembly of browbeaten citizens, angry consumers, disillusioned ideologues, and rebellious nationalities. Long before most others either inside or outside the Communist world, Gorbachev understood that he ruled over a Potemkin Village, which looked powerful and stable from the outside but, in truth, had nothing behind it.

When Lenin died in 1924, Communism was already dying as an ideology in the Soviet Union, though it continued to thrive as a religion in the West. Indeed, many of the most ideologically committed Communists would themselves soon be dead or in exile. But the police state that Lenin had bequeathed to Stalin was firmly established, and thus ideology was no longer as necessary. When ideology was once again necessary—to meet the challenge of Hitler's invasion—it was nationalism rather than Communism that united the country.

The glorious Soviet victory over the Germans and the rapid expansion of Soviet power into Europe and Asia further supported Russian nationalism and transformed it into imperialism. Although nationalism was clearly the motivating force, tactics (and perhaps a degree of sloppy thinking) dictated that many of the symbols of Communist internationalism be maintained as moral justification for aggression. The average Russian took pride in the fact that Russia was the leader of half the world, and he didn't care whether it came about under czars or commissars.

But the half-life of any ideology—even nationalism—is short. Another generation passed, and the average Russian began to think more about the inadequacies of his life and less about the glories of Mother Russia. He began to compare his country with those of the West less in terms of throw weight and barrels of oil per day and more in terms of protein and floor space. The police state was as strong as ever, but the good life remained on the other side of an ever-receding horizon. The average Russian, who never even considered revolt, began to strike back through petty theft, through the black market, through absenteeism, through drunkenness. The bureaucracy began to be "privatized" through corruption, and small patron-client networks began to flourish in typical third-world fashion. Economic growth, which had been remarkable for many years after the war, slowed, infrastructure deteriorated, and the quality of life eroded.

The police state was as strong as ever, but the nation was going backward. There would be no more sputniks, no more Moscow subways, no more glorious advances either overseas or at home. The army that had defeated the Wehrmacht and long held the combined forces of the West at bay was being humiliated by a handful of guerrillas in Afghanistan. The lines were getting longer and the payoffs fewer. Things were bad today and would be worse tomorrow. No one was thinking about revolt, but the nation was going backward and both the people and the leadership knew it.

At the same time, the world outside the Soviet Union was entering a new age. Science and technology were advancing so rapidly that Soviet accomplishments—crude nuclear weapons, primitive computers, unsophisticated rockets—had the ring of oxymorons. If the Soviet economy and scientific establishment could not keep up with those of the United States, how could the country hope to keep up militarily or politically? If the Soviet economy was also falling behind those of Japan, Germany, France, and even Korea, how long could the USSR remain a superpower? What would it cost to catch up? What would it cost not to catch up?

Gorbachev was no slave to Marxist dogma—indeed, at the highest ranks of the party and state, true believers had become relatively rare—but he was a Soviet patriot. He gambled that, by junking much of the old Communist ideology, he could put the country into position to maintain superpower status into the next century. So, following the grand Russian tradition of Peter the Great and Alexander II, he attempted a revolution from above. Turning his back on Marx and Lenin, he began a forced march into capitalism and democracy.

He faced remarkably little *ideological* opposition. Those Russians who opposed him, whether leaders or private citizens, did so not because they were convinced of the ideological superiority of Communism, but because they feared that the resulting instability would do great harm to the country, to their own personal futures, or to both. They did not deny that the edifice was unsound; they only demanded to know where they would live if Gorbachev pulled it down around their ears. Gorbachev eventually came to see that they had a point.

Gorbachev, as a political professional, better understood the weaknesses of the Communist political system than those of the Communist economic system. He assumed that if the Communist political structure were dismantled and democracy were allowed to reign, the economy would automatically come to resemble Western consumer economies after a few years. The imposition of democracy upon a command economy, however, far from producing an orderly transition to market-based prosperity, produced chaos and misery.

Political and economic order began to erode. The people used the freedom that Gorbachev had given them to denounce him for destroying the tenuous economic well-being that they had enjoyed under the old dispensation. Hunger, of the type that the Soviet Union had not known for over forty years, seemed a real possibility. Moreover, the nationalities were in revolt—and Gorbachev, who had been able to throw off Communism without a second thought, remained a Great Russian nationalist. No more than Lincoln was he willing to see a great nation split asunder. A turn back to the authoritarian right seemed inevitable.

Yet it was too late to turn back, even as it remained too dangerous to go on. Gorbachev zigged and zagged, while his country crumbled and his popularity, even in the West, declined. A halfhearted military coup, led by tired right-wingers who had no more belief in the future of Communism than did Gorbachev himself, sputtered and failed. Boris Yeltsin, showing signs of becoming the Soviet Fujimori, rose to the top on a surge of people power. The center could not hold. The nationalities withdrew, one by one, unopposed. The USSR was no more.

In place of the world's second most powerful state, we have a collection of squabbling third-world countries. While some have nuclear weapons, none are superpowers. Some are more viable than others, some are more democratic, some are more peaceable. It will be years, if ever, before any of these states again play a truly important role on the world stage. The greatest empire the East had ever known is now one with Nineveh and Tyre!

CHINA AND THE BLOC

In some ways, Gorbachev was a kinder, gentler version of Chairman Mao. Each leader was instrumental in destroying the Communist system in his country. And each may have believed, in some hazy way, that he was trying to save the system through radical but necessary change. In truth, however, the Russian patriot was trying to save the Great Russian Empire, while the Chinese sociopath was trying to save the revolutionary process. Although both claimed to be Communist, Gorbachev had long since lost his faith and Mao had probably never believed in anything that would have been recognized by Marx or Lenin.

China, with its Middle Kingdom conceit, is one of the least ideological of nations. The party cadres, the companions from the Long March upon whom Mao had unleashed the Cultural Revolution, had little more reverence for received Marxism than had Mao himself. Far from being a religion, Communism was for most only a tool that, once adapted to local conditions, could be used to seize power and effect change. And, after the party bureaucracy had been popularly discredited and physically decimated by Mao's hordes of bloody-handed children, it was a very blunt tool indeed.

Even in Mao's lifetime, the "socialist imperialism" of the Soviet Union came to be seen as a greater threat than the capitalism of the United States. After Mao's death and the rise of Deng Xiaoping to power in 1978,

Communism was dropped in everything but name. Suddenly, "To get rich is glorious!" and the "Four Modernizations" replaced class conflict. The United States was a friend, Vietnam was an enemy, foreign investment was welcomed, and a stock market opened in Shanghai.

Red China was fast becoming an NIC. In the words of Fairbank: "In the 1980's China moved toward a mixed bureaucratic-command and market system. Japan, South Korea, and Taiwan had all done this. . . . Reliance on market forces to spur competition and productivity was part of China's new industrial strategy."[3] And NIC-like economic reform was rewarded with an NIC-like explosion of output and exports. A new economic power—potentially bigger than Taiwan, Korea, or even Japan—seemed to be shaking itself awake.

But that was not to be—at least, not immediately. China's evolution as an NIC was aborted by middle-class assertiveness, by fear, and by the old "hydraulic" imperative toward centralization. Deng's reforms, which had benefited industrious peasants and rural entrepreneurs first and foremost, were resented by the educated Communist middle class. These men and women, the spiritual heirs of the old Confucian bureaucracy, felt that there was something basically wrong with a system in which an illiterate farmer could earn more than a university scholar and a street-corner vendor could have a higher standard of living than a midlevel party official.

Moreover, while the economy grew, inequality increased and corruption burgeoned. Certain, mainly coastal, provinces roared ahead while others stagnated. As the command economy gave way to the market, provincial and industrial hoarding increased. Some (largely state-owned) industries were starved for raw materials and were forced to lay off workers, while some (largely private) firms exported those same raw materials at a handsome profit. Crime and inflation soared, along with the number of Red millionaires. Bribery was a necessary cost of doing business in both the state and private sectors, and the sons and daughters of high officials—the *gaoganzidi* or "cadre kids"—were widely believed to profit from ever-increasing levels of corruption.

These myriad resentments converged bloodily in Tiananmen Square in 1989. The ideology of Communism was never an issue; it was already dead for all concerned. The middle-class students—milling around, shouting insults at high officials, drunk on their own audacity, singing the "Internationale," building a replica of the Statue of Liberty—thought they wanted democracy, when all they really wanted was a return to some of the certainties and privileges they thought were their due. The aging leadership—spouting dusty Marxist slogans that they hadn't used in years, seeing a sinister foreign hand behind every TV camera, feeling cornered by events in the USSR and Eastern Europe, suspicious of each other, not fully trusting their own security forces—feared that the country was coming apart, that a new Cultural Revolution was in the offing, that the Mandate of Heaven was about to be lifted.

The conservative autocoup that failed in Moscow in 1991 was successful in Beijing in 1989. The clock was turned back, and reform appeared to have been stopped in its tracks. But the story is not yet over. The aged Deng still strives with consummate skill to unite political authority with economic liberty to achieve NIC-like prosperity. The old guard is dying, the provinces are becoming more assertive, Hong Kong looms on the horizon, a second stock market has opened, and some sectors of the economy are still in the midst of a capitalist boom. Though far from assured, the future appears brighter for China than for the Commonwealth of Independent States.

The rest of the former Communist bloc is slowly reverting to its pre-Marxist destiny. In some cases it is as if the twentieth century had never happened. Vietnam, having lost its Soviet protector, risks becoming a satellite of its old overlord, China. Ethiopia, Angola, and Mozambique have returned to Africa. Cuba's Castro continues to rule his increasingly miserable island through a mixture of charisma and terror more typical of a nineteenth-century Latin American dictator like Paraguay's Solano López than of a twentieth-century Marxist revolutionary. The Sandinista army, once an effective tool of the Nicaraguan government, is now just another corrupt and power-hungry group of armed men who answer only to themselves.

The once captive states of Eastern Europe appear to have learned nothing and forgotten nothing. Yugoslavia has dissolved in a bitter tribal war. Rumania persecutes ethnic Hungarians and totters on the edge of Iron Guard-like dictatorship. Bulgaria has revived its age-old war with its Turkish minority. Czechoslovakia has split, Hungary shows some signs of renewing its vocation for decadence, and Poland finds a reactionary and very political Church ready and willing to guide it back to the Middle Ages.

The immediate prospects of most of these countries are poor. Sometime in the future, with a lot of luck and a period of enlightened authoritarian rule, countries such as Hungary, the Czech Republic, Estonia, Slovenia, Vietnam, and Cuba may achieve NIC status. Poland may thrive for a period with massive Western aid. Rumania and Bulgaria may or may not be able to re-create the non-Communist police state. Most of the others, never having been truly a part of the second world, will remain in the third. In the more distant future, the more Westernized of the East European states may find a place in a vastly expanded European Community.

THE TRIBAL DEMOCRACIES

The Afrikaners, after having faced down the civilized world for almost forty years, have blinked. More and more explicitly, the majority of Afrikaners have chosen to define themselves not by their language, history, and skin color, but by the territory in which they live. They have made the conscious, political decision to cease being Afrikaners and to become South Africans. They hope, of course, that they will somehow as individuals continue to have a privileged position in a new, first-world, multiracial, democratic South Africa. This, however, is only what they hope, not what they expect.

The decision to move beyond the racially limited democracy of the white tribe to the more inclusive democracy that characterizes the first world has not been an easy one. The Afrikaners had been reasonably secure in their police state. World Communism was in such obvious decline that even the most paranoid of Afrikaners found it difficult to maintain the illusion of vulnerability. The so-called Front-Line States, never very serious in their stand against racist South Africa, were fast giving up even the pretense of opposition. Domestic terrorism—the odd bomb—was hardly even an inconvenience. True, the economy was in a mess and getting worse, but still the average white South African lived as well as or better than his counterpart in Europe, Australia, or the United States.

And the Afrikaners stood to lose much that they considered important. If they did not preserve their language, their culture, their history, their "covenant" with God—in a word, their tribal identity—no one else would. Without a scrap of land to call totally their own, they would have less future than England's Welsh or France's Bretons. In fifty or a hundred years, their blood would be thoroughly mixed with that of other Europeans, in Africa or elsewhere; their vibrant, living tongue would be as dead as Latin; their tales of *voortrekkers* and Boer War heroes would have less connection with living persons than Homer's epics. By moving beyond the tribe, they were willing their own ethnocide.

Yet, having a decent respect to the opinions of mankind, a majority of the white tribe decided to detribalize, to join twentieth-century Western civilization. The Afrikaners' belief that they were doing the West's work in protecting southern Africa from Communism had been hard to keep up in the face of near-universal Western scorn for the apartheid state. Political and economic sanctions, sports restrictions (especially), speeches in the

U.N., books, plays, newspaper articles, had all had their psychological effect. Well before the advent of F. W. de Klerk, Afrikaner leaders and laymen had been quietly looking for a way out. When de Klerk made his move, they were ready to follow.

Despite the goodwill, heroism, and intelligence of men like de Klerk and Nelson Mandela, despite substantial support from the West, the South African experiment with universal democracy may well fail. Tribalism is far from dead. Afrikaner police are increasingly forced to use lethal force on their brothers of the fascist right. Zulus and Xhosas, who a few years back were playing down their tribal differences in order to present a solid front against the white establishment, are now retribalizing to slaughter each other. Crime is pandemic, and apolitical youth is on a bloody rampage. Atavistic Marxism is alive and well, and demands for "economic democracy" threaten to destroy Africa's strongest economy. "One man, one vote" is seen by many whites and blacks alike as a code word for dictatorship of the majority. Success, though not impossible, is far from inevitable.

If South Africa is deemphasizing tribalism to emphasize democracy, Israel—the world's other major tribal democracy—is deemphasizing democracy to emphasize tribalism. The idea of a nontribal Israel—a secular democratic state in which all people would be equal without regard to race or religion, in which the Law of Return would have gone the way of John Adams's Alien and Sedition Acts—is anathema even to liberal Israelis. If white South Africa is risking its Afrikaner identity in a possibly futile attempt to join twentieth-century Western civilization, Israel is resolutely reaffirming the centrality of its Jewish identity even at the cost of maintaining a system that looks suspiciously like apartheid.

Israel may have little choice. The Palestinians, and to a lesser extent the other Arabs, are unlikely ever to agree to a lasting peace with the Jewish state. They recognize that they may not prevail, but they will not give up their grievance.[4] Despite PLO recognition of Israel, the Palestinians as a group are unlikely to be coaxed into a long-term peace by even the most liberal schemes of Israeli doves. And they will not be frightened into peace by even the most Draconian schemes of Israeli hard-liners. Thus the *intifada,* though it may sputter, is unlikely to die as long as any Palestinians remain under Israeli rule. The *Herrenvolk* democratic police state is not a stage, it is Israel's unchangeable destiny.

Yet even this course is fraught with danger. Israel, using its own resources, cannot support either its world-class military establishment or its first-world lifestyle. But if it were to lose either of these two elements, its continued existence would be jeopardized. The military is needed to keep the Arab world at bay, and the subsidized lifestyle is needed to keep

Israelis in Israel. Thus, Israel will continue to depend on the charity of foreign governments and of the world Jewish community. And, like the *Herrenvolk* democratic police state, this is not a stage, it is Israel's unchangeable destiny.

It is an open question whether foreign funding will continue to be provided in adequate amounts. The increased publicity given to Israeli police-state methods, the end of Israel's strategic utility to the West, and the emergence of severe economic problems within the first world could in time undermine the willingness of both governments and private groups to maintain open-ended support. Moreover, the beginnings of a peace agreement will be used by some nations as an excuse to shift aid to other, more needy recipients. After all, even the Crusaders eventually lost their backing.

THE CONTINUING FUNCTION OF THE SECOND WORLD

The second world will remain a slippery stepping-stone between the third world and the first. The third world, though often stable, is essentially ungovernable. It exists, a tangle of private and political relationships, a can of worms, a pudding without a theme. Many authoritarian leaders may try to give direction in this or that third-world state. Some few may succeed and thereby usher their states into the second world.

Often the impulse to effective rule will be ideological. Indeed, in those rare cases, such as Nazi Germany, in which first-world states choose second-world status, the impulse is always ideological. During most of this century, varying forms of Marxism and nationalism constituted the main ideologies. Now Marxism is dead and nationalism, while retaining its ability to create violence in Eastern Europe and elsewhere, is losing much of its effectiveness as a basis for authoritarian government. As the century draws to a close, only Islamic fundamentalism—which, like Christian, Jewish, and Hindu fundamentalism, has recently acquired a new popularity—retains that effectiveness.

Religious ideology, however, tends to work in cycles. Islamic fundamentalism has waxed mightily in Iran and now is waning. The movement remains strong in Egypt, Algeria, Tunisia, Jordan, Lebanon, and many other parts of the Islamic world, but it seems unlikely to revolutionize many if any of these states. It may well die out as a political movement over the next few decades only to rise again sometime beyond 2050. In the meantime, secular nationalistic police states on the model of Hafiz al-Assad's Syria or Pinochet's Chile will continue to pop up from time to time around the world.

Some of these ideological police states, like Franco's Spain, may develop into NICs. Most NICs, however, will very quickly pass through, or even entirely avoid, the ideological stage. Many of these NICs will evolve under military governments, if only because in most third-world states the military is the sole institution, if indeed there is any institution, with the structure and some of the goal orientation of the Weberian bureaucracy.

In time, in the most economically successful of the NICs, the authoritarian political sector, having served its function of protecting the economic bureaucracy from private pressures, may wither away like Marx's state. At that point, the second-world state has passed into the first world. Power—the ability to achieve goals—is now shared between the bureaucracy and the private sector. In this uneasy partnership, the bureaucracy creates progress while the private sector maintains freedom. Both look back over their shoulders at the still posturing political leaders, so essential in the second world and so marginal in the first.

PART THREE

The Dilemma of the Third World

The third-world state is little more than a platform for squabbling private-sector groups. Like a large raft adrift, it is roomy enough to accommodate geniuses, heroes, and villains, and—under normal conditions—it is stable enough to give them all elbowroom. It is, however, impossible to steer. Its helmsman is pure politician—without the power to *do* anything, but with the happy knowledge that he has dominated all his rivals.

Severe political instability, which is relatively rare in the third world, allows the possibility of fruitful change at frightful cost. The costs, however, are more certain than the fruits.

CHAPTER 16

The Nature of the
Third World

The rational bureaucracies that do so much to homogenize the first and second worlds are largely absent from the third. This gives greater scope to the extended families and subnational groups—regions, tribes, clans, castes, religious sects, and patron-client complexes—that constitute the private sector. And this, in turn, makes for a magnificent diversity. Indeed, third-world countries encompass the extremes of poverty and plenty, culture and barbarism, democracy and tyranny. The third-world state is almost always less than the sum of its often spectacular parts.

Third-world subnational groups, while sometimes paying lip service to nationalism, are themselves superior to the nation. The nation, far from being a unifying factor, is booty, the prize in a zero-sum game to be seized by one subnational group and held against all others. To the extent that a national political class—most often the army and most often in the wake of numbing political and social crisis—is able to separate itself from subnational groups, the way is open to the second world.

T he very name "third world" implies a first-world perspective. There is something dismissive about the term. The first world is the eye, the ego, the protagonist, the hero. The second world—whether the Soviets with their missiles or the Koreans with their VCRs—is the threat, the antagonist, the other, the actual or potential villain. The third world is background or battleground, a bit player, essentially unimportant, fit only to swell a progress, start a scene or two.

The first-world eye, looking out upon the third world, sees only what it wants to see or what a priori theory or Eurocentric myth has led it to expect. The Northern liberal sees pervasive class war, noble peasants, brutal landowners, bemedaled generals, rapacious multinationals, heroic liberation priests. The Northern conservative sees leftist subversion, corrupt socialist governments, drug lords, terrorists, religious fanatics, ignorant and lazy populations. Both agree that the third world, unlike the more sophisticated first and second worlds, is a region of stark blacks and whites, heroes and villains.

Both liberals and conservatives see the third world as something qualitatively different, alien, exotic. Both think that an election stolen in Managua is qualitatively different from an election stolen in Chicago, that corruption in Karachi or Riyadh is different from corruption in Tokyo or New York, that police brutality in Algiers or Lima is different from police brutality in Los Angeles or Marseilles, that nuclear weapons in the hands of Indians or Arabs are different from nuclear weapons in the hands of French or Chinese, that the assassination of an Egyptian president is different from the assassination of an American president.

The liberal sees the third world as an opportunity to feel good about himself, while the conservative sees it as an opportunity to feel good about his bankbook or his bases. The liberal—the heir of the heroic and myopic missionaries of the nineteenth century—wants to ally himself with "democratic forces," and, if they do not exist, he pretends that they do. He wants to re-create an idealized version of the first world on third-world territory. The liberal knows that deep down in every third-world peasant there is a socially aware Connecticut suburbanite aching to get out. The conservative, more selfish but less arrogant, is more inclined to exploit foreign cultures for his own benefit or security than to try to remake them in *his* own image for *their* own good. The clever third-world leader is well positioned to use both the greed of the conservative and the missionary spirit of the liberal for his own purposes.

The educated and, to a large extent, even the uneducated third-world observer, looking at the first world, does so with considerably more knowledge and understanding than does his Northern counterpart looking south. The schoolchild in Bombay or Buenos Aires knows U.S. and European history and geography as well as his own. He sees American movies and listens to American music. He knows as much about Superman and George Washington as about Lord Ram or San Martín. His teacher reads newspapers filled with detailed and largely accurate accounts of first-world politics and culture. His uncle down the street worked for twenty years in Manchester or Detroit.

Yet the view from the South is also distorted. On the one hand, there are hordes of what the Mexicans call *malinchistas,* for whom everything foreign is superior to everything native and heaven is a job in Los Angeles.[1] In many less developed countries, much of the rising middle class and even more of the stagnant poor are confirmed *malinchistas.* On the other hand, any third-world country also has large numbers of what one might call *arielista* intellectuals, for whom the first world—and especially the United States—is at the same time an impotent paper tiger and the source of all evil.[2]

No LDC asked to be ranked third, and no LDC agrees with that ranking. The world has no preordained center. Every man is his own protagonist and the eye, whether clear or clouded, has as much right to look north as south.

THE GREEK PARADIGM

The tribe, with its essential egalitarianism, its Darwinian leadership, and its lack of specialization, exemplifies the third-world state at its most basic. The civilizing leg of the triad, the bureaucracy, is rudimentary or even missing, leaving the freedom-loving but calculating private sector in uneasy union with the aggressive and often paranoid leadership. The private sector—the members of the tribe—almost always dominates the union. In this primitive parliament, a leadership-toppling vote of no confidence can come at any time, for any reason.

The tribe, if it is to evolve, will usually do so in one of two ways. In some cases, religious evolution leads to the development of a strong priestly bureaucracy, which, in turn, supports—indeed, creates—a strong and relatively secure political dynasty. In other cases the accidental appearance of a series of unusually capable tribal leaders establishes a tribal kingdom—a "robber state"—strong enough to appropriate the trappings of civilization while avoiding its bureaucratic essence. The city-states of the Nile and the Tigris-Euphrates, which developed into second-world empires, are examples of the first; the more tribal city-states of Greece are examples of the second.

Ancient Greece is indeed an illustration of the third world at its violent and creative best. The Bronze Age city-states of Crete and Mycenae, which constituted the foundations of Greek culture, were almost certainly bureaucratic-political states on the Egyptian or Asian model. Had they been allowed to evolve normally, Greece would probably have ended up as a second-world empire. That was not to be, however. Around 1200 B.C., the Dorian Greeks began their massive migration out of the Balkans, over-running, destroying, and partially absorbing the civilization that they found.

These Dorian invaders, long on hormonal leadership and iron weapons and short on everything else, established a very different type of city-state. Although it superficially resembled the city-state of the earlier era, it was in reality little more than a settled war party. It was made up of quarrel-some leaders and quarrelsome followers. It had culture but no civilization. The addition of slavery, the result of conquest, gutted the old egalitarian democracy, but the leader, although now a "king," was still only as secure as his last military success.

Unstable kingdoms gave way to unstable aristocracies, as the old tribal members tried to reassert their equality by claiming nobility. Within the state, divisions grew up between slaves and freemen, rich and poor, citizens and foreigners, as well as among the various clans and phratries. Increasing poverty gave rise to class war, which, in turn, created dema-gogues, and unstable aristocracy gave way to unstable tyranny. Well-justi-fied paranoia, with its corollary of preemptive violence, reigned within states and between states. Fulsome patriotic oratory covered a lack of civil virtue, and treason was a national pastime.

The political history of ancient Greece is a story of unrelieved failure. Among the 150 or so Greek city-states every conceivable form of govern-ment was tried. All failed in their basic function of providing security, order, and a degree of freedom on a continuing basis. This failure was not due to lack of understanding—indeed, most of the world's stock of good as well as bad political ideas can be traced to ancient Greece—but to lack of bureaucracy. Greece had culture, world-class specialists, but lacked civilization, the structure with which to make full use of those specialists.

As the city-states developed, they tended to take one of two forms. Sparta became a typical inward-looking, conservative, second-world police state (complete with its secret police, the *crypteia*). Athens, on the other hand, became an arrogant and imperialistic *"Herrenvolk* democracy." Nei-ther was a particularly happy place. Both had lost much of the old tribal egalitarianism but gained little in terms of security. Both were sick societ-ies. In Sparta individualism was suppressed, while in Athens egoism ran rampant. War was the highest good in both states, and successful generals and admirals—like their micro counterparts, successful boxers and lawyers —were national heroes, at least until they lost a battle or a bout. Ironically, democratic Athens tended to be much more aggressive than militaristic

Sparta.[3] Indeed, in the Peloponnesian War, it was Sparta that defended the freedom of Greeks from the imperialism of Athens.

Yet, we all know that Athens, even if it was unable to create a civilization, was able to create an admirable culture. Its works of art, literature, philosophy, mathematics, and even science—no less than those of Egypt and Asia—remain an important part of humanity's heritage. Western civilization, however, although informed and enriched by the works of individual Greeks of genius, is a continuation of the broad stream that began at Sumer and that largely bypassed ancient Greece.

The third world of the twentieth century, like ancient Greece, is a creator of culture and a borrower of civilization. Its achievements—and it has numerous writers, artists, and scientists who are equal, and often superior, to those of the first world—are individual; its failures are societal. The great third-world scholars and scientists are almost always found in the universities and laboratories of the first world.

THE IMPORTANCE OF THE FAMILY

The old truism that the family is the basic unit of society actually holds true in the third world. In most of the third world, one's duty is toward the family, one's loyalty is to the family, and one's refuge is in the family. Close family members can be trusted completely, more distant family members less so, outsiders not at all. Morality, law, and politics are nonbinding abstractions; the family is real.

Unlike in the first world where the most important freedom is often freedom "from the family," in much of the third world freedom "for the family" is everything. You use bribery, threats, and influence to keep your brother out of jail, though you detest both him and his crime. You join your family's political movement, though you see nothing to admire in either its leaders or its principles. You inherit blood enemies from your parents and bequeath them to your children. You count for nothing except as a member of the family. Goals are always family goals, never individual, never universal.

The world of the family is a suspicious, near-paranoid zero-sum world, in which one family's gain is another's loss. It accurately reflects the stagnant nature of the society around it. If the pie is not going to get bigger no matter what one does—and that *is* the case in much of the third world—the only sensible goal is to get as big a slice as one can for oneself and one's own.

If, as is often the case in tribal societies, the pie is so small and the families so evenly matched that maneuvering for a larger slice is impractical, the best course is to demand absolute equality so that one's neighbor cannot gain at one's expense. The "primitive communism," so sentimentalized in the first world, is based not on altruism or solidarity, but on envy, the desire to reduce every member of the society to the level of the lowest. This is the obvious reason behind wealth-destroying rituals such as the *cargo* system of the Maya Highland, and similar customs elsewhere.

As the third-world state evolves, the family generally comes into conflict with other groups or institutions. The trick then becomes to suppress this conflict to protect the family or, if possible, to use the broader group to further family interests. This is relatively easy to do when the group is a clan, village, or linguistic unit. It is more difficult when the group is a patron-client complex of one kind or another. It is even more difficult when the group is a transcendent institution or movement such as the military, the established priesthood, a charismatic political party, or a dynamic religious current. When one can pull it off, it can be quite rewarding, however. The mediocre son of Khomeini is still a factor in Iranian politics, just as the mediocre son of Cárdenas remains a factor in Mexican politics. The relatives of the Mahdi continue to be important in Sudan, and throughout the Muslim world the descendants of the Prophet and his son-in-law continue to dine out on their family tree.

TRANSCENDING THE FAMILY

The clan, the tribe, and the linguistic group are weak extensions of the family. While they partake of the zero-sum ethos of the family, they command loyalty only when placed in juxtaposition with more alien clans, tribes, and linguistic groups. In Ethiopia, the Somali-speaking tribesmen of the Ogaden unite against their Amharic-speaking rulers; in Somalia, where non-Somali speakers are few, linguistic unity breaks down and clan fights against clan; in Mogadishu, the Somali capital, even the clan breaks down and subclan fights against subclan. Ali Mahdi and Aideed, the principal rival warlords during the recent unpleasantness, are both members of the Hawiya clan.

Ascendant third-world political leaders, in an effort to increase their power, often try to expand the emotional definition of the family. They do this by raising the specter of alien enemies—other clans, other tribes, other nations—that constitute a grave danger to the enlarged "family." As this fictitious family is based on manufactured emotion rather than perceived benefits, it tends to break down very quickly as the real family reasserts itself.

The battle waxes and wanes. A Saddam Hussein expands from his base of Tikriti kinsmen to rule the "secular and modern" Ba'th Party (in opposition to Communists and Shi'ites and Kurds and Sunni fundamentalists). As his power grows, he transcends the party to become father to the Iraqi nation (uniting Communists and Shi'ites and, to a lesser extent, Kurds and Sunni fundamentalists against the threat of Iran). Then he transcends even the Iraqi nation to lead the Arab Nation against the Persians. Finally, he transcends the Arab Nation in an attempt to champion all Islam against the West and its lackeys.

Each stage of this construction, however, is incomplete and unstable. Built of momentum, success, propaganda, and a very temporary suspension of disbelief, Saddam's Babylonian Tower has no firm foundation. When momentum fails, the structure collapses. Persians and other Arabs pull away, Kurds and Shi'ites revolt, Ba'th Party members plot. Saddam is left where he started—dependent on his Tikriti kinsmen.

Not all patriarchal leaders are as overtly political as Saddam Hussein. The *patrón*, surrounded by his clients, is a far more common third-world father figure. The plantation owner, the union leader, the small-town political boss—themselves the clients of more important patrons—rule over fictitious clans that may be almost as cohesive as the real thing. In those areas of the third world where tribes and clans and linguistic groups have lost much of their importance, such as Latin America and parts of Asia, the patron-client complex is the glue that holds the state together.

States based on patron-client complexes tend to be more stable than those based on tribal confederations, because the patron-client dynamic depends more on cooperation and less on confrontation than does the tribal dynamic. Quasi-familial ties, both up and down, support the status quo, discourage revolt, and suppress egoism in the name of paternalism. Whereas the tribe, the clan, and the linguistic group are exclusive, seeing enemies at every turn, the patron-client complex is inclusive, always on the lookout for new clients to exploit and more powerful patrons to tie in with.

Finally, there are groups that transcend the family by replacing it rather than by mimicking it or building on it. These groups, following the grand tradition of new religion, boldly deny the primacy of the family. Christlike, they preach that one's first loyalty is no longer to parents, children, spouses, or siblings, but to some military or religious hierarchy, to some political or religious guru. "He that loveth father or mother more than me is not worthy of me" could have been said by Kenyatta or Perón or

Khomeini. This is not only the message of the charismatic outsider, it is also the institutional message of the military academy, the religious seminary, and the Asian secret society. It is in this third form of family transcendence that the greatest potential for chaos and for progress is to be found.

THE PRIVATIZED BUREAUCRACY

The patron-client complex, based upon personal loyalty and reciprocal advantage, is in direct opposition to the Weberian bureaucracy, based upon impersonal efficiency and societal goals. In opting for patron-client relationships over bureaucracy as a means of organization, the third-world leader opts for stability over governability. Far from land on a stormy sea is no place to start taking the raft apart to build a clipper.

In the third world, the bureaucracy, far from being in opposition to the patron-client system, is a part of it. It serves neither the state nor itself; it serves its members as individuals and it serves the larger patron-client network. As in Jackson's United States, the primary aim of the third-world bureaucracy is not to deliver mail or inspect meat or devise economic strategy, but to supply "opportunities" for cronies of the powerful and jobs for the politically faithful.

The Northern conservative observing the third world sees the heavy hand of the bureaucratic state everywhere and the healthy forces of the private sector relegated to the sidelines. The Northern conservative sees a mirage. In reality, in most parts of the third world the private sector has taken over the state—lock, stock, and bureaucracy. As in ancient Greece, the state is booty. Its power is used to punish private enemies, and its resources are used to reward private friends. The patron-client complex— the private state within the public state—is strengthened at the expense of those who choose to remain outside, and private goals are pursued under the cloak of public service.

This privatization of the state is much closer to the market than it is to the neomercantilism of Japan, Inc., in which the state makes use of the private sector to increase its own strength, or even to the robber-baron mercantilism of mid-nineteenth-century America, in which private bureaucracies effectively performed state functions. Unlike the Japanese and U.S. cases, with their strong elements of oligopoly, in the privatized state of the third world the market works and everything is for sale to the highest bidder.

This is not all bad. The poorly remunerated petty bureaucrat is paid by the private sector on a "services rendered" basis through bribery. This allows red tape to be cut, unwise laws to be bypassed, and government favors to be allocated in accord with market rather than legal principles— and it does it all without undue strain on state coffers! "Socialist" legislation can be enacted without fear that it will be enforced to the detriment of the economy, and "capitalist" legislation can be enacted without fear that it will be enforced to the detriment of political stability. Government becomes public relations, while the private sector operates happily just below the surface.

The greater boon of the patron-client complex, of which the privatized bureaucracy is only a part, is that it ties the society together. It creates a community of interest, or at least an informal organization, where otherwise there would only be chaos or tribal and family antagonism. Although grossly unequal, it enforces duties and limitations on patrons as well as on clients. Because it unites (even if imperfectly) so many self-interests, it is a strong force for political and social stability. No country with a healthy system of patron-client relationships has ever suffered a revolution.

The great evil of the patron-client system is that it makes effective government almost impossible. The system sacrifices everything to maintaining itself and has nothing left over for achieving greater goals. Indeed, the mere idea of greater goals is a danger to the intricate relationships that make up the system. An honest bureaucracy developing and enforcing wise laws and regulations without favor or exception could send the whole structure toppling and, with it, the stability of the society.

CHAPTER 17

The Dynamics of Discontent

Political and social unrest are, on average, no higher in the third world than in the first world and considerably lower, though often more open, than in the second. Moreover, the forms that such unrest may take are substantially the same in whatever world they may be found. The major difference is that once such unrest passes certain, often rather low thresholds in the third world, it becomes exceedingly hard to contain. This unstable equilibrium allows progress but does not ensure it.

Security, from the very beginning, has been the raison d'être for political organization. Thus, it is only natural that questions of political unrest should have long concerned both philosophers and practical politicians. Indeed, the earliest legal codes were probably nothing more than mechanisms to prevent unrest. And, for most of mankind during most of history, there has been no greater or more practically pressing real-world question than the proper relationship of the ruler, the ruled, and the laws of God or Nature. The proper formula guaranteed peace and prosperity—the Mandate of Heaven—while the slightest mistake could bring revolt and ruin.

Without going back to the ancients or even to Machiavelli, all of whom had much of interest to say on the subject, it is possible to see two major lines of reasoning with regard to the dynamics of discontent.[1] The intuitively obvious dynamic—the "volcano" theory, grinding poverty driving the population into sudden, desperate revolt—is accepted without question by the average person, be he liberal or conservative. It is the basis of the Marxist religion, though greatly modified in the more modern forms of Leninism and Trotskyism. It lies behind the thinking of the Kennedy speechwriter who wrote that "those who make peaceful revolution impossible will make violent revolution inevitable." It is the reason that right-wing first-world leaders demand reforms in third-world client states that they would never accept at home.

The intuitively obvious dynamic—as is so often the case—is wrong. Alexis de Tocqueville was one of the first to note that the poverty theory did not fit the historical record. In writing about the French Revolution, he points out that a "study of comparative statistics makes it clear that in none of the decades immediately following the Revolution did our national prosperity make such rapid forward strides as in the two preceding it"[2] and that "this steadily increasing prosperity, far from tranquilizing the population, everywhere promoted a spirit of unrest."[3] He generalizes this phenomenon in an often quoted passage:

> Thus it was precisely in those parts of France where there had been most improvement that popular discontent ran highest. This may seem illogical—but history is full of such paradoxes. For it is not always when things are going from bad to worse that revolutions break out. On the contrary, it oftener happens that when a people which has put up with an oppressive rule over a long period without protest suddenly finds the government relaxing its pressure, it takes up arms against it. Thus the social order overthrown by a revolution is almost always better than the one immediately preceding it, and experience teaches us that, generally speaking, the most perilous moment for a bad government is one when it seeks to mend its ways.[4]

Tocqueville's insights, largely because they jibe with the historical record in a way that the poverty theory does not, are now accepted with only occasional reservations by almost all non-Marxist students of unrest. There is less agreement, however, on the mechanism behind the facts that Tocqueville observed. Some theorists stress "unequal modernization," others "relative deprivation" or "rising expectations." James C. Davies talks of the "J-curve," and Vilfredo Pareto worried about the "circulation of elites." Mark Hagopian rounds up all the usual suspects and adds a dozen or so more.

I believe, however, that on the most basic level the dynamic that Tocqueville observed can best be explained as a result of an apparent changing of the rules of the game for certain players—that is to say, the *breaking of an implicit promise* to a certain segment of the population.

THE IMPLICIT PROMISE

Stability of expectations is the basis of all other stability. Although expectations differ from country to country, class to class, family to family, and even individual to individual, they nonetheless constitute the foundation of mental well-being. The peasant, accustomed to keeping two-thirds of his crop, feels that he has the right to expect that his share will not be reduced to a half. The mullah, raised to believe in the centrality of religion, feels that he has the right not to see the Laws of God mocked on every street corner. The rising businessman, having attained a certain level of wealth, feels that he has the right to the status that usually accompanies such wealth. The middle-class high school graduate, born into the right family, feels that he has the right to go to college and not to Vietnam.

The abrogation of these "rights," in addition to whatever physical or financial discomfort it may bring to the individual peasant or high school graduate, creates a mental state of victimization. The "victim" has kept his side of the bargain, has accepted his lot (hard though it may have been), but "they"—the powers that be—have not done their part. The world is suddenly without rules; if "they" did this today, what might "they" do tomorrow? Can anyone feel safe once the web of implicit promises—the "social contract" that holds society together—begins to unravel?

Political discontent arises out of social uncertainty, and political unrest is initially an attempt to reestablish acceptable conditions of certainty. Far from reflecting an impulse toward anarchy, it is an attempt to preserve order. It is an attempt to maintain an understandable world, where given causes lead to given effects, where the kid who keeps his nose clean doesn't land in jail, where the university graduate is assured of a job in the bureaucracy, where women don't show their bare faces in public, where blacks don't take "white" jobs, where military men are tried only in military courts, where the currency maintains its value, where the fruits of corruption are fairly shared, where the person who goes along gets along, where the price of a loaf of bread never changes. Political discontent arises when the world of one's fathers, one's childhood, and one's dreams is threatened.

Not all cases of discontent are equally serious from the standpoint of political unrest. The seriousness of a broken implicit promise is generally proportional to: (1) the power of the person or group affected; (2) the number of people or groups affected; (3) the amount of damage done to the perceived interests or ambitions of the person or group affected; and (4) the availability of nonpolitical alternatives for correcting or offsetting that damage.

Thus, for the third-world leader, it is more dangerous to offend the general who commands a tank garrison in the capital than the general who commands a training unit in the provinces, more dangerous to offend a rich landowner (a patron with many clients) than a poor one, more dangerous to offend a student or intellectual than a worker or peasant, more dangerous to offend a charismatic religious fanatic than a humble parish priest. Yet if one offends all the provincial generals and poor landowners, to say nothing of all the workers, peasants, and parish priests, the loyalty of all the generals and intellectuals of the metropolis may not be enough.

Similarly, the rising young politician who is defrauded in his first run for mayor may not be as dangerous as the older politician who sees his last chance for the presidency slip away. The world-famous intellectual whose ideas are suppressed by an ambassadorship to Paris may ultimately be less dangerous than the intellectual whose ideas are suppressed by a bullet in the back of the head. The charismatic prophet laden with awards from the government may be less dangerous than the charismatic prophet recording cassettes in exile. The peasant who loses his land but is given a job at the big house may not be as dangerous as the peasant who is given nothing at all. The man who is willing to settle for second best, however reluctantly, is no revolutionary.

RELATIVE DEPRIVATION

The idea of the broken implicit promise as a cause of political unrest, because it is so broad, is compatible with most modern theories of political instability. I choose to illustrate it with Ted Robert Gurr's concept of relative deprivation (RD), not because I believe RD to be "truer" than other theories, but because it is clear, easy to use, and remarkably free from hidden ideological bias.

According to Gurr, there is always a gap between the expectations and the capabilities of any individual, group, or nation. This condition does not lead to unrest, however, unless the gap becomes wider. This can happen in any of three ways: (1) through "decremental deprivation," in which expectations remain the same while capabilities decline; (2) through "aspirational deprivation," in which expectations rise while capabilities remain the same; and (3) through "progressive deprivation," in which, after both expectations and capabilities have been rising at the same rate over a long period, there is a sudden drop in capabilities.[5] To this list, Hagopian adds a fourth type: "accelerated deprivation," in which both "expectations and capabilities increase at a steady clip, but the former 'accelerates' much faster than the latter."[6]

It is difficult, if not impossible, to find a real-world example of any form of RD that does not entail the breaking of an implicit promise. Under decremental RD, we find examples such as the sudden imposition of special taxes (so important in the American Revolution) and sudden increases in land rents (a usual cause of peasant rebellion). Under aspirational RD, we can list cases such as the effect of decolonization elsewhere in Africa on expectations in Portugal's African colonies and the effect of Soviet *perestroika* on Eastern Europe. Under progressive RD, we note the sudden near collapse of the Brazilian economy in the early 1960s after many years of rapid growth (a major cause of the "Revolution of 1964") and a similar situation in Uruguay (which gave rise to the Tupamaros). Finally, under accelerated RD, we can do no better than to note Hagopian's own example of how the rapid rise in the prosperity of the men who made the French Revolution was exceeded by the even more rapid rise of their ambitions.

Chances are that many forms of RD will be involved in any major case of political unrest. The Mexican Revolution, for example, began with a clear case of aspirational deprivation. The so-called Creelman interview—in which the aged dictator, Porfirio Díaz, stated that, after some thirty years of one-man rule, he was ready to step down from the presidency—suddenly created a "political class" among previously apolitical members of the Mexican aristocracy. These men, the most important of whom was Francisco Madero, suddenly saw the possibility of creating a more or less U.S.-style democracy and attaining power through elections. When Díaz went back on his word, breaking the explicit promise of elections and the implicit promise of democracy, Madero rose in revolt.

A revolt is not a revolution, however. The ground for revolution had already been prepared by radicals such as Ricardo Flores Magón who—disappointed when the promise implicit in what had seemed to be the rapid rise of Mexican syndicalism and class consciousness was crushed at Cananea (progressive deprivation)—had turned from labor organization to preaching armed revolution.[7] At the same time, even those elements of the "Europeanized" middle and upper classes who had benefited under Díaz were becoming disillusioned by the growing gap between the progress that Mexico was making and the progress they thought possible (ac-

celerated deprivation). The country that had seemed on the verge of joining Europe in 1900 appeared to be losing ground in 1910.

Finally, the great masses of Indian and mestizo peasants, who had demanded little except the personal economic stability that a loyal client
could expect from a worthy patron, saw their meager expectations eroded
by the growth of capitalist agriculture and by recession during the last
decade of Porfirian rule. Widespread decremental deprivation provided
the cannon fodder that changed Madero's revolt into the first great social
revolution of the twentieth century.

DEGREES OF UNREST

Most of the time, in most of the third world, the implicit promises are kept
—this is, after all, what traditional society is all about—and consequently
discontent is limited and the unstable equilibrium is maintained. Indeed,
those observers who come to the third world without ethnocentric precon-
ceptions—in contrast to the Kennedy speechwriter quoted above—are
often struck by how "unrevolutionary" the third world actually is. This is
not to say that violence, exploitation, and injustice are absent—they are
present on a massive scale in many parts of the third world—but rather
that they are kept within the bounds of custom.

Most often it is modernization, from without or within, that creates the
opening for equilibrium-threatening unrest. Modernization, by definition,
involves breaking the implicit promises upon which traditional society is
based. It shakes up customary pecking orders, undermines long-estab-
lished patron-client relationships, and casts doubts upon traditional beliefs
and sources of legitimacy. Throughout the society, greater numbers of
people feel deprived, because some are advancing and others are not,
some are advancing less rapidly than they feel they should, and some—
particularly traditional religious and tribal leaders—are disconcerted by
changed definitions of what advancement means.

The *riot* is the least threatening form of unrest. Indeed, riots, like
crime, often allow a discontented population to let off steam and are
thereby stabilizing. They are most likely to occur in response to price
increases in, or shortages of, basic goods and services such as bread and
buses or to rumors or incidents of police brutality. Occasionally they result
in substantial loss of life and property. Occasionally they force minor
changes in policy. Occasionally they mushroom into secession or revolution. But mostly they have no effect whatsoever.

Terrorism is another generally nonthreatening form of unrest. Unlike the riot, which is an unplanned response to real or imagined deprivation by a relatively large group, terrorism is the carefully planned response of a small group. It is often the result of accelerated deprivation, when highly ideological (and usually psychopathic) left-wing individuals fear that their desired Utopia will not be established soon enough, or decremental deprivation, when psychopathic right-wing ideologues fear that their preferred established order is in danger.

Although many terrorist groups, such as the Ku Klux Klan, the Provisional Irish Republican Army, the Abu Nidal Organization, and Irgun, act in the name of ideologies that have broad support, their tactics are generally recognized as counterproductive and their members are usually scorned even by their ideological fellows. Terrorist groups of the first world, such as the Red Army Faction, the Red Brigades, the Japanese Red Army, the Weather Underground, the Symbionese Liberation Army, and the various neo-Nazi groups, usually have little or no community support. They are correctly seen as the functional equivalents of Charlie Manson's bloodthirsty girls wrapped in Che Guevara's cloak.

Guerrilla war, like terrorism, is the planned response of a small group to perceived relative deprivation. Indeed, many guerrilla armies, especially in Latin America and East Asia, began as terrorist groups, and a few retain the typical terrorist psychopathology. Most, however, profit from the country air. Unlike the terrorist group, which depends on secrecy and rational suspicion, the guerrilla group must be open enough to attract new members. It must broaden, rather than narrow, its ideology. It must only commit those acts that it can explain to present and future members.

Although guerrilla warfare, unlike terrorism, is not clearly counterproductive, it rarely constitutes a serious threat to an established government. The well-known victories of Mao, Ho, and Castro are the exceptions; Guevara's ignominious failure in Bolivia is the rule. In most countries of the third world, a dozen or so ragtag insurgencies are under way at any given moment. The regime does not worry about them, the citizens have never heard of them, the tourists are not frightened by them. If the first-world terrorist group resembles the Manson gang wrapped in Che Guevara's cloak, the typical third-world guerrilla group is Bonnie and Clyde hiding under the same garment.

Secession is a planned mass movement. Although such movements fail more often than not, they are rarely undertaken without a reasonable chance of success. Wherever they occur, they constitute a major threat to the continued rule of the central government over a part of its generally recognized territory. Major examples are the colonial wars that brought freedom to the United States, Latin America, and many parts of Asia and Africa. Failed movements include those of the U.S. South, Nigeria's Biafra, and Zaire's Shaba. Although most governments, including many in the former Communist bloc, now see the folly of trying to retain control over areas whose populations prefer independence, a few such as India, Indonesia, Iraq, Israel, Sudan, and some Balkan states have yet to see the light.

The *coup d'état*, like terrorism and guerrilla war, is the work of a small group responding to particular feelings of relative deprivation that may not be shared by other groups within the society. Unlike terrorism and guerrilla war, however, the coup is more often successful than not. The reason for this success is that the military men or palace officials who undertake most coups are in excellent positions to know the odds of success before taking action. Although it is true that many coups have little or no lasting effect (the third-world raft looks much the same upside down as right side up), some—such as those in South Korea in 1961 and Brazil in 1964—ushered third-world states into the second world.

Finally, we come to *revolution*. Revolutions—great tumults such as those that overturned governments and shook societies in France, Mexico, Russia, and China—are extremely rare and, by our definition at least, always successful. They occur when the perceived breaking of implicit promises to different groups by different groups has become so endemic in a society that all hope of restoring the status quo is lost. Unrest, no longer a question of restoring or preserving "rights," becomes a headlong dive into the unknown. Every group and every individual is racked with fears of Hell and hopes of Paradise. Though the fears often outweigh the hopes, it is easier to push ahead than to attempt to turn back. Each true revolution is both planned and unplanned. It changes society, though often not to the degree and occasionally not even in the direction desired by its proponents.

REVOLUTION AS PROCESS AND REVOLUTION AS RESULT

Specialists as well as laymen often appear confused by the different meanings of the word "revolution" as commonly used. For some, revolution is any massive outbreak of violence that engulfs an entire nation over an extended period even if, as in the Bolivian Revolution of 1952, the society ends up little changed. For others, revolution requires a profound change in society even if, as in the Meiji Restoration (or the Industrial Revolution), the change is accomplished with little or no violence.[8] Still others, mesmerized by 1789, demand both violence and change.

Revolution as process—that is to say, massive countrywide violence and destruction, whether or not it is accompanied by profound social change— is a plausible, though statistically unlikely, threat throughout the third world. Colombia's Violencia and prolonged crises in Sri Lanka and Haiti come close to the third-world leader's nightmare of revolution without content.

We are more interested, however, in revolution as result. In speaking of the third world, the result of "revolution as result" is always the centralization of power that presages entry into the second world. Here again, we follow Tocqueville, who believed that "centralization was at once the Revolution's starting-off point and one of its guiding principles."[9] This centralization essentially involves the creation or extension of a Weberian bureaucracy.

In the typical second-world revolutionary state, it is the military and security bureaucracy that is the focus of the political effort. If the revolutionary regime is to survive, it must have an efficient means of protecting itself from internal and external enemies. From the time of Cromwell's New Model Army (one of the first military establishments to embody bureaucratic, rather than martial, virtues), through the age of the Cheka and the Waffen SS, to the era of the IDF, SAVAK, and the well-named BOSS (South Africa's now-disbanded Bureau of State Security), it was recognized that neither ideology nor nepotism could be allowed to get in the way of the efficient protection of the regime and its revolutionary mission.

In the NIC variant of the second-world state, it is the economic bureaucracy that must be created and nurtured. The authoritarian rulers, military or civilian, recognize that economic efficiency, even more than military efficiency, is the ultimate protection of the regime from internal and external enemies. By abandoning ideology, the NICs are able to effect changes far more revolutionary and far more beneficial than those trumpeted by the ideologically bound totalitarian states and *Herrenvolk* democracies.

CHAPTER 18

The Roots of Instability: Conquest

During most of history, conquest has been a reciprocal process. Civiliza-tion ("the second world," to speak in anachronistic terms) expanded outward to absorb barbarian tribes ("the third world") for decades or centuries. But then, inevitably, the tide would turn, the great empires, unable to help themselves, would collapse in slow motion, and barbarian kings would rule where living gods had once reigned. Sometimes the change was for the better; sometimes not.

During the nineteenth century, however, this pattern changed. The first world, though not yet named, came into being. It saw itself—and, grudgingly, was seen by others—as the wave of the future, the model of progress, the epitome of social morality. Europe knew best. In this new Age of Imperialism—unlike previous eons in which the ebb and flow of tribe and empire implied little more than a temporary superiority in arms and energy—conquest became a sign of moral and usually racial superiority. This nineteenth-century imperialism, far more pernicious than that of the Age of Discovery, explains much of the third world's current condition of unstable equilibrium.

The desire to conquer is the most natural of emotions. Man (and woman) shares it with all the higher animals. In its human form, it is the basis of all politics and of much personal interaction in other spheres. In a world long ruled by the sword, the ballot, and the coquettish smile, only the Weberian bureaucrat, to the extent that he or she is able to suppress his or her humanity, sees conquest as a disturbing irrationality, at best neutral, most often harmful.

Conquest, together with the feelings of superiority that conquest often engenders, is a major source of in-group unity and cooperation. On the tribal level, it leads the Greeks to consider all non-Greeks as barbarians, legitimate targets for slavery and other forms of exploitation. On the imperial level, it leads Rome to consider all non-Romans as potential Romans, legitimate targets for incorporation into the empire. On the first-world level, it leads the British to think they have the right (and duty) to suppress slavery in Africa or force China to buy opium, the French to think they have the right (and duty) to suppress tribal warfare in the Sahara or explode nuclear bombs in Polynesia, and the North Americans to think they have the right (and duty) to "open" feudal Japan or stamp out Bolivian coca.

Conquest obliges the conquerors to make certain changes in the societies of the conquered for their (the conquerors') own security and allows them to make other changes for their own comfort—to create a little bit of Rome in the British Isles or a little bit of the United States in the middle of Panama. It obliges them to displace rulers and elevate quislings, to make snap judgments based on accent or skin color or simply "compatibility." It allows them to protect missionaries of the home religion and stamp out local "superstition," to clothe the naked and to instruct the ignorant— even against their will. Conquest changes everything it touches, but rarely does it change anything completely.

FROM THE BEGINNING

Conquest—that is to say, domination—is the basis of leadership on even the most primitive level. Without domination the tribe would not have a leader, and without conquest the bureaucrats of Sumer and Egypt would not have been in a position to create civilization. But most conquest served no useful purpose even in this early period.

Before the advent of the first world, war rarely broke out between grossly unequal opponents. Most major battles were not between empires and tribes, but between empires and empires and tribes and tribes. The frontier between tribe and empire did wobble, however, as imperial captains, bucking for promotion, captured villages beyond the march and as tribal chiefs, lusting for loot, overran isolated garrisons. None of this was of great importance.

On occasion, however, more formidable groups, endowed with unusual energy, leadership, tactics, and (often) novel military technology, would sweep across the steppes or out of the deserts and into settled lands. Dominolike, the barbarian would push the semicivilized, and the semicivilized, part refugee and part conqueror, would surge across the borders of empire. Thus, the Huns defeated the Ostrogoths, who nudged the Visigoths, who eventually sacked Rome and conquered Roman Spain. In similar ways, other barbaric and semicivilized tribes broke through into the empires of China, India, and Persia.

Healthy civilizations were able in time either to regroup their forces and oust their invaders or to absorb and civilize them into a new ruling class. Thus, the Sassanians were able to dislodge the Ephthalite Huns from Persia and the Sui were able to defeat the Avars (Juan-juan) in China, just as at other times India was able to absorb wave upon wave of barbarians from Alexander on and Mesoamerica was able to civilize incursion after incursion of savage Chichimecs. Rome was not so lucky, however. The security bureaucracy—the famed Roman Legions—thoroughly corrupted by politics, was unable to defend the state. Indeed, the army, now more barbarian than Roman, became itself a threat to security. The civil bureaucracy—the makers and dispensers of Roman law—proved itself no match for troglodyte "leaders." Along with economic stagnation and population decline, along with the replacement of imperial universalism with Christian intolerance and transalpine tribalism, Rome was done in by the brutal politics of leaders and would-be leaders that made rational administration close to impossible. Europe, both empire and tribe, had earned its Dark Ages.

None of these conquests or reconquests was without cost. No matter who won, society lost. New rulers, new social classes, new religions, new customs, came to the fore. Relative deprivation was rampant. Where, as in Western Europe, the second-world state did not survive, violence was endemic, bureaucracy died, and civilization guttered. Where, as in Byzantium, the second-world state did survive, the violence was only forced beneath the surface, ready to emerge years or centuries later when the power of empire weakened.

THE AMERICAS

Spain, according to J. Fred Rippy, "embraced the absorption of the natives into the body politic and the creation of a new race. In this respect Spain was the most original of all colonizing powers."[1] Moreover, "the fate of the aborigines of Spanish America was probably more fortunate than that of the backward races subdued by any other modern colonizing power."[2] Finally, to quote Richard M. Morse:

> The growth of the centralized state in Western Europe has been described as a process which undermines local autonomy and initiative and which, by equalizing all citizens before the law and the state bureaucracy, weakens the protection afforded them by community ties and customs. In Spanish America under the Hapsburgs the role of the state was in some respects precisely the opposite. Central to its function was the preservation or creation of Indian communities which would maintain their own way of life, be protected against excessive exploitation, and have independent access to royal justice. . . .[3]

Contrary to the "Black Legend" of Las Casas—still widely believed in Anglo-Saxon lands—the Spanish colonization of America was probably the most humane and certainly the most successful example of imperialism since ancient times. After a disastrous beginning in the Antilles, much of which can be blamed on the Columbus brothers, the Spaniards settled down to creating an empire larger than that of Alexander or Caesar and longer-lasting (and more peaceful) than many of the empires of antiquity. Indeed, the Spanish Empire far outlasted the Spanish dynasty under which it was consolidated.

Although most Europeans of the sixteenth and seventeenth centuries, with the important exception of the Calvinists, were not racists, the Iberians were even less so because they had had more experience with other races. And this experience gave them no false feelings of superiority. The Spanish Christians in the fifteenth century, like the Germans in the fourth century, were in some respects unruly barbarians encroaching upon a declining civilization. While they were proud of their military prowess and confident of possessing the one true religion, they were well aware of the superior splendor of the Muslim-Jewish south. Even the Portuguese, who, as far as Europeans are concerned, virtually invented the African slave trade, regarded the African kings they dealt with as their equals.

The Spaniards carried their Old World standards into the New World and respected the civilization they found there. One has only to read the letters of Hernán Cortés or the "True Relation" of Bernal Díaz to see the respect, even awe, in which the conquistadores held the Aztecs. They admired their art and architecture, their courage, and even their treachery (virtues and vices not unknown to the Spaniards themselves); they hated only their religion. And even that hatred was not absolute. The great clerical anthropologists of this period—Bernardino de Sahagún, Diego Durán, Alonso de Molina, even the often intolerant Bishop Diego de Landa—not only admired and preserved the Indians' culture but also had a grudging respect for their religion.

Although European diseases sharply reduced the number of Indians in Spanish as well as in British America, the Spaniards, unlike the New England Puritans, never praised God for destroying the heathen through disease and, unlike later North Americans, never deliberately introduced disease into the native population. They never doubted that the Indians were humans with immortal souls, and quite without hypocrisy they justified grand larceny and massive exploitation as fair exchange for salvation. This mind-set, in a weakened form, remained even after the end of Spanish rule; it is inconceivable that Latin America could ever have a "populist and democratic" leader like Andrew Jackson who, while defending the common man, clearly excluded blacks and Indians.

In its early days, as Morse has pointed out, the Spanish conquest was a free-enterprise operation of soldiers of fortune with little help or guidance from Madrid. This did not last long, however. The original conquerors were soon dispossessed of their power, lands, and Indians, and the bureaucrats took over. A major task of these bureaucrats was to protect the Indians from the local Spaniards and to keep themselves from being co-opted by these same Spaniards. This was done by "limiting the tenure of royal officials; forbidding officials to acquire family and economic ties in their jurisdictions; using inspectors and spies to supervise all levels of administration. . . ."[4] Spanish America had no place for a Byrd, a Carroll, a Fairfax, a Fitzhugh, a Winthrop, a Penn, or a Calvert.

Thus, political power was separated from local wealth and from local patron-client relationships. No local nobility or enduring aristocracy was allowed to grow up to challenge the political power of the crown. Creole and even mestizo society was remarkably fluid—certainly more so than that of Spain itself. Political power was out of the question, but wealth was up for grabs. Today's storekeeper was tomorrow's landowner, and today's landowner was tomorrow's pauper. It was a great way to run an empire— which, after all, was all that Madrid really had in mind—but a very poor way to prepare a people for independence, which requires the stability of an experienced local ruling class.

The situation elsewhere in America was somewhat different. Brazil, like Tidewater Virginia before the coming of the Scotch-Irish Presbyterians, was indolent and tolerant—the home of the equal opportunity exploiter. Lacking, to a large extent, both the religious fervor and the religious scruples of the Spaniards, without access to precious metals or large numbers of hierarchically organized Indians, with little direction from Lisbon (certainly nothing to compare with Spanish bureaucratic rule), the Portuguese settled down to a life of precarious leisure, exploiting the Indians in the fields and in bed and, after the Indians were dead or absorbed, the black slaves.

The Brazilian, the result of this fusion of races, was less proud, less violent, less religious, and less concerned with abstract justice than the Spanish American. Unlike the Spaniard, but like the North American, he had no qualms about enslaving or even exterminating the Indians—Spanish America had no equivalent to the Brazilian *bandeirante* slave hunter, who was usually part Indian himself—and like the Spaniard, but unlike the North American, he had no qualms about cohabitation or legal marriage with people of color. The Spanish American was quick to take offense, while the Brazilian was quick to take advantage.

The European conquerors of mainland America (though not those of the West Indies) shared at least one trait: they came to stay. Although for centuries they remained loyal to their mother countries, they very quickly began to see themselves as American rather than Spanish, Portuguese, British, or French. In this, they were like the Dutch of South Africa and the British of Australia and New Zealand (and for that matter like the Roman conquerors of Spain or the Moghul conquerors of India) but completely different from the later European conquerors of Asia and Africa. The conquistador has more in common with the nineteenth-century Italian immigrant at Ellis Island than either has with the British administrator in Calcutta or the Belgian soldier in Léopoldville.

ASIA AND AFRICA

The thrust and counterthrust of Islam and Christianity from the seventh century to the beginnings of the nineteenth century was essentially a battle of equals. Crusaders conquered Jerusalem, Islam's third most holy city, and Süleyman's Turks threatened Vienna, the capital of Europe's most important empire. Between wars, scholars and merchants mingled and the exchange of goods and ideas flourished. Enlightened rulers and philosophers respected each other across the religious divide. Christians and Jews in Egypt and the Levant became "Islamized" without ever losing their religions, and Cambridge established a chair of Arabic studies.

This pattern influenced Europe's early relations with India and the Far

East. Travelers such as Marco Polo returned with wondrous tales of wealth and sophistication that seemed to imply a certain superiority to those lands. The Jesuits went to China as much to learn as to teach. From the time the first Portuguese mariners reached Asia to the end of the eighteenth century, trade was the goal and, for the most part, large-scale conquest and colonization were never seriously considered. Trade, however, required secure trading posts—and a monopoly of trade, that old mercantilist ideal, required the destruction of other European trading posts.

Thus, in its origins, the British conquest of India had more to do with countering the claims of Holland and France than with imposing British rule over the crumbling remains of the Moghul Empire. The businessmen of the East India Company, who had been trading with India since early in the seventeenth century, had cozy relationships with many of the local rulers and tried to avoid political entanglements that could get in the way of profits. It was through no desire of their own that their fortified "factories," built on land leased from local princes, became outposts of empire. British Madras, Bombay, and Calcutta, Dutch Negapatam and Cochin, French Pondicherry, Chandernagore, and Masulipatam were little more than "business offices." Their political and strategic competition only made sense in European terms.

European wars were reflected in Indian battles. The British lost Madras to the French in the War of the Austrian Succession, while the French lost Pondicherry to the British in the Seven Years' War. Although the merchants of both nations, with a lack of patriotism that can only be commended, would have preferred profitable neutrality, the political leaders back home—shaking their clubs and bellowing their troglodyte chants—had their way as usual. With fighting men in short supply—there was, after all, a lot of dying to be done in Europe and America as well as the East—both sides made war alliances with Indian rulers and led Indian troops in battle.

Those Indians who objected to having European wars fought on Indian soil became legitimate targets for both sides. Indian neutrality was suspect, and Indian opposition was beyond the pale. Buffer zones had to be protected by other buffer zones. At the same time, some Indian rulers and rebels, with dreams of empire dancing in their heads, courted the Europeans and tried to draw them deeper into Indian domestic affairs. Even the merchants—hitherto an island of relative sanity—began to see that politics, power, and plunder had some advantages over the humdrum world of trade. And East India Company leaders, such as Robert Clive, began to think more in political and military and less in commercial terms. As J. M. Roberts writes:

The obscuring of the company's primary commercial role . . . gave its employees even greater opportunities to feather their own nests. This drew the interest of British politicians, who first cut into the powers of the directors of the company and then brought it firmly under the control of the Crown, setting up in 1784 a system of "dual control" in India that was to last until 1858. In the same Act were provisions against further interference in native affairs; the British government hoped as fervently as the company to avoid being dragged any further into the role of imperial power in India. But this was what happened in the next half-century, as many more acquisitions followed. The road was open which was to lead eventually to the enlightened despotism of the nineteenth-century Raj. India was quite unlike any other dependency so far acquired by a European state in that hundreds of millions of subjects were to be added to the empire without any conversion or assimilation of them being envisaged.[5]

This was not yet a first-world empire. "There was," according to Percival Spear, "little idea of reform of manners or the molding of society. Practices like suttee or widow-burning, hook-swinging as an act of religious devotion, infanticide, Hindu widowhood, and Muslim polygamy were deplored as 'heathenish' but regarded as customs of the country which could not be interfered with."[6] Indeed, the British of this period found much to admire in the old India of the Moghuls.

Early in the nineteenth century, however, the first world came into being, sired by the Enlightenment and born of political and industrial revolution. Suddenly Europe (and the new United States of America) had all the answers. Europe alone had the keys to morality, justice, science, and progress. In a few short years, the rest of the world lost not only its equality (or superiority) but its very humanity. With an arrogance worthy of the ancient Greeks, though slightly more justified, Europe once more split the world between civilization and barbarism, who and whom, the master races and the lesser breeds without the law. Understanding of other peoples and other ideas smacked of going native, and tolerance seemed to hide a selfish reluctance to pick up the White Man's Burden.

The new Age of Imperialism had begun.[7] Never before had greed—for power more than wealth—been so fashionable, so moral. Never before had the troglodytes of government intoned their hymns of domination with such fulsome piety. In a premonition of Orwell, war became "pacification," annexation was undertaken to extend "freedom," native rulers were replaced with Europeans to teach "democracy," millions of people were brought under the European yoke to facilitate "stamping out slavery," once thriving economies were destroyed in the name of "progress," undereducated louts from the slums of Europe and North America lived lives of unexpected luxury in foreign climes and called it "sacrifice," and men were blown from the mouths of cannon to advance "civilization."

Where annexation was impractical, domination would do. From Canton to Cairo, from Tehran to Tangier, nominally independent rulers were expected to follow the dictates of distant masters. Indeed, foreign rulers—no longer the magnificent potentates admired by earlier travelers—came to be seen as the enemies of progress and justice. Like twentieth-century *"sandalistas,"* many British and French soldiers, advisors, ambassadors, administrators, and missionaries saw themselves firmly on the side of the "simple natives" and against the corrupt and tyrannical "black despots" who had the effrontery to be in power. This attitude was equally popular with the people at home—and the press that catered to them—who delighted in being able to bash their "inferiors" and "love" them at the same time.

Africa, which—except for the Cape, the slave coast, and the Arab areas of the north—had been little touched by the first and relatively benign wave of European imperialism, received the full force of its more virulent and racist "first world" manifestation in the last decades of the nineteenth century. The late conquest of Africa was essentially an exercise in filling in the blanks, to color the remaining white spaces on the map British pink before the French could color them green. In some ways, it had as little to do with Africans as the concurrent "conquest" of Antarctica had to do with penguins.

By the dawn of the twentieth century, virtually all of the white spaces had been colored in.

LIBERATION

While conquest was an abomination, liberation was not an unmixed blessing. Indeed, by virtually every measure except that of self-respect, most third-world states were better off during the last decades of colonial rule than during the first decades of freedom. With independence, aspirational deprivation soared to an all-time high; never before had so many expected so much and been so grievously disappointed. In most third-world countries—even in many of those of Latin America that have been independent for almost two centuries—group still eyes group suspiciously, wondering what ever happened to the "freedom dividend."

The most stable countries are those that had either the most or the least direct contact with Europe. Equally fortunate are those such as Japan that were able to avoid Western conquest while absorbing Western material culture and those such as the United States, Canada, Australia, and New Zealand that, through luck or genocide, were able to create culturally unified, essentially European societies. Least fortunate are those countries, largely in sub-Saharan Africa, that saw their political organizations and cultures destroyed by first-world arrogance without in any real sense becoming "Europeanized." In between are countries such as Thailand and Saudi Arabia that were able to avoid conquest at the cost of falling behind in material terms, countries such as many former Spanish and Portuguese colonies that through massive miscegenation achieved a degree of cultural unity, countries such as India and Pakistan that were saddled with an oil-and-water mix of their own ancient cultures and those of their conquerors, and *Herrenvolk* states such as South Africa, Rhodesia, Algeria, and Israel that were (or are) able to control disequilibrium through separation and domination.

The process of liberation also has an effect on later stability. Countries such as Brazil, Canada, and Australia that achieved independence without a war of secession are—all other things being equal—more stable than countries such as the United States, Mexico, and Indonesia that fought for their freedom. Countries such as Cuba, the Philippines, and many in Africa and Central America that had their freedom delivered by third parties or were, essentially, abandoned by their colonizers tend to be the least stable of all.

Most third-world states achieved independence under the leadership of the most Westernized segment of their population. These leaders—the San Martíns, the Bolívars, the Nehrus, the Ben Bellas, even the Kenyattas and Nyereres—often had more in common with the alien rulers they revolted against than with their own people. Their very concepts of nationalism, of revolt, of postliberation political and economic organization almost always had Western roots. They did not want to return to precolonial times; rather they wanted to take control of the colonial state.

Although these leaders were often wildly popular with their countrymen, they and their followers lived in different worlds. The leaders thought in terms of the nation, jealously guarded its arbitrary colonial borders, and found their enemies among the "imperialist," "neo-imperialist," and "social-imperialist" powers; the followers thought in terms of tribe, caste, or religion and found their enemies among the Hindi speakers up north, the Muslims in the next country over, or the Hutus around the corner. The leaders wanted to retain the best of the West defined as secularism and socialism; the followers wanted to retain the best of the West defined as Coca-Cola and Hollywood movies. The leaders saw liberation as an opportunity for the country to become something better; the followers saw liberation as an opportunity for the country to be itself. The leaders, disappointed, accused the followers of breaking an implicit promise of moral and national progress; the followers, disappointed, accused the leaders of breaking the implicit promise of psychological and economic comfort.

The leaders were frustrated that they were unable even to maintain the old second-world state, much less to build upon it. Bolívar was frustrated to see the empire that Spain had been able to administer relatively efficiently break into an ever-increasing number of states that no one could administer at all. Jawaharlal Nehru was frustrated to see that religions and tribes and linguistic groups that had lived together in relative peace under British rule were unable to do so after liberation. New leaders around the globe were frustrated to realize that, under the old dispensation, a colonial administrator with a couple of clerks had wielded more real power than they did with all their armies and sashes of office.

LIBERATION AND UNSTABLE EQUILIBRIUM

Liberation demoted the colony from the second to the third world, from controlled disequilibrium to unstable equilibrium. The new leader, who had expected, like his colonial counterpart, to be a social engineer with all the levers of power at hand, found that he had become a juggler with dozens of balls in the air, using all his skill not to achieve goals, but simply to avoid disaster. The new leader, if he was good, could keep the balls in the air for a lifetime and even, with some risk, pass them on to a friend or rival who was studying in the wings. If, however, he missed a ball, the act was over.

CHAPTER 19

The Roots of Instability: Status

*How a society is organized—the relative status of groups and individuals
—is fraught with dangers to stability. A highly stratified society breeds
envy at the bottom and arrogance at the top. A highly egalitarian society,
on the other hand, breeds frustration among the gifted and ambitious.
Both extremes have the potential to transform discontent into revolution.*

Jefferson to the contrary, the self-evident truth is that all men are not
created equal. This, in and of itself, is not enough to create lasting
divisions within a society. Indeed, by its very random nature, the birth
lottery tends to make lasting social divisions impossible. Over time the
talented children of peasants and tramps oust the sluggish offspring of
princes and tycoons. Social divisions are intended to slow down this process, to give the weak progeny of strong parents an artificial advantage over
the talented but poorly born.

These divisions, being not so much a result of the Darwinian struggle as
a means of taming it, protect the society from chaos in the short run at the
cost of possibly greater chaos in the long run. Whether short-term stability
is transformed into long-term catastrophe depends upon the permeability
of the social structure. A rigid caste society in which status is determined
by birth is obviously more of a pressure cooker than an open class society
in which status is determined by earned wealth.[1]

THE MYTH OF CLASS

Marx, in the course of an ultimately erroneous analysis, makes the useful distinction between a "class in itself" and a "class for itself." The former is an undeniable social reality; the latter is, in the third world at least, largely a myth. While it is possible and often useful to slice a population by income level—arbitrarily assigning, for example, the upper 5 percent of income recipients to the "upper class," the next 35 percent to the "middle class," and the rest to the "lower class"—it is a mistake to postulate that the members of the various groups have anything besides income in common.

As Robert Hughes has pointed out, the first and perhaps the only class to achieve "class consciousness" was the mid-nineteenth-century British and British-influenced middle class.[2] It had "middle-class values" that were superior in its own eyes both to those of the frivolous and slightly immoral upper classes and to those of the often destitute and occasionally dissolute lower classes. Most important, it was singular while the other classes were plural. Whereas the struggling establishment clergyman and the well-to-do merchant held an ethos in common, the besotted East End pickpocket had nothing in common with the sober Methodist mechanic, nor did the wastrel rakehell lord have much in common with the cautious City financier. Apparently, what transforms a class in itself into a class for itself is a shared disdain for the morals of others.

The second-world middle class, as was pointed out in an earlier chapter, is almost always destabilizing. It is a class for itself, impatient, demanding, know-it-all, riddled with ideology and counterideology, ready to upset applecarts, racked with relative deprivation, fearful of the undeserving poor, envious of the unworthy rich, eager for democracy but reluctant to accept responsibility. It is born out of second-world progress but scorns its parent.

The third-world middle class, whether defined by strictly economic criteria or by some combination of economic and social status, is much less dangerous. Tangled in a network of family and patron-client relationships, it has little potential to become a class for itself. Individual members of the third-world middle class—doctors, lawyers, teachers, editors, bureaucrats, merchants, military officers—do of course have revolutionary potential. Indeed, when a third-world state is ushered into the second world, the usher is usually a member of the middle class. (If, instead, the state trips into chaos, the man with his foot out is also usually a member of the mischievous middle.)

The other third-world classes are even less likely to be or become classes for themselves. In the third world, with few exceptions, divisions are vertical, not horizontal. A poor Kenyan Kikuyu has more in common with a rich Kenyan Kikuyu than with a poor Luo. A poor Indian Muslim has more in common with a rich Indian Muslim than with a poor Hindu. A poor client has more in common with his rich patron than with another poor client in a different patron-client complex.

Class conflict in the Marxist sense is not a danger in the third world and never has been. (It is dismaying how many scholars, non-Marxist as well as Marxist, are willing to assume the existence of a class consciousness and a latent class conflict for which there is not the slightest shred of evidence.) Marxists, and perhaps some others, will of course argue that the "objective interests" of the poor Kikuyu are with the poor Luo and not with the rich Kikuyu, that hard economic fact is more important than sentimental cultural ties, that the class in itself will—or at least should—become a class for itself. In the real third world, however, it would be tantamount to suicide to renounce well-tested vertical ties to conform to the crabbily Eurocentric prophecy of a library-bound, chilblain-ridden expatriate *Schriftsteller*.

In the more advanced parts of the third world and in the second-world NICs, status is largely based upon class—that is to say, upon wealth. To the extent that opportunities are open to better one's position—even if only slightly—a class-based society tends to be stable. To the extent, however, that opportunities for economic advancement are lacking, class can take on some aspects of caste and a class-based society can become almost as rigid—and as unstable—as any other. A static economic monopoly, as in Somoza's Nicaragua or Trujillo's Dominican Republic or, for that matter, Nyerere's Tanzania—works against a strong human urge, the Jeffersonian Pursuit of Happiness.

This economic frustration, however, is felt by members of a class, not by the class itself. It can be easily defused by a clever government with money to spend.

ESTATE

Estate, for our purposes, is group-based status that can be achieved through other than economic means. It depends neither upon birth nor upon wealth—though, obviously, both of these factors help—but upon profession or position. It does not depend upon individual merit beyond the merit required to enter the profession or gain the position. A rural priest renowned for his womanizing and a metropolitan bishop renowned for his sanctity are equally members of the religious estate. Good and bad poets, good and bad journalists, good and bad philosophers, all belong to the intellectual estate. Lawyers, doctors, bureaucrats, and engineers—rich and poor—are united by estate. The military officer corps is in many third-world countries the most powerful estate of all.

Each estate has its customary or legally binding privileges. One may be addressed as "mullah," "licenciado," or "mon colonel." One may be allowed to transform bread and wine into Body and Blood or to take 1 percent off the top of all road-construction contracts. One may be exempt from serving in the military, from paying certain taxes, or from going to jail for minor crimes. One may be allowed to speak out against tyranny, when others not of the estate would be imprisoned or worse. One may become virtually untouchable except through the hierarchy of the estate itself.

The privileges of the estate, perhaps unearned by the individual, are on occasion matched by equally unearned dangers. Indeed, certain professions are the objects of an almost racist hatred. Professors as professors, not as individuals, may be lynched by students or executed by death squads, priests as priests may not be allowed to vote, generals as generals may be presumed without trial to be guilty of human rights violations, and journalists as journalists are always in peril of becoming men without names in cells without numbers.

Certain estates—the military in the third world, the clergy in the Islamic world, the press in the first world, and students almost everywhere— see themselves as guardians of the constitution, consciences of the nation, prophets of a better way, protectors of morality or democracy. These estates are elitist, profoundly antidemocratic in the Thoreau sense, putting their vision of what is right above the law, even in cases where the law is democratically decided upon. In the more stable societies, where relative deprivation is not acute, these estates march harmlessly around the civic square, keeping time to their different drummers, growling at the spectators, and generally feeling good about themselves. In less stable societies, other groups may fall in behind one or another of the marchers and coup, riot, or revolution is in the making.

RACE

Race in the status sense is not determined by blood or birth, but rather by caste. In the United States, for example, a very small amount of black blood can make one black, just as in Nazi Germany a very small amount of Jewish blood could make one a Jew. In other societies less influenced by Calvinistic or tribal fears of contamination (even in South Africa), more descriptive categories are devised. In Latin America (and nineteenth-century Louisiana), there are mestizos, mulattos, pardos, zambos, castizos, moriscos, octoroons, quadroons, and dozens of other groupings purportedly based on exact percentages of black, white, red, and (later) yellow blood.

These categories are largely fictions, however, the result of the classificatory mania of a handful of colonial and Peninsular Linnaeuses. In the real world of colonial Latin America (even in the Anglo-led Republic of Texas), it was quite possible to buy or be awarded a piece of paper that would officially turn any degree of black or red into white. Even today, in the Indian countries of the Andes and Central America, the difference between the indio and the ladino is not one of blood, but of language, dress, diet, and custom. Any Indian can cease to be an Indian simply by speaking Spanish and changing his shirt and shoes.

Of course, it is never quite that simple. It is always difficult to leave behind one's culture, language, family, and society—one's very identity— in the quest for social or economic advance. The fact that in some societies many choose to make the transition is both a sign of relative deprivation and a nonviolent means of dealing with relative deprivation. It may also be an indication that a formerly stable social subgroup is coming apart. Those who stay behind feel inferior, and those who cross the line feel treasonous. Each side may be tempted to use violence as a means of self-affirmation.

In Africa and Asia, some of what appears to be racism is really closer to envy, xenophobia, or tribalism. Black hatred for South Asians in East Africa, Malay hatred for Chinese in Indonesia and the Philippines, and the mutual hatreds of Tamils and Sinhalese, Sikhs and Hindus, Punjabis and Sindhis, Arabs and Berbers, Palestinians and Israelis, and Xhosas and Zulus all probably fall into this category. In none of these cases is there a strong, generalized belief in racial superiority or inferiority. True racism, as between some whites and blacks in South Africa, is of course also to be found in these areas.

CASTE

When a race or class or other social division becomes impossible—or nearly impossible—to escape, it can fairly be considered a caste. Although castes exist throughout the third world and throughout the first and second worlds as well, they are most highly developed in India. Percival Spear describes some older theories of their origin.

> Its origin has long been a subject of scholarly speculation. Thus the French scholar Senart thought that caste grew up as an extension of the tribe seeking to maintain its purity. The key for him was the purity of the conqueror. Sir H. Risley based caste on color feeling leading to marriage restrictions. The shortage of women, he thought, compelled the fair-skinned invaders to take dark brides. Aversion to color (still to be found in India) put a stop to the process as soon as the deficiency was made up. This would explain the unique marriage restrictions (exogamy, endogamy, etc.) which are the basis of caste. . . . For Hutton touch leading to pollution was a key, for this explains the aversion of the aboriginals for the invaders as well as of the invaders for the aboriginals. Caste restrictions are mutual, not merely imposed from the top downward.[3]

Spear goes on to list four characteristics of the Indian caste system: (1) occupational restrictions; (2) the "hereditary principle," expressed through marriage restrictions; (3) restrictions affecting diet, touch, and ritual purity; and (4) duty. The restrictions of caste are reinforced by the Hindu religion, which teaches that one's lot in this life, having been determined by one's actions in past lives, must be meekly accepted. One is perfectly justified in scorning the less fortunate and idolizing the more fortunate, because everything that exists is merited.

For our purposes, a caste is any hierarchical social division based on birth and endogamy and recognized by most people inside and outside the caste as *a good or natural thing.* It is often associated with contamination tabus. As Spear says, caste cannot be imposed merely from the top downward. (The caste cannot be completely "in itself"; it must also be "for itself.") The true member of the caste may want his caste to advance relative to other castes, but he does not want to leave the caste in order to advance. In the United States, for example, Martin Luther King, Jr., dreamed of ending caste; Malcolm X—before he became an orthodox

Muslim—dreamed of making his caste stronger relative to the dominant caste. Black student unions and segregated water fountains, black studies programs and burning crosses, "It's a black thing. You wouldn't understand," and "Go back to Africa!" are all designed to make caste coincide with race.

A caste system, while largely benefiting those on top, also has its comforts for those on the bottom. It is a refuge, a cocoon, and a closed shop. In an economy of extreme scarcity, such as that of India, a lowly caste—street sweepers, let us say—may be quite content to forgo opportunities for higher-status jobs in order to maintain a monopoly on sweeping the streets. A Peruvian Indian may find it preferable to remain in the familiar poverty of his caste than to take his chances in the more competitive ladino world.

CASTE WAR

While class war is virtually unknown in the third world, caste war is common. Classes are in no position to wage war. Not only do they lack class consciousness, except on occasion the middle class, but also—because they represent horizontal cuts of society—they lack resources and leadership. Most castes, on the other hand, have their own leaders, if nothing more than village mayors, and their own relatively rich, if nothing more than the ham-fisted organizers and exploiters of the sweepers' trade. A caste is an organized, functional society, whereas a class is little more than a collection of autonomous individuals.

Caste war is most likely in those situations where transcending caste is most difficult. In general and where possible, talented and ambitious individuals leave their caste in order to advance in the world. If, however, such a course is impossible or nearly impossible, these individuals will harness their talent—and their feelings of relative deprivation—to the task of elevating their caste as a whole.

The archetype of the caste war is the Guerra de las Castas in Yucatán, which lasted, with greater or less intensity, from 1847 until the early days of the Mexican Revolution of 1910.[4] Nelson Reed gives a good description of the relative deprivation that led the Mayas to war:

> Independence from Spain . . . made the social situation more explosive. The Creoles, formerly content to enjoy feudal rights under a monarchy that afforded some protection to the native population, became

interested in a fuller use of their human resources. The Church, tribal organization, anything that blocked the drive toward progress was swept aside. But native groups, subjected to greater pressure than ever before, were also more inclined to resist. Enlisted by the Creoles in the cause of revolution, they were awakened by it. They learned something of the military arts, and developed a taste for warfare; their knowledge of social injustice grew as they saw the Creoles break their revolutionary promises; and from small victories at arms, they formed an exaggerated idea of their own strength.[5]

It is worth noting that the more acculturated and less tribal Maya, somewhat better equipped linguistically and culturally to survive in the ladino world, often sided with the Mexicans against their fellow Maya. These acculturated Maya, already caught up in ladino patron-client complexes, adhering to a somewhat more orthodox form of Folk Catholicism, and well removed from tribal authority, essentially opted out of the caste and the war. This caste-transcending option was not available to Indians more distant from the centers of ladino population.

In a sense, the Caste War of Yucatán is not so different from the caste war that may be winding down in South Africa. The Afrikaners, with considerable help from the English, have done their best to create a caste society. True to their Calvinistic fear of contamination, they divided society into a number of endogamous groups based on race and enforced these divisions with the creation of "homelands" and a variety of other racist restrictions. Not only was black separated from white, but the blacks were separated by tribe and both blacks and whites were separated from the Asians and the "Coloreds."

Groups such as the largely Xhosa African National Congress, the Communists, and to a lesser extent the largely British Progressive Party and the Zulu Inkatha Party fought against the caste system. Other black groups, such as the Pan-Africanist Congress, essentially supported the idea of a caste system but wanted blacks, rather than whites, to be on top. Some individuals, including a fairly large number of Asians, a few Coloreds, the Soweto "black millionaires," and the many blacks who work in the South African security services, opted to transcend caste to the extent possible by making it in the white man's world on the white man's terms.

The war has been brutal and indiscriminate in that targets are often chosen by color and by color alone. Yet most of the brutality, whether by blacks or whites, has been directed against blacks. Despite the occasional bomb on a crowded street or the odd massacre of an isolated farm family, whites have been little affected. Indeed, they fear damage to their reputations as members of the "civilized West" far more than they fear for their lives.

The slow dismantling of the race-based caste system from the top under de Klerk threatens to substitute third-world chaos for second-world controlled disequilibrium. Blacks are no longer as united as before and tribalism is resurging. Asians and Coloreds are increasingly fearful. Timid English are putting their passports in order, and *verkrampte* Afrikaners are oiling their rifles. Common crime is up. *Tsotsis* and *"comtsotsis"* and racist Afrikaner punks are on the rampage. The economy is down and the good life is receding. It remains to be seen whether a few men of goodwill in the ANC and the National Party can avoid substituting catastrophic chaos for institutionalized injustice.

In caste-ridden India, there is a tendency to see all divisions as castes or at least castes in the making. A Hindu is as unlikely to marry a Muslim or a Sikh as he is to marry another Hindu of a lower caste. (Like Rajiv Gandhi, he is much more willing to marry a non-Indian where the question of caste does not enter than to marry an Indian of another caste or potential caste.) The Muslim and the Sikh return the compliment. Division becomes natural, group hatred universal, and individuals who choose not to think in caste terms lose out.

The formal Indian castes are almost certainly the fossilized remains of ancient conquests. Some believe that this is reflected in the name (*varna,* or color) that is given to the four broad occupational estates into which the Indian castes are grouped. Spear writes: "Instead of displacing the occupiers, as the Saxons did the Britons in England, they superimposed themselves. Thus arose that special feature of Indian society, the existence of races in social tiers, instead of side by side in contiguous groups. The racial as well as the social division of society was horizontal instead of vertical."[6]

Despite the secularism of the Congress Party that has dominated India since independence, the country remains a Hindu country, and minority religious groups, such as the Muslims, Sikhs, and Parsis, and racial-linguistic groups, such as the Naga, the Khasi, the Gond, and the Munda, are justified in fearing their eventual incorporation into the Hindu world as de facto inferior castes. It has happened before.

This fear of imposed caste at least partly accounts for the brutal civil war that is smoldering or flaring around the ethnic edges of India from Assam and Nagaland in the east to Kashmir and Punjab in the west to Tamil Nadu in the south. As during the Hindu-Muslim riots of Partition, the atrocities on all sides are so great that it is unlikely that the Kashmiri Muslims or the Punjabi Sikhs or the Mongolian peoples of eastern India will ever come to see themselves as Indians. It is even more unlikely that the Hindi-speaking Hindu majority will ever come to see these alien races and religions as their equals. The caste wars will continue.

TRANSCENDING SOCIAL DIVISIONS

As noted earlier, the permeability of social barriers is relevant to the stability of a society. Discontent—that is to say, relative deprivation—is common in permeable as well as in rigid societies and may lead to outbursts of violence, but this unrest is unlikely to spiral into regime-threatening instability. Even if many cannot or do not choose to take advantage of the escape valves, the mere fact that they exist is stabilizing.

To transcend a major social barrier—as British snobs, Marxist ideologues, and black separatists so often point out—is to be a traitor to one's group. It is to cut oneself off, to swim away from the sinking ship, to thrust off the clinging weak who threaten to drown not only themselves but also the strong. (Of course, one has every intention, once one is safe ashore, to go back out with a sturdy lifeboat.) Such a move requires ambition, talent, and a ruthlessness probably inspired by alienation within the group.

As I have already implied, there are three ways to transcend one's social group: by changing race, by changing class, and by changing estate. Changing race can, at times, seem very natural. Many a child enters the mission school as an indio and exits as a ladino, no longer even speaking the language of his parents. In other cases, it is more difficult because it is more final: the adult who turns his back on his village and "goes down to the coast," never to return; the low-caste Hindu who becomes a Muslim or Christian and thus loses his caste; the Sikh who moves to Canada and takes off his turban; the octoroon who one day gets out of bed and decides to "pass."

Changing class in the third world is largely a matter of talent and opportunity. The LDCs are, in general, little afflicted by the castelike restrictions that often grow up around class in the first world. In the third world, if you've got the money, you've got the class. And it matters little whether you inherited it from your grandfather, made it converting coca leaves into cocaine, or brought it back home after thirty years of drudge work in the United States. As long as one is slightly discreet, all money has the same color and the same smell. And a million made by an illiterate *cholo* in prostitution or politics will always top a thousand made by an educated white working in an office.

Changing class is not an escape valve for everyone. Even in an open, highly mobile society, it requires talent, ambition, and luck. (Not every Scots weaver's son is an Andrew Carnegie.) It happens most easily in times of chaos, in the aftermath of war or revolution, when old ways of making money, old business connections, old patron-client complexes, are torn apart by political and social violence. Under such circumstances, the quick-witted man on the spot, with nothing to lose and no ties to tradition, can make his fortune. The less talented and less lucky may still be able to move up a notch or two in economic status by moving to the city or by temporarily taking work abroad. Most people in most societies, however, will have neither the ability nor the opportunity to change class.

Where economic mobility is lacking, either because of castelike classes or because of general economic stagnation, changing estate may be the only option for the talented and ambitious. In much of colonial Latin America and the Islamic world, religion was a way out for the poor but bright. The pious and quick child at the parish school or the town *madrasa* would very likely be noticed and encouraged. After decades of study and service, he might find himself sitting in the episcopal palace or delivering the Friday sermon at the main mosque in the capital. At any rate, he would not be working in the fields with his brothers.

At the other extreme, criminality is an often used way of transcending one's social group in a rigid society. Like the priest, the criminal boss is always on the lookout for the bright kid, the boy who looks like he could be taught when to use a knife and when not to, the girl who with the right clothes and a few pointers could have those rich lechers downtown eating out of her hand. Not every kid recruited will end up a narcotics kingpin or presidential mistress, but for many, crime constitutes a better future than the *favela,* the *bidonville,* or the hardscrabble farm.

Halfway between the religious estate and the criminal estate (and partaking of both) is the political estate. The local machine politician always has an eye out for the person whose virtue, oratory, or thuggery makes him a natural to get out the vote (or who, at the very least, should be co-opted and neutralized). The revolutionary movement, inevitably top-heavy with university students and other upper- or middle-class elements, is always eager to recruit a genuine peasant or worker. Prospects for advancement are poor, however. In sharp contrast to religion and crime, it is relatively rare for someone born into a lower-class home to achieve a high position in either conventional or revolutionary politics.

Finally, there is the military estate. In many parts of the third world, the military is the closest thing to the Weberian bureaucracy that exists.[7] The officer corps, usually scorned by the upper classes, is the domain of the lower middle class, the sons of shopkeepers, moderately well-off peasants, village teachers, and the like. Like religion, crime, and the lower levels of politics, it is open to talent. It is not, however, as likely as these other estates to catch the bright kid at a young age, nor does it have their tolerance for initial illiteracy. Indeed, except in exceptional periods, progress to the upper ranks is generally limited to those who have attended the state military academy, which is rarely difficult for an ambitious member of the lower middle class. But unlike crime, religion, and politics, the military tends to isolate itself from the nepotism and civilian pressures that could prevent it from achieving its goals. It is thus often more open to talent.

It is these goals that make the military dangerous. The officer corps sees itself—often correctly—as the only group that is detached enough from parochial concerns to look out for the interests of the nation as a whole. Representing a broader geographical and economic cut of the nation than any other single group, less selfish than the upper classes, less obscurantist than the clergy, professionally educated, sworn to die for the nation if necessary, the officer corps sees itself as a natural judge and jury for the political sector and for much of the private sector. Convinced that only it is willing to make the hard decisions that others selfishly shun, the military institutes right-wing terror in Argentina, left-wing lunacy in Peru, and revolutionary economic progress in South Korea and Brazil. Though no friend to democracy, the military is the most dynamic—and the most broadly national—group in most areas of the third world.

CHAPTER 20

The Roots of Instability: Religion, I

Religions—and perhaps religion itself—go through cycles in which instinct gives way to ideology, which, in turn, gives way to habit. In some cases, the religion may die. The religion of ancient Egypt, probably the world's longest-lasting high religion, long ago ceased to be even a habit, and the religion of Babylon lives only in our daily horoscope. In other cases, religions or segments of religions complete the cycle, break through the shell of habit, and are born again as instinct. Christianity, at one and the same time, can be instinctive among the Pentecostals, ideological among the Liberation Theologians, and habitual among the Episcopalians.

Instinctive religion does not demand faith; it is believed because it is felt. Ideological religion requires faith—the willingness to believe something that one suspects may not be true. Instinctive religion, though often surrounded by ritual tabus and imperatives, does not concern itself with morals or formal theology. Its purpose is to empower, to comfort, and to explain. Ideological religion often concerns itself with little more than morals and theology. Its purpose is to regulate conduct, not to empower; to call to duty, not to comfort; to enforce an explanation, not to explain.

In general—and the exceptions are frequent—instinctive religion is politically stabilizing, ideological religion is politically destabilizing, and habitual religion is politically irrelevant.

T he first humans, powerless and fearful, developed an instinct for religion.[1] Like the even older and more purely animal instinct for leadership, the instinct for religion probably helped to preserve the race. It gave *Homo sapiens* a feeling of having some power over his fate, of understanding his environment, of being a who rather than a whom. Although this power was a false power and this understanding was a false understanding, the confidence that they engendered—and that they continue to engender around the world—was very real.

It is this instinctive religion—what most Christians call superstition, what Marxists call the opium of the people, what anthropologists call shamanism or animism or magic—that ensures that there are no atheists in the foxholes, that allows Adventists to survive prison camps better than Unitarians, that makes it possible for individuals to fight for life when reason tells them to stop. Instinctive religion is what we believe but know we shouldn't—that Friday the 13th is unlucky, that one can lick incurable cancer—in contrast to ideological religion, which is based on what we know we should believe but really don't—that Christ was born of a Virgin, that one should love one's enemies as oneself.

Ideological religion made some medieval Christians gleefully slaughter Jews and religious heretics. It fathered the Crusades, the Inquisition, and the hanging of the Salem witches. Even today it persecutes scientists and burns books. It hovers behind much of the world's imperialism, racism, and self-righteousness and constitutes a justification for genocide, war, and civil war. It is profoundly antidemocratic in that it elevates morality and right thinking (as determined by the few or perhaps by the One) above the popular will. It is profoundly antibureaucratic in that it elevates morality and right thinking above rationality.

On the other hand, ideological religion made some modern Christians run great personal risks to hide Jews and political heretics in Nazi Germany. It constitutes a rationale for sympathy, charity, and fellow feeling. It freed the slaves, improved the conditions of labor, aided the sick and the poor. On occasion it protects social and intellectual minorities. Most important, it often corrects its own excesses as well as the excesses of its archenemy, instinctive religion.

Instinctive religion, though comforting and empowering, is tribal, antisocial, and obscurantist. It is intolerant not out of principle, but out of feeling—though the result may well be the same. It believes that the sun revolves around the earth, not because God put man at the center of the universe, but because you can *see* that it revolves around the earth. It is ready to kill the stranger, not because he is a dangerous heretic who could endanger the salvation of others, but because he is *different*. It goes unafraid into battle, not because Right is on its side, but because it has a Holy Medal or a special ointment to ward off bullets.

Habitual religion is comforting in a very different way from instinctive religion. It is tolerant, sophisticated, civilized. It gets and gives a warm, comfortable, familiar feeling from going through the rituals, from linking itself to the past. Unlike instinctive religion, it does not believe. Unlike ideological religion, it does not pretend to believe. It chooses not to raise the issue; it pretends to pretend to believe. Although it is convinced that religion is a good thing, it suspects that all religions are pretty much the same and it shies away from those wild-eyed fellows who want to argue the pros and cons of predestination or to free the slaves. It is of no danger to anyone.

Instinctive religion—in the third world and elsewhere—is more powerful than ideological religion simply because what is "known" through instinct is more powerful than what is "believed" through faith. For the "knower," God—white beard and all—is as real as one's own hand, the United States is the Great Satan, homosexuality is pure evil, and the end of the world will come on March 12. For the "believer," God is essentially unknowable, perhaps more a symbol, "Providence," something between a person and a principle, maybe a force, like Love or Community, or, as they say, wherever there is Justice, there is God; though no country is fundamentally evil, the United States has misused its great power; the homosexual is made in God's image too; and, if we had perfect knowledge, we would see that science supports revelation. The "knower" dies for his religion because he has no doubts. The "believer" dies for his ideology in order to submerge his doubts.

MILLENARIANISM

Millenarianism is perhaps the only politically dangerous form of instinctive religion. Hagopian defines millenarianism as "the general category of movements which claim to replace the sinful, corrupt, or soon to be destroyed community with one that is directly inspired and informed by a religious rebirth. It promises a perfect society—'a land without evil'—in the sense of realizing the moral and religious commands of the divinity."[2]

He further defines "messianism" as "the most interesting form of millenarian movement. It is characterized by the exalted position of a charismatic leader or messiah over the community of adepts. The claims of the messiah run the gamut from being the spokesman . . . of the deity to being his direct incarnation. . . . The adept owes blind, unquestioning obedience to the messiah. . . . This may include exemption from further compliance with the moral and legal precepts of the traditional order. . . ."[3] Finally, all "messianic movements require (1) a discontented or oppressed collectivity, (2) hope in the coming of a divine emissary, and (3) the belief in a simultaneously sacred and profane paradise."[4]

Hagopian goes on to note that "subversive messianic movements . . . tend to occur in transitional societies poised midway between a traditional society and more modern forms of social organization. . . . The emergence of the social question is reflected in the predominantly lower-class appeal of the subversive messianic movements. . . . Prophecies that proclaim the complete overturning of class relationships—'the meek shall inherit the earth'—are especially in vogue. It should cause no surprise then that messianic movements of this type often come to practice forms of primitive communism. . . ."[5]

In a word, millenarianism is a desperate attempt to relieve relative deprivation. It responds to the breaking of the implicit promise that a society will remain recognizably the same. It is an instinctive defense against accelerating uncertainty, an answer to alien forces so strong that only magic can prevail against them. Although theoretically backward looking—seeking to restore a Golden Age, to purify a corrupted religion, to bring the people back to the beliefs of their fathers—millenarianism is the womb out of which most, if not all, new religions are born.

Millenarianism is instinctive, not ideological. It is magical, not rational. It feels but does not analyze the tragedy of a great religion corrupted. It feels but does not analyze the shame of a noble people brought under the heel of alien authority. It feels but does not analyze injustice, poverty, and oppression. Its hatred is so strong that it "knows" that chants will turn enemy bullets into water, that mysterious "medicines" will make its own troops invisible, that when all seems lost, God will send his angels to turn the tide of battle and drive the white devils into the sea. Its love is so strong that it "knows" that there is a better day coming, when the enemy will be gone, when war and hunger will disappear, when virtue will reign, when the lion will lie down with the lamb, when "angels would descend to teach . . . Western science and the English language, which they [the faithful] would be able to learn in a single lesson."[6]

While not all millenarian movements favor revolution or war—Christianity and Islam began at opposite ends of the spectrum in this regard but later converged—most bring violence in their wake because they are profoundly disturbing to the status quo. Most modern movements are undone by this violence whether or not they directly provoke it. Either, like the

Ghost Dance warriors of the American West and the Jim Jones cultists in Guyana, they essentially disappear, or, like the followers of Sudan's "Mahdi" Muhammad Ahmed and those of Brazil's Antônio Conselheiro, they are reabsorbed into the traditional religions out of which they came.

Nevertheless, some movements achieve substantial victories before they are snuffed out or otherwise disappear. China's White Lotus and Taiping rebellions threatened to overthrow an empire. The Cruzob of Yucatán's War of the Castes were able to seize a large area of land and hold it for half a century. The Canudos rebels of Antônio Conselheiro defeated expedition after expedition of the large and generally competent Brazilian army before their own final defeat. Sudan's Mahdi crushed the British and Egyptian armies of the famed "Chinese" Gordon.[7] The Mau Mau helped to free Kenya from British rule. Khomeini's Shi'ite fanatics not only overturned a strong, modernizing government but also fought the United States to a standstill before their movement was gutted from within.

Although millenarian movements like other religious movements are cyclical, not secular, and thus have little or no lasting effect in the political realm, they can be massively destructive in the short run. Only in such movements are the powerful forces of instinctive religion turned against the political order. In normal circumstances, instinctive religion "renders unto Caesar" and supports the status quo. Indeed, in the least developed countries, it is probably the principal means of coping with relative deprivation on the personal level.

THE STATE OF THE CHURCH IN LATIN AMERICA

In no area of the world is instinctive religion stronger or more politically stabilizing than in Latin America. The Catholicism that the conquistadores brought from Spain—itself a strange mixture of instinct and ideology—never caught on with the native populations. The Indians and the black slaves who followed them took what seemed reasonable and ignored the rest. The monks baptized en masse, declared a victory, and, in the interest of harmony and stability, averted their eyes from the actual beliefs and practices of the conquered. Fearing that they might uncover a mountain of innocent heresy beneath the thin soil of apparent acceptance, they wisely exempted the Indians from the Inquisition.

To this day, the semiacculturated Indian has no use for any sacrament except baptism, considers priests unnecessary and vaguely ridiculous, knows the San Miguel in his village to be completely different from the San Miguel of the next village, beats his saints' images when promised rain does not come, has no clear idea of who the pope is, finds Latin more powerful than Spanish—and either one preferable to some gringo priest trying to speak Quiché or Aymará—and is more concerned with propitiating the *aires* or fending off witchcraft than with living the moral life as defined by Rome.

In the cities—until recently, at least—it has been different. The Catholicism of the upper- and middle-class Creoles was as good (and as bad) as that of their counterparts in Spain. And the Folk Catholicism of the urban Indians and mestizos was somewhat more orthodox than that found in rural areas.[8] Sons and daughters of some of the best families took up the religious life, talented and intelligent sons (rarely daughters) of the poor turned religious vocations into social stepping-stones, and native-born priests not only filled the many churches of the New World but also established new missionary churches in wildest Asia. Despite its weaknesses in the countryside, colonial Catholicism was a going concern.

That began to change early in the nineteenth century, and well before the century was over, Catholicism ceased to be a major force in most parts of Latin America. (North Americans, perhaps misled by the fact that most Latin Americans still describe themselves as Catholic, are reluctant to recognize this development.) As colonial Latin America gulped down the ideas of the Enlightenment and prepared itself for revolution, the Church fell into disfavor with all classes except the poor, who continued to ignore Catholicism in favor of Folk Catholicism, and some reactionary Hispanophiles. Revolutionary priests like Miguel Hidalgo, José María Morelos, and Luis Beltrán dabbled in Freemasonry much as later Liberation priests would dabble in Marxism. The average urbanite, straddling tradition and enlightenment, justified continued belief in the Church by vicious attacks on the clergy.

Independence in country after country was followed by civil war between liberals and conservatives. The liberals favored nineteenth-century economic liberalism, science, limited democracy, and England, France, and the United States. The conservatives favored corporatism, tradition, authority, and Iberia. But these were side issues; the real battles were fought over the place of the Church in Latin American society. Although sometimes successful on other issues such as corporatism and authority, the conservatives lost badly on the main issue. The recognized heroes of the nineteenth century, from Benito Juárez to Domingo Sarmiento, were almost without exception anticlerical; the villains of the period were suspected (often without adequate reason) of being creatures of the Church.

Although Latin Americans continued to consider themselves Catholic, the atmosphere had changed. In country after country, the Church lost much of its property and privileges. No longer a rich *hacendado,* the Church was unable to maintain patron-client networks and the poor and weak drifted away to stronger patrons. The priest, far from being a figure of wealth, wisdom, or authority even among believers, became the pampered pet of women and an object of mockery to men. Upper- and middle-class families no longer considered the priesthood a fitting vocation for their children, and the churches emptied. Whereas once the Latin American Church had supplied missionaries to the rest of the world, now it was dependent on priests from Spain, Italy, Ireland, and the United States to keep open even a fraction of its churches.

Protestantism acquired a prestige among the upper classes, which it later lost, especially in the countries of the Southern Cone, and it became the religion of preference (after Folk Catholicism but well ahead of orthodox Catholicism) among the poor in many areas. European Spiritualism became popular among the literate, and African-based religions such as Umbanda and Candomblé strengthened their hold on the black poor and made deep inroads into the white middle class. The once orthodox middle and upper classes developed their own form of Folk Catholicism, in which priests should be seen and not heard, Rome should bugger off, and abortion was not a sin. As David Martin puts it:

> Curiously, in view of the stereotypical view of Latin America as securely and devoutly Catholic, the culture of the people has been quite resistant to Catholic teaching. This is very understandable in those areas where subject peoples have maintained an underground resistance to the religion of their masters. But it is also evident among the Hispanic and Creole populations, for whom such practices as priestly celibacy are unintelligible and who regard actual attendance at church as suitable only for the very young, the old and the women. Quite apart from this resistance there have been far more dissident and sectarian movements than is usually realized, especially in Brazil.[9]

Martin goes on to speculate that perhaps "less than 20 per cent of Latin Americans are regularly involved in the church. . . ."

The Church, again contrary to the stereotype, has little political influence, largely because it no longer has the wealth, connections, and patron-client arrangements that made it a political power in the past. (The idea that a "poor" Church would have more clout among the people than a "rich" Church was obviously conceived by someone who had never been in the third world—at least, not with his or her eyes open.) Even pious Catholics pay little attention to priests' political stands. A liberal or radical layman will applaud the liberal or radical pronouncements of priests, bishops, or the pope. A conservative or reactionary layman will make use of the conservative or reactionary statements of priests, bishops, or the pope. Neither liberals nor conservatives will pay the slightest attention to statements that do not further their interests.

There remain, however, two circumstances under which the Church still has considerable political power. The Church may be the only outlet for political opposition. As may be seen from the examples of Archbishops Miguel Obando y Bravo in Nicaragua and Oscar Romero in El Salvador, if other political expression is severely curtailed, a brave and outspoken churchman can attract a wide following. The second circumstance is when the Church has international clout. If the press and the government of the United States or Germany or Sweden decide to treat a Latin American bishop and his president as equals, then for many political purposes they are equal—no matter what the natives of the country think. It is ironic that even as it was losing the respect of Latin Americans, the Church was gaining what it had never achieved before in the Anglo-Saxon North: a favorable press.

LIBERATION THEOLOGIANS AND . . .

Nevertheless, some Latin Americans, braving the ridicule of their fellows, do become priests. Unlike the days of the distant past when the best and brightest of all classes vied to enter the priesthood, today's entrants are often upper-class misfits seeking shelter, not opportunity. Most live out their lives in benign obscurity, doing more good than harm. Some, however—usually the brighter and more worldly—slowly come to recognize their irrelevance, their lack of place in their own society. Profoundly alienated, they become frantic in their search for connections. Some turn to pisco, some turn to paramours, and some turn to politics.

The individual priest who mixes in politics—be he liberal or conservative—gains the illusion that he is once more a leader of the people like his counterparts in centuries past. Even more important, he gains the illusion that he has a firm place in society, that he is as important to the life of his country as if he were a general, an industrialist, a labor leader, or a revolutionary guerrilla.

The particular cause is not important. As one Brazilian remarked, "Anytime there is a group of people marching, some priest runs around to the front and pretends to be leading the march." Much depends upon fashion. Dom Helder Câmara, the radical archbishop of Olinda, Brazil, dabbled in fascism (Integralismo) in the 1930s when fascism was all the rage. In the 1960s and 1970s he moved to the left when Communism was in vogue. If the good padre is still alive, I'm sure that he is now preaching the glories of the free market, privatization, and plural democracy. This has nothing to do with opportunism or cowardice—the archbishop has always been willing to risk prison or worse—and everything to do with a kind of myopic search for relevance.

This nagging anomie constitutes the psychological background for the rise of Liberation Theology, a Belgian-German export to Latin America that is taken very seriously in North America. Although there are many forms of Liberation Theology, some quite tame, what the North American observer, friendly or hostile, generally means by the term is the syncretic mix of Catholicism and Marxism. Unlike what the conservative North American may think, Liberation Theology is not a cabal of Red priests foisting Communism onto the people in the guise of Christianity. Rather it is a loose group of alienated and doubting priests seeking to use Marxism to make their religion and themselves relevant. It is with a certain sadness that one thinks of them hopefully abandoning the storm-tossed but still floating raft of Latin Catholicism to board the glittering *Titanic* of Marxism only moments before it hits the iceberg.

Despite the good intentions of its practitioners, Liberation Theology (here again, I speak only of the radical Marxist version so admired and hated by North Americans) is saved from perniciousness only by its lack of resonance in the community. Its implicit philosophy that ends justify, and even sanctify, any means—the same kind of thinking that led Las Casas to advocate black slavery to alleviate Indian suffering—is corrosive of intellect and integrity. The Liberation priests, already—like Alice's Queen—used to believing six impossible things before breakfast, have no trouble twisting fact, logic, and Scripture to serve the people. As Anatole France might have said, "It's their métier."

Truth takes on a truly miraculous elasticity. Revolutionary violence is not violence at all. The only real violence is "structural" or "institutional violence," Orwellian terms that have little or no relationship to the dictionary definition of violence. Atheistic Communism is not really atheistic but a purer form of Christianity. Indeed, the Christian has a duty to be a Communist and a revolutionary.[10] Christ—he of the parable of the talents, he of "render unto Caesar" and "ye have the poor always with you," he who advocated Mary over Martha, he who would rather have his hair perfumed than give the money to the poor—suddenly becomes a revolutionary!

Closely related in the North American mind to Liberation Theology are the *comunidades eclesiais de base* (CEBs), the base communities intended to give the Catholic poor a greater say and a greater stake in their Church and thereby counteract the attraction of Protestantism. With the support of most sections of the Church (not just the Liberation Theologians), these lay groups have been created throughout Latin America, especially in Brazil. At one time, at least in the North American mind, they appeared to be the wave of the future. Now many—but by no means all—are being abandoned.

A problem, perhaps an insurmountable problem, is bound to arise when an authoritarian, hierarchical institution such as the Church tries to decree democracy from on high. What one gets is Rome's—or the local hierarchy's—idea of what the people would want if they were smart enough to know what they wanted. Moves that are often popular in the first world, such as turning around the altar or doing away with Latin, may be very unpopular in the third world. From the viewpoint of Folk Catholicism, orthodox Catholicism is just another foreign-based multinational corporation making decisions that affect the people without asking the people's opinion.

Thus the paradox of the CEBs: to the extent that they succeed, they fail; and to the extent that they fail, they succeed. The successful CEBs—the ones that last—are the ones that are actually taken over, Protestant style, by the laypeople. Yet these are often a disappointment to their sponsors. In a CEB that Rowan Ireland studied in Campo Alegre, Brazil, for example, the people, much more concerned with the "sin" of the landowner than with the "injustice" of the system, continually refused to allow the priest to push them into political action, did not know what to make of the priest's desire to wash their feet, were much more interested in discussing the Church's position on the Pill than was the priest, and generally preferred to think of Jesus as a lawgiver rather than as a liberator.[11]

This is not to imply that the people of Campo Alegre or elsewhere have no interest in politics or in political solutions, but rather that they go to religious entities for religious solutions and to political entities for political solutions. To the extent that the CEBs escape from the dead hand of the priest and become either purely secular social and political institutions or purely lay Folk Catholic institutions, they will live. To the extent that they remain under the "guidance" of the Church, they will die.

. . . PENTECOSTAL PASTORS

The Liberation Theologian has his antithesis in the Pentecostal Pastor, and the Catholic base communities are in part a response to the phenomenal growth of Protestantism—especially the more fundamentalist forms of Protestantism—in this century. In countries such as Brazil, Chile, El Salvador, Guatemala, and Nicaragua, 20 percent or more of the population is Protestant, and in almost all other countries of the region Protestantism is growing rapidly. These percentages understate the true extent of Protestant penetration because, whereas most Latin American Catholics, including an increasing number of Folk Catholics, are only nominal believers who rarely attend church, most Protestants are religion-obsessed. Moreover, this growth has taken place despite the vigorous opposition of an unholy alliance of the most retrograde sectors of the Catholic hierarchy and the most radical sectors of the revolutionary left.

Both the radicals and the reactionaries see Protestantism as a Trojan horse for U.S. economic or cultural imperialism. They could not be more wrong. Indeed, one of the main appeals of Pentecostal Protestantism is local control. Every church makes its own rules and every man and woman is his or her own theologian. Unlike the Catholic Church, in which educational requirements have made the priesthood almost impossible for the poor, any person—no matter how uneducated—can become a pastor or church leader in evangelical Protestantism. And if one doesn't like the church one is in, one can start one's own.

This "design your own faith" aspect of Pentecostal Protestantism, which seems the very antithesis of true religion to most mainline Protestants and Catholics, is the hallmark of a rapidly growing, instinctive religion. Unlike the Procrustean unity of the mainline sects, the "fragmentation" of the Pentecostals "enables them to stay popular (in the sense of reaching the mass of the people) and to create offshoots which can be offered either to those who are ready for mobility or to those who are already in the middle class."[12] Like the African religions of Brazil, which are also penetrating the middle class, the Pentecostal sects subordinate doctrine and ritual to "felt knowledge." In times of crisis, even orthodox Lutherans and Catholics of the middle class may find power in sacrificing to the *orixás* or comfort in speaking in tongues.

Although the appeal of Pentecostalism is religious, its effects are often social and political. Catholicism and Folk Catholicism are essentially communal, while Pentecostalism is essentially individual. Yet, paradoxically, individual responsibility often appears to have more benefits for the community than organized communal efforts. Against the leveling (but capital-squandering) *fiestas* and *cargos* of Folk Catholicism, Pentecostalism stresses hard work and thrift. Like the Puritans and Quakers before them, the Pentecostals have a reputation for business honesty, and even hostile witnesses admit that Pentecostal communities are generally cleaner and more prosperous than others. Drunkenness (almost a sacrament among Folk Catholics) and wife-beating are largely unknown among Pentecostals.

The Pentecostal community tends to be self-contained. Its dealings with the outside world—aside from that part that it believes to be ripe for proselytization—are correct and honest but cold. Its pastors come from within the group; no middle-class or foreign priest is needed to wash feet or raise consciousness. It creates informal support networks in place of the *compadrazgo* and patron-client complexes of the outer community. It values literacy and, by extension, all education. It sees wealth as a sign of God's favor rather than as prima facie evidence of sin, and its members are upwardly mobile to the extent that the society permits. It is serious and somewhat sad when compared with the colorful and often drunken traditionalism of Folk Catholicism. It has lost much but gained even more.

The Pentecostals are notorious for their support of the status quo—even in cases where the status quo is violent and oppressive. Often pacifist and inclined to "render unto Caesar," too absorbed in maintaining their own virtue and their relationship with God to worry overly much about the virtue of others, mistrustful of promises, they tend to opt out of political life. Aware that their religion is somehow "American" but with no strong connections to the United States, they tend to be strongly anti-Communist and to favor those causes that they identify—rightly or wrongly—with America. The Pentecostals will advance as individuals and not as a caste.

All instinctive religion, however, has millenarian potential. Should the implicit promise of the status quo—that those who support the state will not be molested—be repeatedly violated, it is not impossible that an Antô-nio Conselheiro could arise among the Pentecostals. Religions of the people—in contrast to religions for the people—always contain the seeds of revolt. The charismatic Pentecostal pastor, the Candomblé *pai de santo,* the Folk Catholic messiah—for now tacit allies of the political powers that be—each has a revolutionary potential that the Liberation Theologian can only dream of.

CHAPTER 21

The Roots of Instability: Religion, II

CHRISTIANITY AND ISLAM

Now that Marxism is dead or at least comatose, only two world religions remain—Christianity and Islam.[1] As religions, Christianity appears to be in slow decline, while Islam continues to rise. As civilizations, however, the Islamic is virtually dead, while the Christian (in its "post-Christian" or secular form) is taking over the world.

Christianity is, and always has been, much less of a piece than Islam. Christ and his early followers created an instinctive millenarian movement within the context of the Jewish tribal religion. Perhaps because the end of the world seemed imminent, the movement had very little formal ideological content. Although the writers of the Gospels, along with Saint Paul, who in all probability never knew Jesus, had begun to create an ideology of Christ as God based on some of Jesus' sayings, the real transformer of the Christian ideology was the Roman Empire.

Christianity, like a virus, entered the bloodstream of the empire (a "Republican" empire, in the beginning) at an isolated outpost and was soon—almost certainly against its expectations—carried around the known world. Without the Roman Empire, Christianity would have remained a Jewish heresy, a tribal sect rather than a universal religion. The first Christians were provincials, many at the very bottom of the imperial pecking order, and they were overawed by the imperial structure. Thus began the love-hate relationship between Christianity and Rome that continues to this day. Christ might have the Truth, but Caesar had the civilization and the organization.

Thus, through some combination of will and chance, the early Christians found themselves opting for Rome and against Palestine. From almost the beginning, they abandoned the Hebrew of the prophets and the Aramaic of Jesus for the Latin and Greek of the empire. This change of language was all-important: Latin in the West and Greek in the East became the prism through which the Christian saw his religion. To the mind behind the tongue, Jesus became a foreigner, speaking a foreign language, living in a foreign land, the product of a foreign tradition. The early Christian might be willing to die for his faith, but while he lived, he lived and thought as a Roman.

With Islam, it was very different. Muhammad alone created, or recorded, the Koran. Thus, unlike the Gospels (to say nothing of the other parts of the Old and New Testaments that the Christian is obliged to believe), the Koran is all of a piece. Moreover, Muhammad, the instinctive millenarian "Seal of the Prophets," was also Islam's principal ideologue. In a sense, he was Jesus, Saint Paul, and Caesar rolled into one. Like Moses, he was a leader, a lawgiver, a practical politician, and an organizer.

Whereas many early Christians saw the Roman Empire from the point of view of slaves and proletarians and were both awed and troubled by its grandeur, the first Muslims entered Christian and Hellenic Syria and Zoroastrian Persia as conquerors and, although impressed, they were far from overawed. Muhammad, or his dictating angel, had already set down much of the ideology, the laws, the political structure, the basis, of Islamic civilization; his followers felt free to pick and choose among the elements of the splendid civilizations they conquered, to accept what fitted and to reject what did not. Though Islam became a great urban civilization, much of the original desert ideology remained.

Most important, the conquering Muslims were in a position to retain their language and enforce it upon their converts. From Baghdad to Córdoba, Muslims came to see their religion through the same linguistic prism as its founder. They literally "spoke the same language." (Where the Arabs were unable to spread their language, as in Persia, India, Central Asia, and parts of Africa, they also had great difficulties maintaining orthodox Islam.) Unlike Christ, Muhammad never became a foreigner to his believers. Whereas Christianity piggybacked on an already existing empire to become a world religion—and in doing so embraced not only the trappings but also much of the spirit of the Classical world—Islam created an empire in its own image.[2]

The cultural familiarity of Muhammad for the Muslims worked to make Islam a way of life as well as a religion—indeed, Islam is based as much upon the *sunna* (the Prophet's habitual behavior) as upon the Koran—whereas the cultural foreignness of Jesus worked to separate religion from ordinary life for the Christian. All Muslims became in a sense honorary Arabs, sharing even mundane customs. Christians did not become honorary Jews. They honored only Christ's teachings, not his daily life, not his race, not his language. When the time came, it would be much easier for Christians than for Muslims to relegate religion to "its proper place."

The papacy had little importance during the first three hundred years or so of Christianity, but by the fifth century the bishop of Rome was in a position to challenge the emperors of the declining Western Empire. Indeed, he came to see himself as the preserver of imperial unity and his Church as the successor to the empire. Increasingly, "the Church became aristocratic in structure and autocratic in power, on the Roman imperial model."[3] The bishops, once elected by the people, were appointed by the pope. And the pope, far from being a Jewish high priest (or much less a learned rabbi of the Diaspora), had evolved into something like a Roman emperor. In time, he came to live in the same luxury, patronize the arts in the same way, and indulge in the same types of court intrigue. Moreover, he expanded the frontiers of Christianity much as the more vigorous emperors had expanded the frontiers of empire.

Christianity, which early on ceased to be Jewish and tribal, had finally become Roman and catholic in every sense of the words. All people were potential Christians just as all were potential Roman citizens. And Christianity, like Rome, was willing to accept foreign gods and religious customs —the Mother Goddess, the godlets who cure toothaches or protect travelers, the celebration of the winter solstice and the vernal equinox—as long as the pagans were willing to make a reverence to the Holy See.

Unfortunately from the point of view of both, Rome gained a pope without losing an emperor. Indeed, long after the empire had ceased to exist, there was no shortage of ambitious barbarians eager to claim the title and of popes who thought that the title was theirs to bestow. Both emperor and pope came out of the same imperial tradition, and neither was willing to accept the other on the other's own terms. The pope was, in effect, a rival emperor, claiming political as well as spiritual authority, while the emperor was a rival pope, believing it within his traditional rights to dictate the religious beliefs of his empire.

The emperors, in true Roman fashion, used Christianity as an instrument of politics, adopting or rejecting heresy and orthodoxy in order to achieve the ends of empire. In becoming Christians, they intended to run the Church for the benefit of the state. Like their pagan predecessors, they saw the Church as a national cult and the pope as (properly) a functionary of the state. The popes, reasoning that just as God was superior to all men so his vicar on earth was superior to all rulers, determined to render unto Caesar as little as possible. Eventually they fought each other to a standstill. Against the will of both emperor and pope, Church and state became separate and equal.

This constituted a religious and political first. Through all previous history, religion had been the support—not the rival—of the state. Though the religious establishment was often able to manipulate the ruler, it had to work through him, not against him. It neither had nor claimed political power in its own right. While Hebrew prophets might rant against Hebrew kings and Confucian bureaucrats might warn Chinese emperors of the fragility of Heaven's Mandate, they never claimed equality with the ruler, who was himself almost always heavenly ordained. ("King-makers" like Samuel were not prophets at all. Rather they were politicians, backroom manipulators who would have been at home in Kelly's Chicago.)

The political authorities of the empire and later Christian states never in their hearts accepted the validity of the Church as a political rival of the state. If God had wanted some priest to tell them how to run their kingdoms, he wouldn't have made them kings by divine right! Indeed, the Protestant Reformation was in part an effort by some German princes to return the bishop of Rome to his rightful subordinate place. However, once the Church—or any church—was seen as subversive or potentially subversive, it could never again be trusted. It had to be kept at arm's length. Secularism, for the first time, became not only possible but inevitable.

Nothing like this happened in the early days of Islam. The victorious Arabs, even as they conquered city after city and cast down emperors as magnificent as those of Rome, remained true to the consensus politics of the desert. They needed no pope, no ersatz Roman emperor to relieve their feelings of inferiority. They needed no priest to tell them what to believe. Anything that could not be decided by the Koran and the *hadith* (the codified "Traditions" of the Prophet) could be decided by *ijma* (the consensus of the faithful). Between authoritarian revealed law and democratic consensus, there was no room for a priestly estate.

Thus, in the Islamic world, there was no separation of Church and state and no need for purely religious professionals.[4] The early caliphs (the "successors" of Muhammad), much like tribal chiefs, came to power through a combination of rough democracy, treachery, and force of arms. They were anointed by no pope, and they claimed no unique religious authority. In a world where religion permeated political and all other life, they—like other Muslims of whatever estate—bowed to God and to the rules of their religion but to no churchman. Like Protestant Christians of a later date, the Muslim, ruler or ruled, had all the tools he needed to be his own religious authority.

Something of this spirit of simplicity, austerity, religious independence, and political consensus (*cum* skullduggery) still reigns among the more fundamentalist Sunni Muslims, such as the Saudi Wahhabis. With the Shi'ites, the matter is different. If the Sunnis have or at least had an austere, unadorned religion much like that of the seventeenth-century Puritans, the Shi'ites have a rich, complex religion like that of the Renaissance Catholics.[5] Whereas the religion of Muhammad was and is rigidly monotheistic, the religion of the imams gives quasi-divine status to Ali, Husayn, Fatima, and a host of others. Whereas the religion of Muhammad was egalitarian, the religion of the imams is hierarchical and status-proud. Whereas the religion of Muhammad was scornful of ostentation and intolerant of most art, the religion of the imams created a rich and sophisticated civilization marked by glorious artistic achievement.

At the time of Muhammad, the great Persian Empire, which included parts of Arab Iraq, was, unlike that of Rome, very much a going concern. Yet the glorious armies that were a match for the best of Christian Byzantium were struck down by the rabble from the desert, and the Persians—and to a much lesser extent the Iraqi Arab heirs to Babylon's splendor—still smart from the shame. The implicit promise of eternal superiority of the old civilizations collapsed into a void of relative deprivation. Shi'ism is essentially the Persian way of accepting and adapting the religion of Muhammad while proudly rejecting the culture of the desert Arabs.

Shi'ism is not, like Protestantism, a reform movement that eventually took on political overtones. Rather, it began as a purely political movement among those generally urban Arabs (the Shi'a or "partisans" of Ali, Muhammad's son-in-law) whose interests would best be served by a strictly hereditary caliphate. Originally it had no particular religious content, but the Persians, who flocked to the movement for political and psychological reasons, took the opportunity to add their own pre-Islamic religious and political ideas. *Ijma* was cast aside in favor of a powerful priesthood ruled over by a sinless, infallible, and quasi-divine imam descended from Ali. The twelfth imam disappeared, or was "occulted," in 872 and is expected to return sometime in the future to restore the rule of the just. In the meantime, a status-proud religious establishment that stems from Persepolis, not Mecca, rides high.[6]

During the centuries when Islamic civilization was at its height, it was tolerant and vibrant, eager to borrow, eager to create, eager to preserve. And, although religion pervaded life, it was not an excessively religious civilization. Indeed, it was far less God-tormented than Europe during the same period. Science and exploration, commerce and engineering, art and literature, philosophy (even atheistic philosophy) and linguistics thrived. Jews and Christians of talent were honored, Saint Louis and Saint Francis of Assisi were welcomed at (and impressed by) the Ayyubid court, and, despite the Koran, wine and speculation flowed freely. Indeed, just as the spectacular Christian civilization of the Renaissance elbowed the Christian religion to the back of the picture, so the grand Islamic civilizations of India, Persia, Central Asia, Iraq, Syria, Egypt, the Maghreb, and Spain paid only superficial attention to the Muslim religion.

Europe, with a bit of Muslim help, eventually woke from its dark ages and shook off the monsters of the sleep of reason. Renaissance popes learned to subordinate religion to culture. Reformation firebrands proved that Christianity was infinitely divisible. Counter-Reformation intellectuals trimmed the fat out of theology and ethics. Enlightenment philosophers dethroned faith and installed reason. The Industrial Revolution transformed the physical world, while political revolution ushered in democracy and socialism. Western self-confidence exploded, and imperialism and racism were reborn as the White Man's Burden.

The Islamic world was not prepared. In the ensuing clash, Islamic civilization withered because it was incapable of protecting itself by its own means. Because there was no separation between Church and state—indeed, there was no Church at all—the Islamic countries were unable to adopt the tools of Western progress without betraying their own civilization. Islam was a way of life, not just a religion. It could be betrayed by wearing a fedora, by adopting a political constitution, by attending an opera, or by building a factory. Unlike the Japanese of the Meiji Restoration (for whom religion in the Western sense was unimportant), who were able to adopt Western ideas wholesale and somehow become even more Japanese in the process, the political reformers of the Islamic world tore their culture apart.

Islamic civilization withered with every machine gun and European mercenary imported to protect its borders. It withered with every Algerian studying administration at the *Grandes Écoles,* with every Pakistani studying strategy at Sandhurst, and with every Iranian studying physics at MIT. It withered with every intellectual discussing Sartre in a Beirut café and with every revolutionary reading Marx in a Cairo slum. What good was this "glorious" Islamic civilization if it couldn't stamp out cholera or produce a nuclear weapon?

Like the early Christians facing the grandeur of the Roman Empire, present-day Muslims are overawed by Western civilization. But, unlike the early Christians, who essentially had no civilization and thus were able to appropriate Classical civilization for their own purposes, the Muslim can only adopt Western civilization by rejecting his own.[7] But adopt he has, and adopt he must. He can pretend to "Islamize" factories and fedoras, but he sees through his own pretense. Either all the answers are in the Koran and the *hadith* or they are not; the leaders of the Muslim world— the fundamentalists of Iran and the Sudan as well as the secularists of Algeria and Tunisia—have all cast their vote for separation of Church and state, for the creation of a civil sphere, against the way of the Prophet. And in their hearts, they know it.

The implicit promises of value and continuity have been broken. Cultural treason is a condition of survival, and relative deprivation reigns among rich and poor alike. Although the glorious civilization is no more, one can still turn back to the religion.

THE ISLAMIC WORLD TODAY

Instinctive religion is the opium not only of the masses but also of anyone who is in dire need of a painkiller. The Islamic world faces a series of brutal operations that will either modernize it or kill it—and it needs all the painkillers it can get. Whereas the triumphant Islamic civilization of the Middle Ages could guzzle wine and honor a philosopher (Averroës or Ibn Rushd) who preached that Aristotle was superior to Muhammad and speculated that life ended with death, the shattered Islamic civilization of the present is turning in its pain to a faith so narrow and reactionary that it would scandalize Harun al-Rashid or Akbar and probably trouble even the Prophet himself.

"Fundamentalist" Islam—which is not really fundamentalist at all—is not a movement of the villages. In many cases, it is not even a movement of the urban poor. The villagers and many of the urban poor have their own instinctive religion, a Folk Islam that serves their purposes very well. In rural Iran, for example, where life itself rather than the West is the challenge, the villagers have traditionally scorned the mullahs ("On the Last Day 70,000 mills will be turned by the blood of bad mullahs") and do not support the rule of the ayatollahs in Tehran.[8] Yet their religion, largely self-administered, heavy with magic, continues to comfort and empower.

Fundamentalism is more a movement of the middle class, of those who have had extensive and bruising contact with the West. In most countries, it is strongest in the universities and has its greatest following among students of the hard sciences. It is strong among the intellectuals, merchants, and religious professionals who see their traditional position eroded by Western publications, corporations, and experts. It is strong among the children of the Westernized elite, who confuse generational conflict with religious principle. It is strong among the new workers, who could comprehend the weather cycle that once threatened their crops but not the business cycle that now threatens their jobs. It is strong among the Pakistanis of England and the Algerians of France. It is strong wherever a Muslim has been made to feel inferior abroad; it is even stronger wherever he has been made to feel inferior in his own country.

It comforts, it simplifies, it empowers. It returns the Muslim to a position of superiority. It allows him to believe that Western civilization is crumbling with drug-fed criminality and selfish materialism ("Even your own philosophers admit it") and that Islam is being increasingly accepted as the wave of the future ("Your blacks, they are all Muslims now, are they not?"). It allows him to believe that all the wonders of Western science can be derived from the words of Muhammad or the book of Lugman. It allows him to blame all evil on the United States, Israel, and the Devil— whom God allows to triumph now but will cast down in the future. It allows him to feel the thrill of solidarity and the rush of adrenaline as he joins his voice to the millions screaming against the Great Satan. It makes life bearable.

When all is said and done, however, Islamic fundamentalism, at least among the Sunnis, remains more of an opiate for the people than a threat either to their rulers or to the West. Like seventeenth-century Puritanism, Sunni Islam provides a justification for totalitarianism on the one hand but makes it impossible to put into effect on the other. Where every man is his own priest and the Book is there for all, religious and political conformity, no matter how desirable in theory, is almost impossible to achieve in practice. The structure of authority just isn't there.[9]

Although individual rulers in the Islamic countries are wise to respect their religious opposition, the Western fear of a fundamentalist tide advancing unchecked across the Islamic world seems to be unjustified. The country people from Mindanao to the Maghreb are well sedated by Folk Islam, and while they may revolt from time to time, such revolts are unlikely to be for religious ends or under religious leadership. The urban

masses, seething with relative deprivation, may thrill to the example of a
Khomeini, much as they did earlier to the secular Nasser and later to the
secular Saddam Hussein, twisting the tail of the imperialist dog, but they
would rather be spectators cheering from the sidelines than active partici-
pants. Indeed, the example and the cheering are all they need to relieve
their relative deprivation. They have no need for risky political action.

The religious establishment even in Shi'ite countries is not all of one
mind; in the Sunni countries there is no unity whatsoever. Fundamentalists may mutter about Saudi or Indonesian corruption or about Egypt's
opening to Israel, but in all three countries many of the most important
religious professionals have been heavily influenced, not to say co-opted,
by the government. Some may cast aspersions on the Moroccan monarchy,
but others find it hard to fault King Hasan, who is after all a descendant of
Ali. In Lebanon, Syria, and Iraq, various varieties of Sunnis, Shi'ites,
Druze, Christians, and secularists are further divided by clan, tribe, and
"nation." In Pakistan, bitter disputes among Sunnis, Shi'ites, Ahmadis, and
mystics of various stripes are only part of the problem; Punjabi distrusts
Sindhi, who distrusts Baluchi; immigrants from India vie with refugees
from Afghanistan as well as with natives; soldiers and civilians eye each
other with mutual scorn; and secularists have enough clout to make a
woman head of government.

The situation is only partly different among the Shi'ites. True, they have
the hierarchy and the millenarian tradition and a lust for martyrdom for its
own sake. (Indeed, the Iranian obsession with blood—one's own or that of
the enemy or preferably both—as necessary to feed the growth of the
religion strikes me as more Aztec than Islamic. The "hanging" Ayatollah
Khalkhali, obsidian knife in hand, would feel perfectly at home atop a
blood-covered Mexican *teocalli*.) But they also have an alternate tradition
of quietism and respect for civil authority. As the failure of the Islamic
republic becomes more obvious, this tradition—pushed authoritatively by
an alternate set of ayatollahs—may well come to the fore. The Shi'ites of
Iran, Iraq, and Lebanon would once again become the model citizens that
they have so often been in the past.

This is not to say that Islamic fundamentalism will have no impact. A
few extremists can always murder a president or even create a war. Public
opinion can force secular or even nominally religious regimes to slow modernization or adopt counterproductive laws. Emerging democracies can be
faced with the dilemma of freely elected totalitarianism. But there is no
clear trend. As fundamentalism rises in one country, it declines in another.
The Muslim Brotherhood, largely defanged in Egypt and partially tamed
in Jordan, may still be a threat to the state in Syria. But that too will pass.

THE FUNDAMENTALIST CYCLE

Fundamentalism in any religion appears to run in cycles. This does not mean that the ardent believers, suddenly disillusioned by the failure or moral turpitude of a Khomeini or a Swaggart, renounce their beliefs of a lifetime. No, the United States will continue to be the Great Satan and the Bible will continue to be "inerrant"—but, somehow, it will no longer matter as much. Enthusiasm will wane, life will get back to normal, secular concerns—family and work—will become more important. The end of the world may not come tomorrow, but even if it does, I've got to feed my family today. Let the mullahs and the preachers worry about such things; that's what they're paid for. After every Great Awakening, there is a Great Period of Exhaustion and then, very often, a Great Sleep.

Fundamentalism is both belief and catharsis. The belief may be stable or evolve only slowly over time. It is a worldview, a framework for life and thought. It tells the believer who he is, where he is, and why he is—and then allows him to get on about his life. The catharsis comes only when needed. It may be personal. The dozing believer is suddenly shaken awake. He loses his wife, his child, his job, he wakes up drunk in a gutter or comes out of an argument, surprised, with a bloody knife in his hand. In a flash of light, he sees God, and everything else becomes unimportant. Working for the Lord, his deprivation is eased.

Catharsis may also be societal. The woes of a society may become so great that the mass of believers sees no alternative but to renounce their sinful ways and return to the God of Old. God inflicts the shah upon us because we do not veil our women. God will not smile upon Israel until the Law of Return is amended to allow only the Orthodox. The problems of Indian society cannot be solved until we destroy the mosques and rebuild the Hindu temples. How can we ever expect to catch the Japanese when nobody goes to church, men sleep with men, girls get abortions, and pornography is on every newsstand? Let's all do what we know God wants us to do!

There is a surge of emotion and a flurry of activity. Some people usually die. The shah is gone—but another is undoubtedly waiting in the wings. Israeli law becomes more orthodox—but the people continue to become more secular. A few mosques are torn down brick by brick—but thousands remain in India. The First Amendment is nibbled at—but the United States remains a secular country. The believers all feel better—but nothing has really happened. The catharsis has worked. The Great Awakening is over, and civilization has once again survived.

Because *Homo sapiens* has a religious instinct, fundamentalism as belief will remain and, from time to time, grow. Islamic fundamentalists are doing well in sub-Saharan Africa, and Christian fundamentalists are doing well in Latin America. Individual believers in need will continue to find catharsis in religion. Fundamentalism, like other forms of instinctive religion, will continue to empower and explain.

Because *Homo sapiens* also has a mind, fundamentalism as political catharsis on a society-wide scale will be spasmodic and short-lived. It may eventually die out altogether. It never succeeds in achieving its broader aims, it is always destructive, it is always a costly diversion from a rational solution to the societal problems that brought it forth.

Although the beliefs involved may change, the cycle of fundamentalist belief—the seesaw of comforting faith and productive reason—will probably never die. Nor should it. When a problem cannot be solved, irrational belief can at least comfort while impotent reason only creates frustration. The "good name" of fundamentalism as social catharsis, however, is slowly being undermined by the evolution of society and morality. The cycle of political fundamentalism—the ebb and flow of lynch-mob religion into and out of the political sector—may eventually be broken. We can hope.

CHAPTER 22

The Roots of Instability: Economics

In the unstable equilibrium that characterizes the third world, poverty more often contributes to the surface equilibrium than to the underlying instability. Poverty, "age-old" poverty, "changeless" poverty, "numbing" poverty, saps the will to revolt or even to progress. Some of the most tranquil societies in the most tranquil periods of history have been marked by such poverty. But such societies are static. If the leadership of such a society wishes to have an effect on the domestic scene or to be noticed on the international scene, it must stimulate economic discontent in its own people in order to create the national wealth necessary to finance political ambition.

But not all third-world societies are poor. Some are rich. Their wealth, however, based as it always is on primary products, is itself unstable, and the loss of such wealth, whether gradual or sudden, inevitably leads to political unrest.

Over the long run, economic change—though not necessarily economic progress—is inevitable. And the political and societal costs are high.

Although never the Edens pictured by romantics of the past, during much of history many parts of the third world—before it was labeled as such—were hotbeds of apathetic content. Tribesmen warred, hunted, procreated, and died. Peasants worked hard, feared witchcraft, found solace in religion, beat their wives, and created remarkably

little economic surplus. Landowners lived lives of pride, poverty, ignorance, and sloth, rarely bestirring themselves except to sire large numbers
of children who would grow up to be even poorer and lazier. Politicians—
those cursed with the leader's lust to dominate—played a bloody but en-
tertaining chess game in the national capital. But it was only a game; the
presidential sash or its princely equivalent had no power behind it. The
unspoken but comforting assumption was that human labor, though part of
one's lot, had little effect on outcomes. What would be, would be.

Although many in the third world were as obsessed with money as any
in the first world, money actually played a very small part in the organization of economic life. (Perhaps this accounts in part for the romantics'
idealization of the non-Western world.) Tradition, not any rational effort to
increase wealth or avoid poverty, determined both one's calling and how
one conducted that calling. Tradition, not the market, determined the "just
price" for goods and labor. Change, even the thought of change, threatened order in this world and salvation in the next.

This world, so much like that of the medieval West, has tended to hang
on, to resist change under a veneer of "progressive" jargon. Yet, despite its
conservatism, it is a world being eroded by many of the same factors that
brought the West out of the Middle Ages. The transistor radio can be as
revolutionary as the printing press, Coca-Cola as enticing as the spices of
the East, the crusade against Communism as upsetting as the crusade
against Islam, J. R. Ewing as potent a role model as Marco Polo. Over
time, the individual counts for more and tradition for less. (And the romantics, not totally without reason, mourn the loss.)

In the beginning, Western imperialism did little to change traditional
attitudes of comforting hopelessness. After all, conquerors were part of the
nature of things, like earthquakes, drought, storms, and locusts. People
who had survived the Incas, or the Mongols, or the Macedonians were not
overawed by sixteenth-century Europeans. As in other cases of conquest, a
command economy was at least briefly superimposed on the traditional
economy, but the commands reached the masses only through many filters
of tradition. If, during the first few weeks of the new order, one could
avoid becoming part of an exemplary pyramid of skulls, one's life could go
on much as before. This too would pass. Although there was good luck and
bad luck and God would have his jest, nothing ever really changed.

Yet, with late Western imperialism, something was changing. The nineteenth-century imperialists, unlike their predecessors of the sixteenth and
seventeenth centuries, were driven by the idea of progress. Almost without
thinking, they divided the world into modern and primitive, first and third,
human and apprentice human. They were the leaders and all others (if

pigmentation allowed) were destined to follow in exactly their path. No more blaming God or Nature or Bad Luck! No more *Inshallah!* No more *Si Dios quiere!* One's future was in one's hands. Get a move on! Progress or perish! Fatalism, that final and most comforting weapon of the conquered against the conqueror, was powerless against these new crusaders.

Economic progress became a possibility and, once a possibility, it became a duty. The traditional world, though extremely difficult to change, became impossible to live with. Squirming under the smug gaze of the North, Europeanized leaders blamed the inadequacy of their peoples, and consumerized peoples blamed the inadequacy of their leaders. Leaders lusted for nuclear-backed respect, and peoples lusted for Hollywood lifestyles. Relative deprivation was rampant.

Leaders, lacking the bureaucratic instruments to effect economic change, resorted to the magic of words and symbols. Like the creators of the post–World War II cargo cults of the Southwest Pacific—in which docks and landing fields, complete with bamboo radars and palm-frond control towers, were constructed to conjure G.I. abundance back to savage isles—these leaders adopted the semblance of economic strategy without its content. In the nineteenth century, a frock coat or an opera house or a streetcar line in the capital was somehow expected to transform a stagnant tropical subsistence economy into a European powerhouse. In the twentieth century, a well-thumbed copy of Marx or a steel mill rising in the jungle was expected to serve the same purpose.

During most of the twentieth century, socialism has been the cargo cult of the third world. Leader after leader has declared his country "socialist" and then sat back and waited for the magic word to have its effect. But only the Soviets and the Americans were fooled. The state still had no power. A Soviet-style command economy could be proclaimed but rarely could it be enforced. Bureaucrats (of a distinctly non-Weberian type) became proficient in leftist jargon but had no real interest in transforming anything. Economic life either remained traditional or was slowly absorbed into the Western market system. Class continued to be submerged by tribe or caste, and the masses remained only masses. To encourage such a "progressive" nation, the Russians might build a dam or the Scandinavians might create a fishing cooperative—only to see it destroyed bit by bit for family or tribal gain.

Now socialism is out of favor. The magicians of the latest cargo cult talk of "markets" and "privatization." But the state still has no power. The bureaucrats, now citing Friedman rather than Marx, still have no interest in transforming anything. Economic life is still being absorbed into the Western market system at the same slow rate. The only difference is that the leaders have renounced socialism for capitalism. They still fumble for the right incantation that will magically elevate them to first-world status.

Western advisors—and to the third world the West seems to consist largely of advisors—are busy hawking their own incantations from "economic empowerment" and "basic needs" to laissez-faire capitalism and democracy. Like the nineteenth-century robber baron who attributed his rise to wealth to his religious principles and not to the skullduggery that was actually the cause, the pundits of the West, as they preach to the third world, conveniently forget how European and North American industrialization was really achieved. The economic rise of the West was built upon inequality, deprivation, mercantilism, and authoritarianism. As Mae West might say, "Goodness had nothing to do with it."

THE END OF COMPARATIVE ADVANTAGE

Capitalist governments often pretend to believe that if (other capitalist) governments would just refrain from interfering with international trade, the world would soon reach a nirvana in which all countries would produce only those products in which they had a comparative advantage and import whatever else they needed. All countries would then have the highest feasible standard of living. While no government believes this strongly enough to institute it as an across-the-board policy (some have a far better record than others), many governments feel that it is a good doctrine to preach to the third world.

In the nineteenth century, comparative advantage seemed to work. Countries of "recent settlement" such as the United States, Canada, Australia, New Zealand, Argentina, Uruguay, and to some extent Brazil, Chile, and South Africa appeared to thrive by exporting agricultural and mineral products to Europe and importing European manufactured goods. The English worker got cheap food and raw materials, while the American farmer got cheap cloth and tools. Mississippi planters and Argentine *estancieros* were able to afford a very comfortable lifestyle, while mine owners in Australia and South Africa amassed world-class wealth. It was hard to argue that the third world was being shortchanged.

Yet the seeds of progressive and cumulative economic inequality were being sown. Demand for primary products—everything from corn and rubber to oil and copper—is inelastic in the short run. A reduction in supply, through a typhoon or a strike, for example, can send prices and earnings soaring. An increase in supply, through putting new land into cultivation or improving mining technology, can destroy entire economies. Depending on what is happening elsewhere in the world, a frugal, well-run, one-crop economy can go broke, while a profligate, chaotic, one-crop system can go from wealth to wealth. Industrious ants may be exterminated, while spendthrift grasshoppers are rewarded.

In the world of primary producers, outcomes are detached from inputs and economic life is a continual crapshoot. A bumper crop in one country can trigger disastrous price drops around the world, a labor dispute in Chile can boost copper earnings in Zambia, the end of a war in Korea can devastate the market for wool in Uruguay, a move to spur economic growth in the United States can make gold prices soar in South Africa. Entrepreneurial effort and wisdom on the individual level, like sound fiscal and monetary policy on the national level, count for little or nothing. Virtue has no sure reward, nor is vice consistently punished. It's all in God's hands.

In the short run, inelastic demand makes primary product production a crapshoot; in the long run, it's a mug's game with the odds strongly favoring the house. Counterintuitively, the growth of technology leads to a secular decline in demand for raw materials relative to supply and, therefore, to a similar decline in the real prices of almost all primary products. Fiberglass replaces metal in everything from telephone lines to automobiles. Engines are built from ceramics. Scrap metal becomes so abundant that it is cheaper to recycle than to mine. Plant genetics create Green Revolutions that stave off starvation at the same time they destroy marginal farmers. GNP per unit of energy soars across the board. Raúl Prebisch proves to be wiser than David Ricardo. Ant and grasshopper are equally squashed under the boot of technological progress.

As Eric D. Larson, Marc H. Ross, and Robert H. Williams have pointed out in a highly illuminating article in *Scientific American,* "economic growth is no longer accompanied by increased consumption of basic materials."[1] After documenting the truth of this statement, they offer two explanations: more efficient use of materials; and saturation of markets. The saturation of markets, which they consider to be the more important factor, is the result not only of overbuilding—the world, generally speaking, has the highways, factories, and cities that it needs and only requires replacement, not new construction—but also of a change in consumer preferences:

> The affluent tend not to spend additional income on more of the same—yet another car, for example. Instead marginal income is often spent on items such as a video-cassette recorder, a personal computer

and the accompanying software, membership in a health club, better health care or a service that provides stock-market information. Although such goods and services are disparate, they are characterized by a low materials content per consumer dollar. There are now no significant new markets for consumer goods having a high content of materials per dollar.[2]

It may be argued that even if the first world is saturated, most people in the third world would still like to own their first car. Their market for highways, factories, and, unfortunately, even cities is far from saturated. To this, the first world blithely but quite sincerely answers that "growth is not the same as development," that cars cause global warming, and that the third world should stop being so materialistic and start thinking about preserving the rain forests. Typically, once the first world is sated, it decides that it is time for *everyone* to go on a diet. Perhaps fortunately for the earth, but certainly unfortunately for the third world (and for industrial workers in the first world), the developed West still has the power to call the tune.

In truth, the third world, though not everyone in the third world, benefited from the first world's orgy of consumption. Despite the rantings of the dependency theorists, more often than not first-world waste put money into third-world pockets, the center supported the periphery. Now the first world, smugly virtuous in its newfound simplicity, is spending its money for spring water rather than Volvos and turning out the servants to starve. Small is beautiful, indeed!

CORRUPTION

Just as one man's terrorist is another man's freedom fighter, so one man's corruption is another man's ingenuity. Corruption is nothing more or less than an unorthodox means of solving problems, and the problems solved range from how to support a mistress on a junior clerk's salary to how to save the country from military takeover. Depending on the nature of the problem that corruption solves, and the efficiency with which it solves it, corruption can be either good or bad, politically stabilizing or destabilizing, economically beneficial or harmful. In general, though there are exceptions even here, corruption that has some other aim than personal enrichment has the best chance of being beneficial.

In an article in *The American Political Science Review,* J. S. Nye—while noting that "one of the first charges levelled at the previous regime by the leaders of the coup in the less developed country is 'corruption.' And generally the charge is accurate"—gives a persuasive list of corruption's real-world benefits, including economic development, national integration, and governmental capacity. He then shows how, under certain circumstances, corruption can undermine these same benefits.[3]

Nye believes that corruption is most likely to be beneficial in a society characterized by: "(1) a tolerant culture and dominant groups; (2) a degree of security on the part of members of the elite being corrupted; (3) the existence of societal and institutional checks and restraints on corrupt behavior." Rationalizing that these three conditions are relatively rare in the third world, he concludes that in most cases the costs of corruption will exceed its benefits. The reader comes away with the feeling, however, that Nye made a stronger case for corruption than he was happy with and that, at the last minute, he twisted amoral facts into a slightly more moral conclusion than may have been justified.[4]

On reflection, I am convinced that this is not the case. Putting Nye's analysis into our third world/second world framework, what he seems to be saying is that moderate corruption can be both politically stabilizing and economically productive in a relatively placid third-world country. After all, corruption is the lifeblood of the patron-client structures that give most third-world countries their surface equilibrium. Moreover, in the third-world context, it is to everyone's good for a potentially productive enterprise to buy its way around senseless bureaucratic obstacles. Just as it is to everyone's good for the government to spend a million bribing its generals rather than to spend a billion bribing its army with unnecessary weapon systems.

Corruption, unless excessive or grossly mishandled, has a certain calming influence in the third world. As the reader will recall, the third world is characterized by the dominance of the private sector—family or tribe or company or patron-client complex—and to a lesser extent the political sector. There is no independent bureaucratic sector. Through corruption the political sector protects the wealth of the private sector, while the private sector keeps the politicians in office. Each of the two major sectors gets what it wants, and the overall stability of the society is enhanced.

Corruption, however, while it may facilitate political tranquillity and even individual economic progress in the placid third-world state, is deadly for the kind of sea change that bumps the restless third-world state into the second world. In the goal-oriented, positive-sum game of the second world, an honest and effective bureaucracy is essential. I believe this is close to what Nye had in mind when he wrote of corruption's potential either to reduce or to increase administrative capacity. Corruption makes the third-world state easier to run but harder to change.[5]

Whatever its benefits or costs, corruption—in the third world as in the first—has a bad sound to it. It makes a good scapegoat. Wherever people riot, wherever governments are overthrown, corruption is given as an explanation and a justification. Western journalists nod sagely and file their stories, never wondering why there were no riots in previous years when corruption was just as great or why the even more corrupt country next door is still at peace. When corruption is working properly—that is, when it is relieving relative deprivation—there is no cry against it.

Corruption, nevertheless, can be a factor in the more serious types of rebellion. While the politicians, the family patriarchs, the patrons and their clients, and the citizens on the street may be quite willing to live with corruption, this is not true of the nascent ideological leaders or the budding Weberian bureaucrats. These people, often military officers of the lower middle class, are more interested in progress (as they would define it) than in stability. The political sector may be content with impotent titles and the private sector may be content with stagnant wealth, but these people want power. They want to get something done! And they need an honest professional bureaucracy, both military and civilian, to use as a tool.

Their methods are revolution, coup, and autocoup. They are Caesar and Napoleon, Peter the Great and Atatürk, the samurai of the Meiji Restoration and the Founding Fathers of the United States, Nehru and Hitler, Herzl and Lenin, Sun and Mao, Chiang, Park, and Lee, Castro, Pinochet, and Fujimori. They prefer the noose to the bribe, the regulation to the wink, the policeman to the "fixer." They bring not peace, but the sword. And, for better or worse, they do get things done.

DEMOGRAPHY

Just as Raúl Prebisch proved to be smarter than David Ricardo, so Julian Simon—when it comes to resources, at least—is proving himself smarter than Thomas Malthus. To the great disappointment of the Club of Rome and the "Limits to Growth" people, despite the Luddite maneuverings of Greens around the world, wealth continues to increase faster than population. Like others whose religion demands a belief in the imminent end of the world, these worthies are not shaken by defeat. They put down their placards, tuck up their robes, and go back to their computers. And they emerge twenty-four hours later, still unshaken in their faith, to inform us that, due to a misplaced decimal, the Apocalypse previously scheduled for yesterday will actually take place next week. They have never been right before, but this time they have rechecked their figures and there is no possibility of error!

Apart from any demographic pressure on resources, many first-world observers worry that rapid third-world urbanization could be politically destabilizing. So far, this does not appear to be the case. The misery of the city slums is nothing compared with the misery of the countryside—it is only more visible to the middle class. All of the studies that I am acquainted with indicate that, for the first generation of migrants at least, rural-urban migration is stabilizing.[6] Although the data are not yet in for later generations, the relatively deprived among these groups appear to be solving their problems through crime rather than through political action. Urban riots still happen, of course, but—like plagues in isolated towns— these are generally self-limiting. When the rioters have destroyed everything within reach, they get tired and they go home.

This tells only half the story, however. While the macroeconomics of demography continues to defy the doomsters, the microeconomics of population growth can be devastating at particular times and in particular places. Largely unpublished research by Gary Fuller of the University of Hawaii shows a high correlation between the existence of a "Youth Bulge" —20 percent or more of the relevant population in the fifteen-through-twenty-four age group—and political unrest.[7]

Youth Bulge analysis has proven to be an accurate tool—at least in "predicting the past." In Sri Lanka, for example, the Sinhalese revolted when their Youth Bulge emerged and stopped their revolt roughly when it subsided. By that time, however, a Tamil Youth Bulge had emerged and the Tamils were in full revolt. As the fifteen-through-twenty-four cohort grows up—roughly by the end of the century—we can expect the Tamil rebellion to simmer down. This type of analysis seems to work well for various levels, for nations, ethnic groups, cities, or neighborhoods. It can shed light on everything from tensions between secularists and fundamentalists in the Palestinian movement to the future of Chinese student rebellion.

Although Fuller speculates on the social and economic nature of the relationship between the Youth Bulge and unrest, his formulation remains something of a black box. Jack Goldstone, in an exceptionally wise study of revolution, gives a much more complete theory of the demographic connection. As Goldstone notes: "Grasping how population changes and their impact on prices simultaneously unbalanced a wide range of state, elite, and popular social institutions allows us to predict the timing of early modern state breakdowns all across Eurasia, and with greater precision and understanding of their particular features than any existing theories of revolution or early modern crises."[8]

While convincingly denying that he is preaching demographic determinism, Goldstone arrays a mass of statistical evidence to show that revolution often occurs under certain relatively restrictive conditions that are themselves forced by population change:

> In this theory, revolution is likely to occur only when a society *simultaneously* experiences three kinds of difficulties: (1) a state financial crisis, brought on by a growing imbalance between the revenues a government can securely raise and the obligations and tasks it faces; (2) severe elite divisions, including both alienation from the state and intra-elite conflicts, brought on by increasing insecurity and competition for elite positions; and (3) a high potential for mobilizing popular groups, brought on by rising grievances (e.g., regarding high rents or low wages) *and* social patterns that assist or predispose popular groups to action (e.g., large numbers of youth in the population, increasingly autonomous rural villages, growing concentrations of workers in weakly administered cities). The conjunction of these three conditions generally produces a fourth difficulty: an increase in the salience of heterodox cultural and religious ideas; heterodox groups then provide both leadership and an organizational focus for opposition to the state.[9]

Goldstone goes on to point out the disheartening but historically observable fact that the demographic and economic conditions that cause revolution are rarely cured by revolution. Thus France, after its "great" revolution of 1789, had another stab at revolution in 1830, another in 1848, another in 1870, etc. It is at least arguable—though Goldstone does not make the argument—that Gorbachev's "revolution" of the late 1980s responded to the same unsolved problems as the Rebellion of 1905 and the Revolution of 1917.

Goldstone goes perhaps too far, however, in arguing that revolutions are not only futile but often counterproductive in that they stifle the democracy necessary for innovation and economic progress.[10] Goldstone appears to equate democracy (the ability of the individual to have an effective say in the running of the state) with freedom (the ability of the individual to live his life with minimum interference from the state). A high degree of the latter is indeed necessary for economic progress; too much of the former historically has served as a brake on such progress. England of 1770, the United States of 1870, and South Korea of 1970 had little effective democracy but plenty of freedom—and their economies benefited greatly.

The typical third-world state, unlike the NICs of the second world, has neither freedom nor democracy as they are generally conceived. While the private sector—the clans and the patron-client complexes—is often effectively free from government control, this freedom is severely limited by tradition, by competition from other elements within the private sector, and, in many cases, by chaos or the fear of chaos. At the same time, the democracy of the "democratic" third-world states is a sham democracy, just as the tyranny of the "dictatorial" third-world states is a sham tyranny. Only in rare cases can either the democratic president or the tyrannical dictator make his authority felt much beyond the suburbs of the capital—and often not even there. The strength of the private sector, even though its freedom is inhibited by tradition, makes effective government of any kind difficult, if not impossible.

For economic transformation to take place, the political sector must become strong enough—usually through a military coup—to dominate the private sector and to protect and nourish a Weberian bureaucracy of economic experts. This rarely happens, however. The NICs are few and far between. Usually the strong political leader—always most at home sucking the marrow out of a nice femur back in the cave—is more interested in ideology and domination for its own sake than in economics and freedom for the sake of progress. We are more likely to end up with a Mao than with a Park.

CHAPTER 23

Democracy and the Third World

It is a dirty little secret—known to some, suspected by many, denied by almost all—that a third-world state cannot achieve first-world status by democratic means. It must go through a period of second-world authoritarianism. In the best of cases, it will be a mild authoritarianism, like that of postwar Japan, that can pass for democracy, if the observer is willing to close one eye and squint the other.

The political and social instability that lies beneath the surface equilibrium of most third-world countries offers the possibility of progress of a sort. Once the equilibrium is disturbed, by whatever trigger, there is no self-correcting mechanism. The resulting chaos, war, and revolution —the experience of Mexico, China, Korea, Russia, even Germany after World War I—leave the population exhausted, looking for hope, willing to accept authority. The private sector is destroyed, the old traditions are gone, the future is open.

Success is not assured. The police state is more common than the NIC, North Korea more typical than South Korea, Cuba more typical than Mexico. For every Spain that rises into the first world, there is a Soviet Union that collapses back into the third.

Democracy is not foreign to the third world, but it is a different sort of democracy from that found in the developed countries. It is not a democracy of laws, because effective laws require an effective bureaucracy, which, by our definition, the third world does not have. And it is not a democracy of individuals, because the individual in most cases only has importance as part of a larger group.

It is a democracy because the various elements of the private sector, while unable to control each other, can control the government. All the vested interests—the tribes, the unions, the companies, the students, the urban mob—have a veto on government action where their priorities are concerned. Their say in government accurately reflects their strength and passion with respect to the issue involved. Where two sectors are in conflict over an issue—unions and companies over the minimum wage, for example—the government generally has no choice but to let them fight it out and then to certify the winner. What could be more democratic?

If the men of 1776 could see the third world of today, they would undoubtedly be dismayed by the sway of irrational tradition that so limits individual freedom, but they might well be pleased by third-world political life. What the leaders of the American Revolution tried to do through structure in the United States has happened through serendipity in many parts of Asia, Africa, and Latin America. Even without formal separation of powers, government is emasculated and potential tyrants are defanged. Even without a Bill of Rights, mob rule is avoided. Even without property or literacy qualifications, the rich and educated carry more weight in political decisions than do the poor and illiterate.

The thirteen American colonies, once part of the second-world British Empire, chose to become part of what we would now call the third world. They chose to favor agriculture over industry, to turn their backs on centralized government, to promote democracy over efficiency, to accept political corruption rather than risk political tyranny. Although the United States eventually reversed its course, and some like Hamilton and Clay mistrusted this course early on, who is to say that the original aims of the men of 1776 were wrong?

Who is to say that the democracy of groups so typical of the third world —though corrupt, inward looking, and resistant to change—is not superior to the open or disguised dictatorships of the second? Who is to say that government, especially efficient government, is not the evil that the Founding Fathers believed it to be? Who is to say that the chance of eventual first-world status is worth the tyranny involved in passing through the second?

Only the people themselves.

THE POPULAR CHALLENGE
TO DEMOCRACY

"The long-awaited 'revolution' arrived on April 1, 1964—not from the left as anticipated, but from the right in the form of a military coup.

"The squatters, who by then represented 15 to 45 percent of the population of every major city, had been counted on by leftist theorists to play a supportive role in the expected overthrow of the government. But partly because they had been hardest hit by the chaotic conditions and rampant inflation of the Goulart period, and partly for other reasons, a good number of them descended from their hillsides and marched alongside businessmen and housewives in support of law and order, tradition, family, and private property. A number of my Brazilian friends had their personal lives so heavily committed to a different outcome that the double shock of the coup and its popular celebration pushed them into psychic breakdowns."[1]

As this account of the right-wing "Revolution of 1964" that brought Brazil into the second world shows, nondemocratic movements may receive broad "democratic" support. Indeed, it is extremely rare that a successful military coup or other violent seizure of power is not warmly supported by the "people," at least for a time. This support clearly crosses class lines. Just as the poor, for a time, cheered the Argentine and Brazilian generals, so the rich, for a time, rallied behind Castro and the Sandinistas. Khomeini was, for a time, supported as enthusiastically by the wealthy and secular as by the destitute and religious. Gore-soaked nihilistic guerrillas—RENAMO, the Khmer Rouge, Sendero Luminoso—attract educated apologists. Roberto D'Aubuisson of death-squad fame was, until his death, the most broadly popular politician in recent Salvadorean history.

Like Janice Perlman's sophisticated Brazilian friends (undoubtedly an enclave of first-world thinking in a third-world country), we in the North have trouble understanding this. This is not the way things are supposed to work, not the way people are supposed to think. People are supposed to cherish democracy and recoil from brutality. People are supposed to instinctively choose the golden mean, to avoid the extremes of anarchy and tyranny, passivity and revolt, blind hatred and blind obedience. But it doesn't work that way.

In truth, although democracy has a good press throughout the world, it is mainly valued by those who don't have it. Except for the testosterone-driven few, political participation can be as onerous as political suppression. Hungarians and Czechs who risked their lives to achieve democracy can't be bothered to vote once democracy is a fact. While democracy may still have meaning for Chinese, Tibetans, and Burmese, for black South Africans, Lebanese Shi'ites, and West Bank Palestinians, for Cubans, Thais, and Kashmiri Muslims, it has largely ceased to be an issue for Russians, Ukrainians, Paraguayans, Nicaraguans, and Chileans. Once obtained, democracy is almost always a disappointment. It neither butters material parsnips nor relieves psychic relative deprivation.

When all is said and done, democracy is not very empowering for the average person. The individual does not feel that he or she is running the country. The individual vote in the most scrupulously fair election seems no more potent than the same vote in a blatantly rigged election.[2] In times of tranquillity, the third-world citizen is more likely to feel empowered by his or her "connections" than by his or her vote. In times of crisis, the citizen is likely to find his or her empowerment in a crowd cheering a would-be dictator or in a mob looting stores or slaughtering age-old enemies.

Because it lacks an effective bureaucracy, the typical third-world regime is unable to respond to a crisis. No amount of honesty or dishonesty, corruption or idealism, brutality or patience in the presidency or legislature can change that fact. The wheel is not connected to the rudder. In the zero-sum game of third-world politics, any politician who tries to take a broader, more national view, who tries to solve problems rather than stir emotions, who tries to act like a manager rather than a leader, is trampled underfoot by all the others. He and his constituents lose out. And all for nothing. Power is beyond the possibility of politics, but profit is not—so why not go with the flow? The *Titanic* has excellent champagne.

The citizen senses this, that corruption is not so much an unfortunate accompaniment of third-world democracy as it is an integral part of it. While this is good enough in tranquil times (especially if the citizen is getting his or her share of the loot), it is not good enough in times of fear and trouble. In such times, the citizen is willing to listen to those who convincingly promise to sweep away the old "so-called democracy" of corrupt parliaments and presidents and institute a "true democracy" of honesty and discipline and expertise. The citizen is willing to listen to anyone who he thinks may solve the problems of the nation.

THE NATIONALIST CHALLENGE
TO DEMOCRACY

The third-world state is the tribe writ large, and nationalism is nothing more than updated tribalism. It is a powerful—but exceedingly bloody—tool for boosting a developing country into the second world. It plays on the feeling that the people in my cave are better than the people in yours, that God likes me and mine better than he likes you and yours, that despite or because of our superiority, all the world is conspiring against me and my kind, that we have some powerful scores to settle. Nationalism, much more than democracy, makes the little man feel that he counts.

Nationalism calls for organization and sacrifice, for settling disputes among one's own in order to better confront the enemy other. It calls for unity, strength, and honesty, and it scorns division, selfishness, and corruption. Nationalism is idealistic. The true nationalist is willing to spend his fortune or his life to expand the borders of Serbia or Israel, to cleanse Rwanda of Tutsis or Germany of Jews or the American West of Indians, to restore the Islas Malvinas to Argentina or Ulster to Ireland. Nationalism's great potential for evil lies in the very virtues that it attracts.

Nationalism that is ideologically inclusive is, of course, superior from the ethical point of view to nationalism that is exclusive. The melting pot is superior to the gas chamber. The nationalism that turned Norwegians and Irishmen and Jews into Americans (whatever its failures with Indians and blacks), Italians and Syrians and Welsh into Argentines, and Indians and Malays and Chinese into Singaporeans is obviously superior to the nationalism that makes third-generation Koreans foreigners in Japan, Kurds second-class citizens in Turkey, and Turks suspect in Bulgaria.

In the end, the ideology and the goals of nationalism are more important than how well they are achieved. The WASP may feel more at home in the United States than the Chicano, and the white Brazilian certainly has advantages over the black Brazilian. This inequality is lamentable and should be corrected, but the important thing is that the inclusive American and Brazilian ideologies at least *call* for equality. In contrast, Pakistan would lose its reason for existing if non-Muslims were given equality with Muslims, just as Israel would lose its purpose if it made non-Jews as welcome as Jews.

Nationalism, when it is not based on ethnicity, can be a strong factor in overcoming the divisions of the private sector for the benefit of the state.

It turned Irish convicts and English jailers into Australian citizens. With luck, it can make Zulu, Xhosa, Afrikaner, and English into South Africans. And someday nationalist ideology may even win out over subnational prejudice to unite India's multitude of races, languages, religions, and castes. So far at least, inclusive nationalism—for all its failures—has been the only ideology to achieve much success in overcoming racism and religious and ethnic prejudice.

If any of the republics of the former Soviet Union—all of which now clearly meet our definition of third-world states—are to return to second-world status, either as an end in itself or as a stepping-stone to the first world, it will be through nationalism. The various elements of the private sector, now drunk with freedom and apparently shunning all responsibility, may well decide to cede some of their political rights for the greater glory of Russia (or one or more of the other republics). This could be through a violent and noisy turn to the left or right—complete with oppression at home and threats abroad—that would rightly terrify the rest of the world. Or it could be through a Lincolnesque series of "emergency measures," carefully explained in soothing tones by Boris Yeltsin or another, that the world would decide is nothing more than a "tough love" form of democracy.

Some, perhaps most, third-world states will fail when they try to achieve second-world status through nationalism. The politicians, even if they have a vision of the nation, will be unable to create the bureaucratic tools to give that vision body. The private sector—the tribes, the patron-client complexes, all the vested interests—will remain too strong and too committed to the zero-sum view of the world. The third world has never been short of admirable statesmen—it has its Washingtons, Jeffersons, and Lincolns in abundance—but it is woefully short of honest and efficient "faceless" bureaucrats.

The states that fail—all the regimes and revolutionary movements of all the would-be Washingtons and Hitlers who cannot muster the power to match their visions—will see their surface tranquillity torn apart for no good reason. It will be a story of chaos, starvation, and massacre without hope and without purpose. All middle ground will be erased, suspicion will become the law of the day. Ideology will be forgotten, and salvation will be found by seeking shelter with the strongest and most efficiently brutal. It will be a story not of lack of vision, but of lack of bureaucratic tools. It is already the story of much of Central America and much of sub-Saharan Africa.

THE RELIGIOUS CHALLENGE
TO DEMOCRACY

The higher religions are, of course, the natural enemies of democracy. Democracy is based on the idea that what is popular is right, while religion is based on the idea that what is moral is right. Democracy looks to the people for its laws; religion looks to God. This is what gives religion its political power. The average person, in his heart of hearts, knows that he is not competent to run the country—and his neighbor across the street is even less so—but Somebody is competent. That Somebody is All-Wise and All-Knowing. He is the Christian God as interpreted by Jim Jones, the Islamic God as interpreted by the Ayatollah Khomeini, History as interpreted by Marx, or the German Race as interpreted by Hitler. He may be a hard taskmaster, but he eliminates uncertainty.

Like nationalism, religion is psychologically empowering for the little man. To be among the Elect or the Chosen, to be a part of the wave of the future, to be right when others are wrong, to have History on one's side, makes the little man feel a giant. He possesses the Knowledge that obviates thought. He knows, because bigger brains than his have thought about the question and this is what they say. It's right here in the Bible, the Koran, *Das Kapital*!

How can choosing the lesser of two evils in a voting booth compete with this? How can worrying impotently about imperfect candidates with imperfect policies, balancing goods, balancing evils, coping with huge areas of gray, feeling responsibility without power, juggling ethics against interests, personalities against platforms, and wondering what does it all matter compare with the certainty that God's in his Heaven and all's right (or soon will be) with the world?

Unfortunately, while political religion can boost a third-world country into the second world, it puts up almost insurmountable barriers for the next step, into the first world. In going from the second to the first world, the political sector must give way to the private sector and to the market. And the market, being completely amoral, is incompatible with enforced religion. The market would not collectivize Russian peasants or build Jewish housing in "Samaria and Judea" or set up an "Islamic" bank that charges no interest. The market cares nothing for ideology or the Will of God. The market favors freedom—even the freedom to do wrong if one can afford it. The market, for better or worse, empowers the private sector against the government. The market can be suppressed, but only through police-state methods.

In the end, it is often the market that destroys the religious state. When it becomes obvious that the ideology is not paying off, that being right with God and a buck will get you a cup of coffee, that the New Day is as far away as ever, that the heathen still rage, and that evildoers still prosper, the leadership of the religious state begins to hedge and then to defect. These defections at the top allow those on the bottom to think what had hitherto been unthinkable. The private sector reasserts itself, the bureaucracy becomes privatized, politics loses its ideological caste, choice once again becomes a virtue, Mammon wins out over God, and the country sinks back into the third world.

The police state, like the sailboard, depends upon control rather than inherent stability. Once that control slackens, the state collapses. It is rare indeed that the ideological police state—God's Earthly Realm—can be used as a stepping-stone to something higher. But it does happen. Every first-world state was once a second-world state. Franco's Spain, Chiang Kai-shek's Taiwan, and Pinochet's Chile are following a path set centuries ago by the unconscious apostates of Puritan New England.

THE ECONOMIC CHALLENGE TO DEMOCRACY

In the short run, economics does not have the emotional force of nationalism or religion. A man who would struggle to his feet to defend flag and faith will quietly allow himself to starve. Even food riots and land invasions —where they are not purely opportunistic—tend to be driven by ideological, not economic, concerns. It is hatred for the rich (or the assumed rich such as German Jews or East African Asians), not material want, that brings crowds to the streets. While many people became Communists because they saw *other* people starving, few if any became Communists because *they themselves* were starving. The empty belly has more important concerns than the Future of Society.

In the long run, however, economics is a major cause of relative deprivation. It is what in most people's minds defines the third world, and the third-class status that goes along with being a third-world nation is galling. It is especially galling to the educated elite. The more timid minds of the educated elite will rant about "imperialism" and spout the tenets of crude Marxism or crude dependency theory or both (often not realizing that the two are logically incompatible). These poor souls, not smart enough to be thinkers, are condemned to be leaders. Eschewing problems in favor of enemies, they can be found writing "think" pieces in most third-world newspapers or staggering under the weight of AK-47s in most third-world jungles.

Another element of the educated elite, equally galled by the humiliation of third-world status, sees economic backwardness as a practical problem to be solved, not a political issue to be raised. These people are reluctant to accept theories that tie their hands, that underrate national assets, that make "international injustice" all powerful, that are quick to assign blame but slow to offer a plan for progress, that leave the future of the nation dependent on an unlikely first-world change of heart or an equally unlikely world revolution.

Despite the occasional Fujimori or Salinas, these leaders tend to be military men. There is a good reason for this. In most third-world countries, the military is the institution that comes closest to being a Weberian bureaucracy. Although some officers have yet to emerge from the cave—we have only to look at Central America and sub-Saharan Africa for examples—the proportion of troglodytes is not nearly as great as among civilian politicians. The militaries of the more advanced third-world countries are used to thinking like bureaucrats, to working together as a group to solve problems, to obeying orders without seeing their manhood threatened, to having orders obeyed without threats or bribes, to seeing actions end in results, to having the wheel connected to the rudder. Unlike the civilian politicians, they do not see their colleagues as their enemies. Unlike civilian politicians, they are sworn to put their country before themselves—and a number take that oath seriously.

Expertise—the very stuff of bureaucracy—is valued in the military as it is nowhere else in third-world society. The army officer, usually of lower-middle-class background, is typically the product of a military academy, where he is given a heavy dose of science, mathematics, and martial mystique. He learns tactics and strategy, the art and science of solving problems. He analyzes the successes and failures of Alexander and Hannibal, Caesar and Pompey, Napoleon and Wellington, Lee and Grant, Rommel and MacArthur without looking for heroes or enemies. He learns from military history that knowledge can overcome great obstacles, that discipline can multiply numbers, that God favors the army with the best technology. He learns to think in a very different way from other elements of the elite.

The military officer also has a much more profound knowledge of his country than do civilian members of the elite. As a junior officer, he is stationed in the boondocks. He spends years in jungles or mountains that civilian politicians visit for a few days at most. He learns the problems of the people who live far from the capital. As a midlevel officer, he goes abroad, to the United States or the United Kingdom or the former Soviet Union, to study foreign ways of doing things. He comes to know his own country better by having another country to compare it with. Throughout his career, he commands draftees from all areas, social classes, and ethnic groups. He deals with the "People," whereas other members of the elite deal only with the upper 5 percent or so who make it into the university.

The expertise and understanding of the military officer do not necessarily translate into virtue and action. Indeed, the typical officer, like the lawyer who uses his knowledge to pervert the law or the priest who uses his calling to pervert the altar boy, is too often content to use his position to bully the civilian elite and to milk the rest of the population. Outside of his military unit, he ceases to be a manager and becomes a leader, as eager to find and destroy enemies as his civilian counterparts. Moreover, unlike most civilian leaders, the military officer has lethal force at his command and thus is more dangerous.

Nevertheless, in a number of countries from Ottoman Turkey to postwar Korea, atypical officers have taken power not to aggrandize themselves, but to boost their countries along the road to the first world. They are not always successful. Many, such as those who came to power with Juan Velasco in Peru, are overly enamored of faulty but popular economic schemes or simply listen to the wrong advisors. Others find that their countries lack the physical and human conditions for rapid economic growth. Still others are overcome by internal or external enemies, often working to "restore" democracy, before their programs can take effect. A few turn paranoid and become more concerned with preserving their rule than with continuing to advance the country. Power still corrupts.

Those military or other authoritarian regimes that are successful do not attempt to run their national economies. Nothing in the military academy has prepared them for that. Instead, they choose private-sector technocrats and protect them from the very private sector out of which they came while they attempt to work their magic. The workers, the consumers, the businessmen, the foreigners, are told that it doesn't have to be a zero-sum game unless they refuse to cooperate—in which case they have already lost. Relying on their economic brain trusts, the military gives the private sector the freedom to do business but withholds the democracy that could destroy business. And, as we have seen, a new model of economic progress is born.

This model, which third-world states and peoples around the globe correctly see as their only hope for progress, is incompatible with democracy.

THE FUTURE OF DEMOCRACY IN THE THIRD WORLD

The third-world democracy of groups, which effectively keeps government on a short leash, is not seen by the first world to be democracy at all. Its inefficiency, its corruption, its built-in gridlock (so true to the spirit of 1776), are seen as the very antithesis of democracy. And, of course, the third world will buy the first world's definition. Many third-world regimes will try to suppress the power of the groups, by force if necessary, in order to become more "democratic." Such progressive states will be aided and encouraged by the first world.

Most of the time, it won't work. Some states will be unable to muster the force to dominate the private sector and stamp out the zero-sum mentality. Others will lose first-world support as the bodies begin to pile up and—puzzled by first-world inconsistency—turn away from their efforts to achieve a "rule of law" by force and retreat back into the chaotic democracy of groups. Still others, having once achieved a toehold in the second world, will thumb their noses at the first and become police states pure and simple. Only a few, blessed with both bureaucratic potential and self-limiting authoritarian political leadership, will achieve the rapid economic growth that could eventually take them through the second world into the first.

PART FOUR

The Twenty-First Century

Far from being a divinely ordained arrow in the blue, beyond gravity, destined to rise to ever-greater heights, democracy is an earthbound, human creation subject to the entropy of all such creations. It now travels a course of declining relevance much like that of European monarchy from the power of Elizabeth I to the impotence of Elizabeth II. As we enter the twenty-first century, democracy finds itself about halfway through its Victorian era. Queen Victoria, at the apogee of her reign, was honored, influential, arrogant, and self-assured. No one was willing to say a word against her, but no one, least of all the old girl herself, thought she was up to the serious business of running the empire. Democracy, like the queen, is gradually ceasing to be a force and becoming a symbol. It is a flag you carry in a parade, not a leader you follow into battle.

CHAPTER 24

The Marginalization
of Democracy

*During the past two hundred years the evolution of social organization
in the first world has progressed in ways that would both gratify and
puzzle the revolutionaries of 1776 and 1789. Individual freedom, including freedom from arbitrary government action, has advanced beyond the
fondest dreams of the Americans, while government power—exercised in
the name of something very like the "general will"—has reached heights
of efficiency that easily surpass the totalitarian visions of the French.
Moreover, this marriage of incompatibles has been made possible not
through political leadership—that great engine from which revolutionaries on both sides of the Atlantic expected so much—but through market
economics and bureaucratic organization.*

As the century draws to a close, it is becoming increasingly obvious
that wealth—economic power—is the defining characteristic of
the first-world state. Neither size nor military power matters if a
nation lacks economic strength. Russia, spanning a continent and a half,
with many thousands of men under arms and the world's second largest
store of nuclear weapons, is not a part of the first world; Switzerland is.

Recognition of the overwhelming importance of economic power relative to all other national strengths has led quite naturally, but largely unconsciously, to a deemphasis of the political sector in favor of the bureaucratic and private sectors. Conflict—the drive to achieve domination—is
the total content of politics in any age and under any system. Political

power is achieved through conflict—elections, revolutions, or wars—and it is maintained through conflict. To the extent that cooperation is involved at all, it is a temporary and wary cooperation among potential enemies against momentarily greater enemies. Alliances in domestic politics are much like military alliances among nations. At best they resemble the alliance between the United States and the Soviet Union in World War II; at worst they are like that between the Bosnian Muslims and Croats.

Politics has everything to do with achieving power and nothing to do with using power. Indeed, the very traits that allow the politician to achieve power—Tamerlane's hair-trigger brutality, Reagan's empty-headed amiability—prevent him from making effective use of it. Aside from the exceptional few—men on the order of Augustus and Asoka who, after securing their power bases, were able to make the switch from leader to manager—the politicians get in the way of effective administration by politicizing it. That is the only thing they know how to do, the only way they know how to think. What matters is not whether the administrator can do the job, but whether he is a Republican or Democrat. What matters is not whether a policy can restore the economy, but whether it will advance one party or the other. What matters is not solving problems, but defeating enemies.

By destabilizing the economic environment, conflict—that is to say, politics—undermines economic progress. Those countries that continue to make economic progress are those that are able to channel conflict into unimportant areas, that are able to transform politics from a civil war over life-and-death issues into an emotionally satisfying but essentially meaningless sports event. Led by Japan, all of the current first-world states are well along the road to the marginalization of politics. While the gladiators fight it out in the arena to the cheers of the crowd, the bureaucrats and businessmen go quietly about their business of running the country and the economy. They supply the bread while the politicos supply the circuses.

THE CYCLICAL FIRST WORLD

The evolution of the first world from its very beginnings in the nineteenth century has been the story of politicians giving way to bureaucrats in time of crisis. These bureaucrats, in order to solve the crisis, in turn are forced to use the strengths of the private sector. Once the crisis is in hand, the politicians take back some, but not all, of their power. Thus, over time, the authority, but not the legitimacy, of the political sector is undermined, while that of the other two sectors grows. Although both bureaucrats and businessmen hesitate to mention it, it becomes increasingly obvious that the emperor has no clothes of his own but must wear those of his servants and subjects.

On occasion, the politicians, nostalgic for the caves of yesteryear, revolt, take back their power, once more don the imperial robes, and, dominating a strong but compliant bureaucracy, re-create the second-world state. This happened in Nazi Germany. On other occasions, the revolting politicians opt for more egalitarian dress, unite with elements of the private sector to dominate a cowed bureaucracy, and drag the nation back into the third world. This came close to happening in post–World War II England and did happen in Perón's Argentina and Gorbachev's Soviet Union.

In most cases, however, the evolution is not aborted. The first-world voters—and, indeed, the politicians themselves—come to prefer bureaucratic competence and stability over political conflict and excitement. In an ever-wider range of governmental functions, they begin to demand the same degree of professionalism that they have always demanded from other institutions. Even the politicians are heard to mutter that the government should be run "more like a business." Given that the successful corporation is a hierarchical organization of specialists—a bureaucracy without a trace of democracy about it—they are asking for their own obsolescence, to sit on the board of directors rather than to have a real say in running the concern. Thus, with the complicity of the political sector, most first-world states continue to strengthen their first-world characteristics and thereby to maintain their stable equilibriums and their positions at the head of the international table.

Yet, if there is anything that history has made clear, it is that no nation, no society, no civilization, can remain dominant forever. Among current first-world states, some will continue to evolve in such a manner as to maintain their first-world position for a while longer, others will come under the sway of charismatic leaders and consciously opt for the harsh idealism of the second world, and still others will be hamstrung by the private sector and fall back into the third world.

The reason for this fragility of status is simple. Economic power, the defining characteristic of the first-world state, rarely comes as a by-product of some other goal. If a society wants to be rich, it must aim to be rich. If, having become rich, it changes its goals—and puts conquest, piety, justice, ecology, art, leisure, or some other value ahead of production—it will lose its place to other societies that continue to hold production as their major goal. The economic rise of the United States began in the middle of the last century, when the businessman displaced the politician and the general as the American ideal. The seeds of its economic decline were sown in the post–World War II period, when the anti-Communist and the anti-anti-Communist replaced the businessman. By the 1960s Americans were too concerned with dropping bombs and dropping acid, with burning villages and burning draft cards, with saving democracy and saving the whooping crane, to worry about productivity. This decline, though still in its early stages and not yet irreversible, continues.

If one idealistic movement or another reaches the critical mass needed to take over government, the nation slips out of the first world into the authoritarian second. The political sector unites with the bureaucracy to enforce an ideology on the private sector. As ideological purity is always the enemy of productivity, living standards begin to slide. On the other hand, if various idealistic movements split the private sector into antagonistic groups that fight both each other and the political sector to a standstill, the nation sinks gently back into the third world, the Darwinian democracy of the cave from which we all came.

Once in motion, the process of idealism is hard to reverse. Even as a nation sees its economic position deteriorate and its standard of living decline, it finds it difficult to return to the old materialistic moneygrubbing. It seems more worthy to fight for women's rights or to bomb abortion clinics or to enjoy a sunset than to put all one's being into making the marginal buck. Its citizens kid themselves into thinking that they have earned the right to turn their backs on economics and go on to the things that "really matter." They kid themselves into believing that in such a rich country they should be able to have it all. Only a major cataclysm, such as happened to Japan and Germany as a result of World War II, can shake a nation back into reality once it has tasted idealism.

The wealth that breeds idealism also breeds feelings of entitlement. The citizen who once found the meaning of life in work now finds it in consumption and leisure and "respect." Workers, businessmen, professionals, bureaucrats, investors, women, minorities, all demand that not only their living conditions but also their psychological well-being be maintained at whatever cost to the broader interests of society. Everyone wants a subsidy, be it material or psychic, and no one in government—least of all in democratic government—is going to say no. Discipline is lost. The totally irresponsible borrow and squander; the slightly less irresponsible tax and spend.

One fine morning the nation wakes and finds itself back in the third world. The old positive-sum world of the individual, the market, and economic progress is gone, replaced by the zero-sum democracy of groups.

The individual ceases to be an individual and becomes an oilman, a doctor, a woman, a black, a cotton farmer, a lesbian, an automobile worker, a teacher—a member of a group that has a claim on the national treasury, a group that is not going to have its rights trampled upon, a group that is suspicious of all other groups, a group that is willing to shut down the country if necessary. The bureaucracy is privatized, captured by special interests. It ceases to be a machine for progress and becomes a conduit for passing out subsidies. The politicians, now with no other function than to pander to the groups, mud-wrestle for a cardboard crown and a meaning-less title.

This is the world that Mancur Olson warned us about. In his book *The Rise and Decline of Nations: Economic Growth, Stagflation, and Social Rigidities,*[1] he essentially explains how first-world countries fall back into the third world (though he does not use those terms). He notes that, especially under conditions of democracy, states with a long history of stability and prosperity tend to break down into "distributional coalitions," or special-interest groups, that are willing, at least unconsciously, to sabo-tage the nation as a whole in order to achieve even minor benefits for themselves. Such a group "can best serve its members' interests by striving to seize a larger share of society's production for them. This will be expedi-ent, moreover, even if the social costs of the change in the distribution exceed the amount redistributed by a huge multiple; *there is for practical purposes no constraint on the social cost such an organization will find it expedient to impose on society in the course of obtaining a larger share of the social output for itself.*"[2]

Olson goes on to note that "it follows that countries whose distributional coalitions have been emasculated or abolished by totalitarian government or foreign occupation should grow relatively quickly after a free and stable legal order is established. This can explain the postwar 'economic miracles' in the nations that were defeated in World War II, particularly those in Japan and West Germany."[3] Because distributional alliances—the democ-racy of groups—are even more characteristic of the third world at rest than of the first world in decline, the equivalent of "totalitarian government or foreign occupation" (generally chaos and revolution followed by authori-tarian government) is more necessary for the third-world state that wishes to achieve first-world status than it is for the Japans and Germanys of the world that only wish to regain such status.

While the fate that Olson foresees for all developed countries may well be inevitable with time—one can see signs of the "British disease" not only in the United States but also in Japan and Germany—important counter-trends exist. As has been pointed out, many citizens and politicians, sensing, more than understanding, the dangers of unrestrained conflict and entitlement, are voluntarily restricting their own powers. Both politicians and voters know that they are no better equipped to solve the complex economic problems upon which the future of the nation depends than Queen Victoria was to lead British troops into battle. While the politician and the voter, like the queen, are reluctant to cede their ultimate authority, they are increasingly eager to cede control.

Both the politician and the voter are willing to cede power to "faceless bureaucrats" that they would never cede to their political, economic, or social rivals. All they ask is some assurance that they are not playing a positive-sum game in a zero-sum world, that they are not being taken for suckers. Thus, both Democrats and Republicans are far more willing to let the "undemocratic" Federal Reserve make important economic decisions than to allow them to be made by their democratically elected opponents. Thus, both sides of the abortion issue are more willing to trust the "unelected" Supreme Court than their democratic representatives. Indeed, the main complaint against the Fed, the Supreme Court, and other bureaucracies from the CIA to the IRS is not that they lack democratic control, but that they are too likely to allow themselves to be "manipulated" by elected officials. The people demand, correctly, that bureaucracies start acting like bureaucracies.

The political sector will not disappear in the postdemocratic world, nor will it cease to have important functions. First, it will legitimize bureaucratic management, much as the British monarchy legitimizes Parliament. Second, by hogging "name recognition" and most other perquisites, it will keep the bureaucrats from turning into "leaders" in their own right, with all the evils that that would entail. Third, it will act as ombudsman for individuals (though not for groups) who have some quarrel with elements of the bureaucracy. Fourth, under some conditions, it will help to resolve disputes among bureaucracies. Fifth, it may serve to channel societal conflict away from violence and into relatively harmless areas.[4] Finally, if under bureaucratic administration things go too far wrong (and they will from time to time), the political sector can respond to popular unrest by removing the Mandate of Heaven from the bureaucracy. In such cases, after a period of chaos, the old bureaucracy would be replaced by a new bureaucracy with a new outlook (though probably made up of many of the same individuals).

Although in individual cases the politicians may prove wiser than the bureaucrats, over the long run the experts will triumph over the amateurs, the thinkers will beat out the emoters, the problem solvers will best the enemy bashers, competence will win out over charisma, and the "soulless machine" will prove more reliable than the testosterone-driven troglodyte. Those societies that continue to allow themselves to be administered by individuals whose only qualification is that they were able to win a popularity contest will go from failure to failure and eventually pass from the scene.

A century from now, several national cycles will have passed and many of the present first-world states will have lost their importance. Others almost certainly will have risen. Barring the advent of a new Dark Ages, however, a first world will still exist. There will still be arrogant, pathfinding nations that other nations will both resent and copy. While it is impossible to predict the characteristics of the twenty-second-century first world, it seems safe to say that expertise will be honored, freedom will be preserved, and political conflict will be kept within bounds.

THE STRIVING SECOND WORLD

The second world of the twenty-first century is likely to continue to be a stepping-stone both toward and away from the first world. Third-world nations that attain first-world status will pass through the second world. At the same time, some developed nations, faced with seemingly insoluble problems, will reject the relative rationality and freedom of the first world and, taking refuge in ideology, find a home in the second. Other nations will, of course, go straight from the first world to the third.

It seems safe to predict that the leaders of some NICs, following the pattern of Spain under Franco, will voluntarily cede authoritarian rule, correctly confident that their societies have permanently passed out of the zero-sum world into the positive-sum world. The leaders of other NICs, perhaps including those of Brazil, will find that they have ceded authoritarianism too soon. In these cases, with rational administration no longer protected by the newly "democratic" political sector, economic progress will falter, the old zero-sum democracy of groups will reassert itself, and the state will effectively drop back into the third world. The leaders of still other NICs, playing for additional time to transform their societies, will openly or covertly resist "democratization." These leaders, despite their original good intentions, may become addicted to authoritarian rule and gradually push their governments across the blurred border that separates the NIC from the ideological police state.

Even as some NICs drop back into the third world, some third-world states will achieve NIC status. It is likely that many of these will enter the second world as police states and then slowly evolve into NICs, as their leaders come to realize the overwhelming importance of economic power in the twenty-first century. Indonesia, Thailand, and Malaysia may follow this route. Many current second-world police states, such as China, will almost certainly transform themselves into NICs.

Despite the increasing popularity of the NIC model, I do not expect the attractions of the ideological police state to diminish. Indeed, as has already been mentioned, one or another of the current first-world states, faced with rising crime, cultural disorientation, and wave after wave of "barbarian invasions," may turn against freedom and opt for a racist, nationalist, or religious ideology under a charismatic leader who "is not afraid to break heads." In some cases, the "aroused citizens" may use democracy to demand an end to permissiveness, to tolerance, to "corrosive intellectualism," a return to faith and tradition, a "restoration of meaning to life." When a frustrated people clamors for police, prisons, and punishment, there will be no shortage of frustrated leaders to offer them Gestapos, gulags, and guillotines.

While some current first-world states will almost certainly slip into the second world, most of the new police states will arise out of either the old Communist second world or the tribal third world. With the collapse of the Marxist universal religion, which was marked by at least a theoretical tolerance, the once-Red peoples have rediscovered nationalism and racism. Although some fortunate states—China, Hungary, the Czech Republic, and possibly Poland, Russia, Estonia, and Ukraine—are likely to achieve NIC status in time, and others, like many of the Central Asian republics of the former USSR, may stay contentedly in the third world, the greatest number will probably opt for tribal brutality. A few like Serbia and perhaps Georgia may go straight to fascism, while others will choose *Herrenvolk* democracy of the Israeli/South African type.

The second world in the twenty-first century will continue to provide a home for those heroes and idealists who are equally repelled by the chaos and selfishness of third-world democracy and by the materialism and "soullessness" of the postdemocratic first world. Some heroes and idealists will strive for economic progress and the personal freedom that is necessary for such progress. Other heroes will fight for ideological, racial, or national domination, and they will be aided by idealists who will justify their savage causes. Hitler and Khomeini will have their successors as surely as Park and Lee. As long as men and women thrill to the promise of battle and dream of molding a recalcitrant world into a better place, so long will the second world prosper.

THE THIRD WORLD AND THE
NEW VÖLKERWANDERUNG

The twenty-first century is unlikely to be kind to the third world. The end of the Cold War, the secular decline in the relative value of commodities, and the advent of the knowledge-intensive, postindustrial world economy all work against third-world prosperity. The third world—no longer seen by the North as a source of raw materials or as a field for ideological battle —is likely to become little more than an object of inadequate charity and spasmodic anthropological interest. At best, the North will try to bully and bribe the South into ecological responsibility. But the bribes will be small compared with those of the Cold War. In the capitals of the North, the environmental fate of the planet is unlikely to receive the priority that its political orientation once did.

The citizens of the third world—inhabitants of the Global Village if only as pariahs—will feel relative deprivation as never before. And they will put unprecedented pressure on their governments. Those governments with wise leaders and nascent Weberian bureaucracies may be able to enter the ranks of the NICs. This will become increasingly difficult, however; the world can only use a finite number of automobiles, televisions, and VCRs. Other governments will try to buck up morale with ideology or to protect their peoples behind isolationist walls. Dr. Francia's Paraguay may be as good a model as Khomeini's Iran. Some will try to divert their peoples by warring on their neighbors for the economic resources that they cannot get any other way.

Of course, some third-world societies will be able to find their own economic niche that allows them to prosper even as they (more or less) maintain their cultural "identity." These states will trade on their "quaintness," on their very difference from the rest of the world. (But will this be enough in the century of Disneyland—to say nothing of "virtual reality"?) Other states may well provide an escape from morality, much as Bophuthatswana's Sun City provided a refuge from Calvinism and racism for white South Africans in the last decades of the twentieth century.

In the third world, the twenty-first century is likely to be a century of short tempers. Unemployment, starvation, desertification, disease, ethnic cleansing, war and civil war, have already begun to upset the traditional third-world equilibrium. In the future, societies that had once seemed stable may well spiral out of control. Old structures—extended families and patron-client complexes—may prove inadequate, even as old religions fail to comfort. Ancient alliances will crumble, though ancient antagonisms will survive. The individual will be on his own as never before in traditional society.

The twenty-first century is also likely to be a century of movement. Borders are already beginning to blur as individuals and groups migrate in search of water or food or safety. From the Balkans to sub-Saharan Africa, boundaries fixed by nineteenth-century colonial advantage or by post–World War I whim now exist only in the atlas. Without even a nod to weak central governments, refugees and fighters, Kurds and Tuaregs, Armenians and Tatars, Palestinians and Afghans, live out their often short lives in foreign refugee camps, in alien cities, on the road or in battle. These great blind migrations are certain to intensify.

This new *Völkerwanderung* has not and will not remain confined to the third world. Fleeing fear and starvation, seeking opportunity and safety, invited and uninvited, begging and threatening, the cream of the brain drain and the dregs of society, the citizens of the third world are washing over the borders of the first. Like the barbarian tribes that eroded, served, saved, conquered, and eventually destroyed the Roman Empire, the virile and the desperate have nothing to lose and everything to gain. The first wave has already arrived: Turkish *Gastarbeiter* in Germany, Algerians in France, Pakistanis in England, Albanians in Italy, Bosnians in Austria, Vietnamese in Hong Kong, Haitians and Cubans in Florida, Mexicans in Texas, Filipinos in California, Arabs in Michigan. The ethnic and religious makeup of Western Europe has probably changed more in the past twenty-five years than it had in the previous five centuries. It is certain to change even more in the century ahead.

The new barbarians do not come empty-handed. The new migrants, like all migrants, are a select group biased in favor of the educated, the intelligent, the daring, the young, the healthy, the hardworking, and the ruthless. They bring a work ethic that is fast being lost in the Germany of the thirty-five-hour week and the America of the three-martini lunch. Like the ancient Greeks who enriched Persia and Rome, they bring talents, and often genius, that cannot be effectively utilized at home.

Despite or because of their genius and hard work, the new migrants will be fought every step of the way, but they will not be stopped. Just as water will find its own level, the hungry will inexorably move to where there is food, the unemployed to where there is work, the fearful to where there is safety. Trenches along the U.S. border with Mexico, skinhead violence in Europe, and xenophobic laws in Japan will at best only delay the flood.

In the end, the migrants or their children will be assimilated. Before the next century is out, the United States will have a Spanish-surnamed president (who will speak no Spanish) or an Oriental president (who will have no memories of Asia). France's president will extol his country with Gaullist fervor—before he retires to the mosque to pray. The queen will knight ever more descendants of Pakistanis and Jamaicans for their contributions to Albion's wealth, culture, and science.

Although the cultural and ethnic makeup of the first world will change in ways that are impossible to predict, these changes will probably be beneficial. The danger exists, however, that third-world culture and vigor could in time overwhelm first-world civilization and sobriety. If this were to happen, charismatic leadership would reassert itself, rational decision-making would be undermined, and the zero-sum world would be re-created. If this were to happen across the first world as a whole, a major calamity would result. So fell Rome.

Such a calamity, though possible, is unlikely. But, even in the best of cases, beyond the marches of the first world, now defended more by assimilated barbarians than by its own troops, the third world will remain a mystery and a threat. Like the Asian steppe of centuries past, always ready to send forth a new wave of Huns or Mongols, the third world (however defined) will almost certainly continue to exist and continue to exert moral and physical pressure on the rest of the planet.

THE TWENTY-FIRST CENTURY AND DEMOCRACY

For all three worlds, the twenty-first century will be a time of repeated crises. And, as we have seen, democracy does not deal well with crises. In case after case in the past, once it was clearly understood that a crisis existed, the politicians and the citizens "freely and democratically" ceded government to the bureaucrats for the duration of the emergency. Those governments—more often monarchies and dictatorships than democracies —that did not cede power to the bureaucrats generally perished.

Assuming that the politicians and citizens eventually come to see budget deficits, racial divisions, declining productivity, decaying infrastructure, and the like as the "moral equivalents" of war, this cession of power is likely to become permanent. Those countries that are slow to take this step will fall behind, and those countries that refuse will in time cease to exist as major states.

The states of the first and second worlds, though not without risk, are relatively well positioned to make the structural adaptation to a century of crisis. The third world, suspicious to the bone and democratic to the marrow, will find the new century much more difficult. Overall, the twenty-first century will see many more Singapores and many more Beiruts.

CHAPTER 25

Tribe and Empire

Throughout history, the world has gone through cycles of nationalism and internationalism, moving from tribal culture to imperial civilization and back again. The great empires—those that are more than short-lived exercises in tribalism writ large—stress what mankind has in common and what can be gained by working together. The great empires, believing in the essential equality of all those who come under their sway, bestow citizenship and benefits far and wide. Britons and Arabs who never saw Rome were nonetheless well served by Roman roads and Roman law. The great nations, by contrast, are those that foster the individual tribal genius and protect it against all comers.

As the twentieth century comes to a close, the world of nations appears to be tottering between tribe and empire.

T he defeat of Fascism by Democracy and Communism in World War II may be seen as a victory of universalist imperialism over tribal imperialism. Unlike the Germans and the Japanese, who saw themselves as unique master races well suited by blood and culture to direct the affairs of lesser peoples, the Americans and the Russians saw themselves as custodians of almost magical doctrines that they freely offered to all mankind for its benefit, not their own. Needless to say, the world soon proved to be too small for two mutually exclusive doctrines of universal salvation. Conflict was inevitable.

Conflict breeds leadership, however, and leadership breeds nationalism.

A generation of American leaders hammered home the idea that what was good for the United States was good for Democracy. (Indeed, could social-ist England and Scandinavia be considered democratic at all?) Soviet lead-ers made it equally obvious to many Russians (though apparently not to many Yugoslavs, Chinese, and Albanians) that the fate of world Commu-nism hung on the fate of the Soviet Union. The nations of the world reluctantly chose up sides, muttering under their breath of American and Soviet imperialism. Truman and Eisenhower jousted with Stalin and Khru-shchev before a sullen but not uninterested audience.

Now the Cold War is over, Democracy and the United States have won, Communism is in deep disfavor, and the broken Soviet Union has sunk piecemeal into the third world. Yet, despite the hopes and fears of many in the United States and abroad, no universal American Empire has emerged nor is likely to emerge. Even with its still unparalleled wealth and military power, the United States is perceived by many around the world to be a tottering giant lacking both the moral fiber and the economic sinew to direct the affairs of the planet. Some Americans, politicians and citizens alike, appear to agree. In the old bipolar world, America was surrounded by allies and potential allies; in the new monopolar world, America stands alone, beset by enemies on all sides. Americans, for the first time in fifty years, are turning their backs on the outside world to huddle fearfully around the tribal campfire.

THE NEW TRIBALISM

Across the globe, the end of the Cold War has led to a largely unexpected, and very virulent, outbreak of tribalism and nationalism. From Serbia and Kurdistan to Scotland and Quebec, the tribes are on the move. From the parliaments of the NATO countries to those of the CIS republics, national chauvinists are pounding the table. Values once shared—in part out of desperation, coercion, or fear of worse evils beyond the horizon—are be-ing dropped by the wayside. In country after country people and politi-cians are deciding that it is better to commit crimes in the name of the group than in the name of humanity as a whole. People's Republics are replaced by ethnically cleansed republics. Militant Capitalism and Democ-racy are replaced by fearful Japan-bashing and the "lessons of Vietnam." The One Big Enemy is replaced by a thousand little enemies. The crime goes on; only the idealism behind it has narrowed.

Given that the tribe was the first democracy—and perhaps still the archetype that lies in humanity's subconscious—it should not surprise us that the victory of Democracy has resulted in a surge of tribalism. What could be more tribally democratic than for the majority to kill, enslave, or dispossess the minority? This concept is held not only by some Serbian nationalists and Israeli radicals but also by many members of South Africa's Pan-Africanist Congress. Democracy is seen not as a mechanism for governmental cooperation toward shared goals, but as a means of accomplishing a revolution, of rectifying a wrong, of putting those on top who deserve to be on top.

Under such circumstances, safety lies in aggression, separation, and migration. It is safer to be a majority in a tiny enclave than a minority in a powerful nation. It is safer to flee or to fight (or to exterminate) than to coexist. It is taken as self-evident that blacks have no true rights in the white United States, that Scots are discriminated against in the United Kingdom, that a Russian is not safe in Estonia and a Tatar is not safe in Russia. Can a Kurd or a Jew (or, for that matter, a Gypsy) ever feel secure until he or she has a secure homeland? Only a fool gives up his guns. Enemies are everywhere, and it is no more than common sense to pre-empt alien aggression by striking first.

Under these circumstances, Great National Leaders spring up like noxious weeds. A Great National Leader is an all-or-nothing patriot, a fighter, not a compromiser, a tribal man driven by love of his people and hatred for all others. (Even now, some Afrikaner Moses plans to lead his countrymen into the safety of a barren promised land in the northern Cape or the Transvaal, some skinhead defender of the *Heimat* bashes third-world heads in Rostock, some U.S. congressman gives a new twist to long-discredited theories of the Yellow Peril.) The Great National Leader is a throwback to the days when war was the only function of leadership. He will always lead his people into battle, because that is his passion and his calling.

Great National Leaders, ever watchful over their peoples' safety, are quick to recognize any imperialism except their own. And they see the threat of imperialism as coming not only from other tribal nations but also from international institutions. These overarching institutions could well be the empires of the twenty-first century and are recognized as such by the Vercingetorixes of the new age. Under such leaders, the Americans have come to fear the U.N., the French to fear NATO, the British to fear the E.C., and the Japanese to fear GATT. These leaders did—and do— their best to convince their peoples that their national "sovereignty," their "dignity," their "respect," and their "institutions" are being trampled by "international bureaucrats."

What the Great National Leaders, in fact, fear is that a new age is aborning, an age of internationalism—an age of empire, if you will—in which the national is swallowed up by the universal and the leader is replaced by the manager.[1] They see a time when McDonald's will crowd out the local pub, when Turks will actually feel at home in Berlin, when barbarian invaders from south of the border will sop up Social Security and make California's streets unsafe for white women. Inches and pounds will go the way of cubits and dunums, the Flag will stir only a yawn, the Language will be debased by foreignisms, the Heroes of the Past will be forgotten, and that Old-Time Religion will be smothered by some new cult out of Asia. These leaders see the day when some unelected wiseass in the U.N. will tell better men what to do. They will fight such an outcome to the last drop of their people's blood. Their jobs are on the line. Indeed, the ancient and honored calling of Great National Leader itself could disappear!

THE INTERNATIONALISM OF THE PRIVATE SECTOR

Some powerful counterforces work against this trend toward tribalism. One of the most powerful is the attitude—profit-driven as always—of the most dynamic elements of the private business sector. Businessmen around the world, no matter how narrowly chauvinistic they may be in their private lives, have come to realize that they must internationalize or perish. The Taiwanese executive with plants in Communist China sees things differently than does his KMT brother. The Japanese executive with plants in the United States and potential customers in Europe begins to suspect that what is good for Japan may not always be good for his company, and vice versa. The German executive whose main markets are outside Europe finds that his attitude toward E.C. agricultural policy is much less "German" than that of his more political countryman.

Indeed, in much of the manufacturing sector, the very concept of nationality is rapidly losing its meaning. A Ford may be built to a Japanese design in a Mexican plant, while a Toyota may be "made in America by Americans." In one not terribly unusual case, the "Japanese" company, Brother Industries Ltd., after eighteen years of being sued by the "American" company, Smith Corona Corp., for dumping typewriters on the U.S. market at abnormally low prices, has turned the tables by claiming that it is really the American company because its machines are assembled in Tennessee from largely non-Japanese parts, while Smith Corona is the foreign company because it is 47 percent British-owned and assembles its machines in Singapore from partially non-U.S. parts.[2] Protectionist politicians can no longer be sure what to protect!

Reflecting this confusion of national economies (with a slight degree of hyperbole), Robert B. Reich begins *The Work of Nations* with the declaration that "we are living through a transformation that will rearrange the politics and economics of the coming century. There will be no *national* products or technologies, no national corporations, no national industries. There will no longer be national economies, at least as we have come to understand the concept."[3]

This Global Village is inhabited so far mostly by businessmen. The banker in Tokyo finds it easier to talk to his counterpart in New York or London or even Manila than to the Japanese man on the street or the politician across town. Not only have modern communications inverted distance—it is now easier and quicker to hold a "teleconference" with colleagues in Sydney, London, and Frankfurt than to take a taxi to a meeting in one's own city—but they have also led to a homogenization of thought. While it is true that the American businessman can never fully understand the Japanese businessman, or vice versa, it is equally true that the two businessmen may understand each other better than either does his nonbusiness compatriot.

What divides the American and the Japanese businessmen, and their counterparts elsewhere, is the national culture of the past; what unites them is the universal culture of the future. Both are slowly, and largely unconsciously, leaving the tribe to become citizens of the empire. Each retains a sentimental attachment to his nation—a memory of childhood, the taste of a special dish, the residue of a shared experience, a somewhat faded sense of outrage about Bataan or Hiroshima—but their futures are in the same international sphere. They share the same international rice bowl. Each may worry much more about political and bureaucratic decisions in the other's country, or in a third country, than in his own. Each may be coming to the heretical conclusion that what is good for the world (at least as the world is represented by international business) is good for the nation, rather than the reverse.

Businessmen, however, are not the only ones to dwell in the Global Village. Indeed, the Global Village has become the home and refuge for *déracinés* of all types: the world-class Indian scientist who can't find a world-class laboratory in India; the U.N. bureaucrat who rests in New York between assignments in Patagonia and Siberia and no longer even thinks of his home in sub-Saharan Africa; the Russian Jew who, after a spell in Tel

Aviv, ends up in Los Angeles; the much-deported political exile who knows the slums of a dozen European capitals better than he does his own hometown; even the international terrorist for whom borders and homelands have lost all meaning. The barbarian invaders from East and South who breach the walls of the first world are themselves people who have opted to leave the tribe and join the empire.

But, more important—because more numerous—than the *déracinés* of the world, the world's laborers and consumers are also becoming internationalized. The redneck employee of a Japanese auto company in Kentucky may still wave the flag on the Fourth of July, but his viewpoint is much more international than that of his brother in Detroit. The Canadian nationalist and the French intellectual defy political decrees and patriotic sentiment to watch U.S. television productions. The right-wing politician in his Mercedes-Benz joins the union leader in his Hong Kong–made sports shirt to demand that Americans "buy American." As always, the worker looks for the best job and the consumer looks for the best product, even if it involves abandoning domestic companies and domestic brands, and the chauvinistic appeals of politicians fall increasingly on deaf ears.

Countries and peoples who, for reasons of nationalism, are willing to accept domestic second best over foreign best will always lose out over time. It is hard to find even one example of an inward-looking society that has had long-term economic or political success.

THE HESITANT NATIONAL BUREAUCRACY

First- and second-world bureaucrats, recognizing that their nations' health and relative position in the world pecking order depend upon the strength of their private business sectors, are hesitant to put roadblocks in the way of the new private-sector internationalism. They realize, as clearly as their counterparts in the private sector, that, just as all politics is local, all economics is international. At the same time, they also recognize that these new trends in the private sector undercut their power to guide the national economy and could, in time, make their preferred neomercantilist policies impossible.

The bureaucrat, for all his virtues, has the major vice of stubbornly wanting to achieve whatever goal he has adopted or been assigned. This is why—to cite only one example—hundreds of sincere, talented, and dedicated military and scientific bureaucrats beg for just a few more billions and a few more years to develop the Star Wars system. They don't claim, by and large, that it is needed, only that it can be done. They were given the almost impossible job, and, Ahab-like, they want to finish it. Around the world, wherever Weberian bureaucracies exist, you will find many of the best and brightest using great creativity to solve yesterday's problems. The true bureaucrat can rise to almost any challenge—but he finds it most difficult to accept the challenge of dropping one job half-finished in order to take up another of greater importance.

In its simplest terms, the still unfinished job of the national bureaucrat is to maintain, and, if possible, increase, the power and prosperity of the nation. This is the goal beyond his immediate goal of devising international strategy or collecting local taxes. The bureaucratic sector is the only sector to have such a goal. The private sector, except for the fearful and reactionary has-beens, is fast renouncing the tribe for the empire. It pays only lip service to the parochial interests of the nation. The political sector, by its very nature emotional and tribal, thinks that it is increasing the power of the nation whenever it shakes its club and grunts its troglodyte grunts. The *"uns über alles"* boys of the political sector are equally the despair of nationalist bureaucrats and internationalist businessmen.

In the best of cases, the national bureaucracy will provide an element of ballast as the nation-state sails into an internationalist future. Bureaucratic expertise (and the natural distaste of the goal-oriented thinker for the enemy-obsessed emoter) should allow the state to avoid the rocks of tribalism, while the bureaucratic penchant for finishing old jobs (and the distaste of the goal-oriented for the profit-oriented) should slow it enough to find a passage through the most dangerous whirlpools of lost sovereignty.

Under such a scenario, national bureaucrats would tie in with the international bureaucratic sector in much the same way that national businessmen tie in with the international business sector. Central bankers already pay at least as much attention to the views of their foreign counterparts as to those of their domestic political leaders. National and international health professionals see themselves as part of the same team fighting to achieve the same goal of world health. Many other domestic and international bureaucrats (including those of nongovernmental organizations) share goals in the areas of nutrition, human rights, labor conditions, agriculture, weather, population, and environment. In all these areas, most national bureaucrats most of the time—despite contrary pressures from politicians and the suspicions of the public—see international cooperation as a positive-sum game. What is good for the empire is good for the nation.

There is no assurance, however, that this will always be the case in all countries of the world. The experience of the past has shown us that the internationalism of businessmen and bureaucrats, like that of proletarians, is often hollow and can evaporate in times of war or international tension. And international tensions we will have. Under a worst-case scenario, the national bureaucrats would unite with the political leadership to suppress the "antipatriotic, moneygrubbing" internationalism of the private sector. This would require a return to the second world. Although in times of extreme international tension many businessmen would be willing to put tribal feeling ahead of profits, others would not. The latter—and all the others who put their faith in the empire over the nation—would have to be held in check by police-state methods backed up by a police-state ideology.

Many bureaucrats would welcome this. It would allow them to continue to work on old projects of making the nation strong and prosperous—if only in the short term and at the expense of the rest of the world. They would be ready and willing to follow a Great National Leader into total economic war. And if that were to lead to real war, they would eagerly put their organization and expertise into the goal of achieving victory. Bureaucrats, and bureaucrats alone, have the power to change a harmless madman into a global menace. The difference between Idi Amin and Adolf Hitler boils down to the difference between the bureaucratic resources that each controlled.

EMPIRE AND THE POLITICAL SECTOR

On balance, it appears likely that the forces of internationalism will ultimately prove stronger than those of tribalism. One reason is that the United States, the only nation currently capable of creating a *tribal* empire —which would ignite the latent tribalism of the rest of the first world— shows no signs of doing so.

The one remaining superpower, having won the international political competition, has apparently decided that it has no taste for running the world. Being the world's policeman is an expensive, thankless, and dangerous job. Successes are few and partial; failures are trumpeted. You are unpopular both at home and abroad. You get shot at from both sides. You, the scarred and broken hero trying to live up to your "global responsibilities," are scorned both for your presumption and for your ineffectiveness. Lesser—"more civilized"—powers look down their noses at your "cowboy" antics and smugly count their profits. Who needs it?

Moreover, the military superpower—the backbone of any tribal empire —is an anachronism in a world that has decided that all important power is economic. The Germans and the Japanese—indeed, almost all of the first-world powers—have made it quite clear that they have no interest in military power, that they see money spent on arms as money largely wasted, that they do not want to rule the world even for its own good. The United States gains little honor from being the acknowledged world champion in one game, when everyone else—except perhaps Saddam Hussein—has opted to play a different game.

A second reason for believing that internationalism will triumph over tribalism is that internationalism appeals to the self-interest not only of much of the private sector (increasingly laborers and consumers as well as businessmen) and of that part of the bureaucratic sector whose goals are international in scope but also of a large minority of politicians.

The new empire, unlike those of the past, is not a direct threat to politicians. It has no political leader, no Caesar before whom lesser politicians must bow. Rather it has a group of "world managers"—city managers writ large—who are hired and fired by the national politicians as a group. These world managers, of whom the secretary general of the United Nations is only one, are no more threatening than the plumber or electrician who is called in by the modern homeowner to perform a specific job. The homeowner may admire the professional's expertise and admit that he himself could never have done the job, but he is far from overawed. Once the current is back on and the water is out of the basement, the homeowner can get back to the serious business of running the household—deciding which TV programs the kids are allowed to watch.

Since the end of the Cold War, internationalism has become pragmatic rather than ideological. If the president of the United States is no longer vying with the chairman of the Communist Party of the Soviet Union to bail out the world's flooded basements, he is no longer sure that he even *wants* to bail out the world's basements. And the political leaders of the rest of the world, while not wanting to take up the job themselves, would also like to see the American president out of the plumbing business. The solution, for the politician as for the homeowner, is to hire a professional. Once such trivial "housekeeping" problems as world peace and world prosperity are farmed out to Empire Professional Services, Limited, the politicians can get back to such important national issues as harmonizing the abortion laws of East and West Germany.

In essence, the new empire, if it comes to pass, will be administrative rather than political or ideological. It will be run by Kelly Girls rather than by living gods. The nation will not disappear, any more than it did under the Persians or the Romans or the Ottomans, but it will become less important. The local rulers will be allowed to keep their thrones, and their quaint local religions and barbaric customs will be tolerated. (There are limits, however. The international community may well force capital punishment to go the way of the slave trade.) The local satraps may rule, even despotically, so long as they bow to international law, do not greatly outrage international opinion, and, in general, do not disturb the greater interests of the empire.

U.S. politicians, like the other leaders of the first world, do not want to have to solve the problems of Bosnia and Kashmir, of African starvation and Asian population growth, of human rights and international trade. They do, of course, want these problems—and all the other problems that are in the newspapers and that the voters care about—to be solved. They are willing to do their part, but they do not want to do it alone, to take the lead, to play the heavy, to pay all the bills, and to take all the blame for failure. Moreover, U.S. and other Western politicians who once thought they had the answers (Democracy and Capitalism) to all the world's problems, now know that they do not. Like the homeowner who throws down his pipe wrench in exasperation, the politicians are now ready to call in the experts.[4]

The national politician begins to see international law and international institutions as refuges rather than roadblocks. To some extent, they allow him to take the hard measures that he knows are necessary but that the voters are unlikely to accept. To some extent, they allow him to deal with the devil when dealing with the devil is necessary. Both Iran and the United States could accept the decision of the "powerless" International Court of Justice, when neither could have accepted even the most generous proposal of the other side. To a very great extent, they allow the national politician to avoid international problems that he has neither the resources nor the intellect to solve.

Except for a few atavistic Great National Leaders still trying to right ancient tribal wrongs and a few ideological gurus still trying to impose one or another political religion, the national politician has a great deal to gain and little to lose from joining the empire. The pay is good, the honors are numerous, and the workload is light. Perhaps it is time to copy the constitutional monarchs, to sit back and reign while the hired hands run the show both at home and abroad.

THE YEAR 2050

By the year 2050, those of us who are still alive will be living in a very different world—probably far more different from the world of the present than the present world is from that of the revolutionaries of 1776 and 1789. While it is impossible to predict what form political and economic life will take in the middle of the next century, much will depend upon the relative strengths of tribal and international forces.

One could outline a scenario under which tribalism continued to gain strength until most of the world consisted of Serbias and Georgias, Colombias and Cambodias, Israels and Lebanons, Somalias and Sudans, locked in bloody, never-ending battles to right ancient wrongs and restore ancient privileges. Under such a scenario, in most of the world one's hand would be against every man and the life of man would indeed be solitary, poor, nasty, brutish, and short. The first world would consist of a few dozen isolated fortresses, more often groups of cities than whole nations, rich, bureaucratic, and technologically advanced, linked to each other by culture and commerce. Contact between the tribal world and the truncated international world would be limited. It would be an age that only Conan the Barbarian could love.

It is more probable, however, that rational empire will win out over irrational tribe. It may well come to pass that both the totalitarian-democratic impulse of the Enlightenment, based on the optimistic French idea that human nature is good and only society is bad, and the libertarian-democratic impulse, based on the fearful American idea that human nature is bad and that power corrupts, begin to be seen as hindrances to political development. Under such circumstances, the rational impulse of the Enlightenment, based on the idea that human nature, despite its affinity for the irrational, can be made rational, could come to the fore in politics as it has in science and business.

Under such a scenario, the three worlds would continue to exist. The first world—perhaps a very different lineup of countries than at present—would have largely retired its politicians. The internal affairs of the country would be run by faceless but expert bureaucrats under the general supervision of equally faceless representatives of the population as a whole. These representatives, perhaps selected by lot, would have the responsibility for safeguarding freedom while not getting in the way of efficiency. Leadership, like a physical organ made unnecessary by evolution, would atrophy. The national bureaucracy, like the business sector, would be closely tied in with the international administration.

The international administration—staffed largely by highly qualified citizens of the second and third worlds—would be built around the United Nations, the International Court, and a variety of other specialized organizations.[5] It would establish and monitor the rules of the game in international economic and political relations. It would also establish certain minimum standards for human rights within countries. Genocide and the grosser forms of torture would be proscribed. The international administration, with only a small standing army, would generally move cautiously and tailor its initiatives to what it believed the first-world bureaucracies would be willing to accept. As national experts would be dealing with international experts—speaking the same professional language—without the intervention of politicians, worldviews would generally coincide, and agreement would not be difficult in most cases.

The first-world nations and the international administration would constitute the heart of the empire. The second and the third worlds would constitute the periphery. These countries would generally play by empire rules—the only international law around—but would retain more independence. Outside the first world, leaders and politicians would continue to exert an influence. In the second world, NICs would work their way through authoritarian-bureaucratic rule to eventually achieve entry into the first world. Police states would continue to enforce tribal or ideological supremacy at the cost of freedom and prosperity. In the third world, families, clans, and tribes would maintain the destructive zero-sum democracy of groups.

The nations of the second and third worlds would go to great lengths to avoid invoking the displeasure of the empire, while the international administration would generally turn a blind eye to the lesser domestic sins of these nations. Only when the acts of one or another state of the periphery threatened the physical, political, or economic well-being of the planet as a whole, or when such acts created a high degree of revulsion among first-world newspaper readers, would the empire take action. Such action, if it required more than a few troops, would depend on levies from national armies.

WILL IT HAPPEN THIS WAY? No, most assuredly not. We can no more predict the twenty-first century than the seers of 1776 and 1789 could predict the twentieth—or even the nineteenth—century. Will the world of 2050 have some elements of the above scenario? Very possibly. There are, however, two things that can be predicted with a high degree of confidence: (1) the form of government of most states in the middle of the twenty-first century will have very little resemblance to what we now call democracy; and (2) it will be called democracy.

Notes

Chapter 1

1. Shepard B. Clough, *The Economic Development of Western Civilization* (New York: McGraw-Hill Book Company, 1959), pp. 207–32.

2. J. Bronowski and Bruce Mazlish, *The Western Intellectual Tradition* (Harmondsworth, Middlesex: Penguin Books Ltd., 1963), p. 344.

3. R. H. Tawney, *Religion and the Rise of Capitalism* (Gloucester, Mass.: Peter Smith, 1962), p. 131.

4. Ibid., p. 117.

Chapter 2

1. William H. McNeill, *The Pursuit of Power* (Chicago: University of Chicago Press, 1982).

Chapter 3

1. Max Weber, *Economy and Society* (Berkeley: University of California Press, 1978), p. 1393.

2. Martin Albrow, *Bureaucracy* (New York: Praeger Publishers, 1970), p. 31.

3. Weber, p. 225.

4. Ibid., p. 1393.

5. This definition was taken from Friedrich's article in the *Encyclopedia Americana.* James Q. Wilson, who has written the most authoritative study of U.S. bureaucracy—*Bureaucracy: What Government Agencies Do and Why They Do It* (New York: Basic Books, Inc., 1989)—unfortunately gives no definition.

Chapter 4

1. See James Q. Wilson's *Bureaucracy: What Government Agencies Do and Why They Do It* (New York: Basic Books, Inc., 1989). (Or, for a lively gist of the argument, read Tom Peters's review in the November 1989 *Washingtonian.*)

Chapter 5

1. By the private sector I mean more than simply "business" but less than the nongovernment population as a whole. For the purposes of this book, the private sector includes all groups that wield nongovernmental power: largely businesses, labor unions, professional associations, and advocacy groups in the developed world but, in the third world, expanding to include patron-client structures, clans, tribes, religious sects, linguistic groups, and extended families.

2. See Karl Wittfogel, *Oriental Despotism* (New Haven: Yale University Press, 1964).

Chapter 6

1. Max Weber, *The Protestant Ethic and the Spirit of Capitalism* (New York: Charles Scribner's Sons, 1958). For a somewhat similar treatment of the same subject, see R. H. Tawney's *Religion and the Rise of Capitalism* (Gloucester, Mass.: Peter Smith, 1962).

2. From Thomas Jefferson Wertenbaker, *The First Americans, 1607–1690* (New York: Macmillan Company, 1927), excerpted in George M. Waller, ed., *Puritanism in Early America* (Boston: D. C. Heath and Company, 1950)

p. 34. Also see Wertenbaker's *The Puritan Oligarchy* (New York: Grosset & Dunlap, 1947), especially chapter 2.

3. My understanding of Lincoln and the various elements of the Republican Party is derived largely from Richard Hofstadter, *The American Political Tradition* (New York: Vintage Books, 1961), and from R. B. Nye and J. E. Morpurgo, *A History of the United States* (New York: Penguin Books, 1955).

4. Reprinted in Edwin C. Rozwenc, ed., *The New Deal: Revolution or Evolution?* (Boston: D. C. Heath and Company, 1949), pp. 34–44.

Chapter 7

1. Max Weber, *The Religion of China* (Glencoe, Ill.: The Free Press, 1951), p. 27.

2. To the consternation of some of my colleagues who are true Far Eastern experts, I am following the example of a number of writers on China and using a combination of the Wade-Giles and the pinyin systems in rendering Chinese names. For me at least, "Chou" evokes images that "Zhou" does not.

3. Weber, p. 137.

4. Edwin O. Reischauer and Albert M. Craig, *Japan: Tradition and Transformation* (Boston: Houghton Mifflin Company, 1989), pp. 40–41.

5. Ibid., p. 91.

6. Chalmers Johnson, "MITI, MPT, and the Telecom Wars: How Japan Makes Policy for High Technology," in *Politics and Productivity: The Real Story of Why Japan Works,* ed. Chalmers Johnson, Laura D'Andrea Tyson, and John Zysman (Cambridge, Mass.: Ballinger Publishing Company, 1989), p. 187.

7. Reischauer and Craig, p. 226.

Chapter 8

1. Edwin O. Reischauer, *The Japanese Today* (Cambridge, Mass.: Belknap Press of Harvard University Press, 1988), pp. 104–5.

2. Bill Emmott, *The Sun Also Sets* (New York: Random House, 1989), p. 214.

3. The best studies of the modern Japanese bureaucracy that I am acquainted with are B. C. Koh, *Japan's Administrative Elite* (Berkeley: University of California Press, 1989), and Chalmers Johnson, *MITI and the Japanese Miracle: The Growth of Industrial Policy, 1925–1975* (Stanford: Stanford University Press, 1982).

4. Emmott, pp. 238–39.

Chapter 9

1. The "social contract" has, of course, no literal existence. I use the term, as did the political thinkers of the Enlightenment, as a shorthand expression for the slow evolution of attitudes that must have taken place as the tribe was absorbed into higher forms of political organization.

2. Hedrick Smith, *The Power Game* (New York: Random House, 1988).

3. As we will see in a later section of this book, the case is exactly the reverse in a situation of extreme instability. In many parts of the third world, for example, the trend is to move to the extremes and leave the center as a free-fire zone.

4. In the words of Hedrick Smith (Smith, pp. 573–74):

Basically, politicians and bureaucrats represent two different personality types, playing two different games. By nature and function, they are bound to clash.

Success for each group requires strikingly different behavior. For starters, the foreign policy bureaucrat has a passion for anonymity and the congressman a passion for publicity. The reasons are simple: The keys to survival and advancement for a bureaucrat are operating efficiently in private and staying out of trouble. The key to reelection for a congressman is making a name for himself, often by making a public fuss. The bureaucrat benefits by blending in; the congressman by speaking out. The bureaucrat makes his way by developing professional expertise; the congressman by being a quick-study generalist who can jump from field to field, exploiting political openings.

Chapter 10

1. As will be shown in a later chapter, the bloated redundancy of the typical third-world bureaucracy, far from indicating independent strength, is a sign of its subservience to private or narrow political (as opposed to governmental) interests.

2. I use the term "police state" in a descriptive, not a pejorative, sense. A police state depends on the effectiveness of its police, rather than some other factor, for its internal stability. The police state is not a state in which the police are out of control or dominate the government, but rather a state in which the police are an obedient, effective, and much used tool of the govern-

ment. The existence of so-called death squads is an indicator not of a police state, but of the inability to develop an effective police state.

Chapter 11

1. I have followed the political and economic evolution of one or another of the NICs since the early 1950s, when I was an undergraduate in Mexico City. During this time, my ideas have been formed by numerous books, articles, and conversations—most of which I can no longer identify. Some of the more recent titles that I have found useful include Frederic C. Deyo, ed., *The Political Economy of New Asian Industrialism* (Ithaca: Cornell University Press, 1987); Gary Gereffi and Donald L. Wyman, eds., *Manufacturing Miracles: Paths of Industrialization in Latin America and East Asia* (Princeton: Princeton University Press, 1990); Enrique Pérez López et al., *Mexico's Recent Economic Growth* (Austin: University of Texas Press, 1967); Gordon White, ed., *Developmental States in East Asia* (New York: St. Martin's Press, 1988); K. T. Li, *The Evolution of Policy Behind Taiwan's Development Success* (New Haven: Yale University Press, 1988); John P. Lewis and Valeriana Kallab, eds., *Development Strategies Reconsidered* (New Brunswick, N.J.: Transaction Books, 1986); and Luiz Carlos Bresser Pereira, *Development and Crisis in Brazil, 1930–1983* (Boulder, Colo.: Westview Press, 1984). In a somewhat different category, I have found the works of Guillermo O'Donnell, particularly *Bureaucratic Authoritarianism: Argentina, 1966–1973, in Comparative Perspective* (Berkeley: University of California Press, 1988), to be especially stimulating.

2. Gereffi and Wyman, p. 10.

3. Despite all the theoretical—and real—beauties of the free market, government aid and protectionism appear to be essential for successful industrialization. The United States, during the post–Civil War period of rapid industrialization, relied heavily on government favors and protectionism. The United Kingdom, France, and Germany, for their part, all achieved their industrial takeoffs under mercantilist administrations.

Chapter 12

1. When I first wrote this assessment of Mao in the late 1980s, Mao was still regarded with considerable reverence even by anti-Communists, and I quoted a long list of sources—most particularly, Lowell Dittmer's *China's Continuous Revolution* (Berkeley: University of California Press, 1987)—with the caveat that "I am sure that none of these authors would completely agree with my

interpretation." Now I find that I am preaching to the choir. The dean of U.S. China scholars, the late John King Fairbank, in his last major work, has stated that his earlier enthusiasm for Mao was "an outstanding example of sentimental sinophilia," while Jonathan Spence has written, "What a long way indeed many of us have come, from our absorption with the visionary leaps and passions of China's Maoist version of socialism. . . ." See John King Fairbank, *China: A New History* (Cambridge, Massachusetts: Belknap Press of Harvard University Press, 1992), p. 176, and Jonathan Spence, "The Other China," *New York Review of Books* 39, no. 17 (Oct. 22, 1992): 12.

2. For some telling examples of the shah's religious experiences, including a meeting with the Hidden Imam on a street in Tehran, see James A. Bill and Carl Leiden, *Politics in the Middle East* (Boston: Little, Brown and Company, 1979), pp. 209–10.

3. The Iranian Revolution, though it clearly had the support of most classes, was not a peasant or worker revolution; it was the work of the clergy, the merchants, the students, and the intellectuals—all members of the middle class in the Iranian context. If the middle class had not grown so sharply relative to the other elements of Iranian society—the direct result of the shah's modernization program and its lavish oil-fired financing—a shah (perhaps of a different upstart dynasty) would probably be sitting on the Peacock Throne today. The relationship of the middle class to political instability will be discussed in a later chapter.

Chapter 13

1. Leonard M. Thompson, "The South African Dilemma," in Louis Hartz et al., *The Founding of New Societies* (New York: Harcourt Brace Jovanovich, 1964), p. 182.

2. For an excellent description of the hardships and injustices that the Afrikaners suffered before 1948 (in a book that is basically unsympathetic to the Afrikaner position), see David Harrison, *The White Tribe of Africa* (Johannesburg: Macmillan South Africa, 1983), pp. 1–83.

3. Thompson, p. 203.

4. Quoted in John Quigley, *Palestine and Israel* (Durham: Duke University Press, 1990), p. 5.

5. Meron Benvenisti, "The Turning Point in Israel," *New York Review of Books*, Oct. 13, 1983. Benvenisti likened the system to South African apartheid.

6. Quigley, p. 133.

7. Jacobo Timerman, *The Longest War: Israel in Lebanon* (New York: Alfred A. Knopf, 1982), pp. 72–76.

8. Bernard Avishai, *The Tragedy of Zionism* (New York: Farrar Straus Giroux, 1985), pp. 72–78.

9. E. Ramón Arango, *Spain: From Repression to Renewal* (Boulder, Colo.: Westview Press, 1985), p. 76.

10. Ibid., p. 126.

11. Although it is true that neither E.C. nor NATO membership is in itself sufficient to assure first-world status—witness Greece and Portugal—Spain clearly sees itself and is seen by other European countries as being a "member of the club."

12. Jonathan Kandell, "Prosperity Born of Pain," *New York Times Magazine*, July 7, 1991, p. 17.

13. Alfred D. Chandler, *Scale and Scope: The Dynamics of Industrial Capitalism* (Cambridge: Belknap Press of Harvard University Press, 1990), pp. 531–33.

Chapter 14

1. When a long period of economic growth is followed by a prolonged and deep economic crisis, the middle class does not shrink—rather it becomes impoverished. It still retains its middle-class aspirations even as it realizes that it no longer has the means of attaining them.

2. Carlos H. Waisman summarizes Argentina's past achievement very well in his *Reversal of Development in Argentina* (Princeton: Princeton University Press, 1987), p. 5:

In the second half of the nineteenth century, Argentina was fully incorporated into the international division of labor as an exporter of temperate agricultural commodities. This period from the seventies up to the Depression was one of rapid economic and social change. The population was 1.7 million in 1869, but from 1870 to 1930 it was engulfed by over six million European immigrants, over half of whom eventually remained in the country. At the end of the century, Argentina had attained a relatively high level of economic development: "As early as 1895," according to Michael M. Mulhall, "the Argentine per capita income was about the same as those of Germany, Holland, and Belgium, and higher than those of Austria, Spain, Italy, Switzerland, Sweden, and Norway." And Lewis writes that Argentine exports grew "at an average rate of 6 percent per annum, making Argentina compete with Japan for the title of the fastest growing country in the world between 1870 and 1913." From the beginning of the century up to the Depression, the GDP grew at a rate of 4.6 percent per annum.

3. The Mexican situation—indeed, the situation of all the NICs—is much more complicated than I have pictured it here. The strand that I emphasize—how sudden oil wealth allowed a more-than-rhetorical emphasis on social (and even political) democracy, permitted destabilizing levels of corruption, aborted a promising turn to manufactured exports, undermined fiscal discipline, and brought economic growth to a standstill—is by no means the only strand involved in Mexico's political and economic crisis. It is, however, what I believe to be the most important strand.

Chapter 15

1. It has been my privilege to know a number of (mostly Protestant) ministers and theologians. I have found that these professionals, who take their religion very seriously, are much more likely to have doubts than are the lay members of their flock. It is, after all, their profession; they think about it all the time.

The professionals in any realm, not ordinary citizens, are usually the first to doubt. Revolutions in physics, economics, or psychology are made by physicists, economists, and psychologists—even though these professionals have the most to lose by the disruption of their profession—and not by laymen, who have other more pressing concerns. Thus, we should be no more surprised by a Gorbachev or a de Klerk than by an Einstein or a Keynes. Such revolutions in thinking are first and foremost intellectual exercises that almost always begin among those who know the most rather than among those who have the most to gain.

2. Samuel P. Huntington, *Political Order in Changing Societies* (New Haven: Yale University Press, 1968), p. 1.

3. John K. Fairbank and Edwin O. Reischauer, *China: Tradition and Transformation* (Boston: Houghton Mifflin Company, 1989), pp. 531–32.

4. The Palestinians see themselves as the victims of an international mugging. Although the realists among them may be willing to cut a deal, the majority are unlikely to let bygones be bygones in exchange for what they see as a few coins from their own purse.

Chapter 16

1. From Malinche, Cortés's Indian mistress and interpreter, who played a pivotal role in the Spanish conquest of Mexico.

2. José Enrique Rodó's 1900 pamphlet *Ariel* (Buenos Aires: Editorial Kapelusz, 1966), influential throughout Latin America in its time, is still a good

characterization of the way many third-world intellectuals see the first world. For Rodó, the third world (or at least Latin America) is, like Shakespeare's Ariel, *"la parte noble y alada del espíritu,"* representing the dominion of reason and sentiment over irrationality, the symbol of generosity, altruism, wit, intelligence, and culture, whereas the first world (or at least the United States) is like Caliban, the almost-animal symbol of sensuality, materialism, and intellectual sluggishness.

3. Democracy is associated with many of the worst vices of ancient Greece. Weber points out in *Economy and Society* that war was conducted with extraordinary ruthlessness in the democratic period "in contrast to the chivalrous conduct . . . in the patrician period" (pp. 1361–62) and that "the fullest expansion of the exploitation of slaves in ancient Greece fell precisely in the periods of Democracy" (p. 1343). And, of course, it was Athenian democrats who gave the hemlock to Socrates.

Chapter 17

1. The literature on political unrest is extensive and fascinating. It ranges from readers like Jack A. Goldstone, *Revolutions: Theoretical, Comparative, and Historical Studies* (San Diego: Harcourt Brace Jovanovich, 1986); Harry Eckstein, *Internal War: Problems and Approaches* (New York: Free Press of Glencoe, 1964); and James C. Davies, *When Men Revolt—and Why: A Reader in Political Violence and Revolution* (New York: Free Press, 1971), through such old classics as Crane Brinton, *The Anatomy of Revolution* (New York: Vintage Books, 1959); George Pettee, *The Process of Revolution* (New York: Harper & Row, 1938); and Lyford P. Edwards, *The Natural History of Revolution* (Chicago: University of Chicago Press, 1970), to more specialized works such as John H. Kautsky, *The Political Consequences of Modernization* (Huntington, N.Y.: Robert E. Krieger Publishing Company, 1980), and Eric R. Wolf, *Peasant Wars of the Twentieth Century* (New York: Harper Torchbooks, 1973). One of the very best books on the subject—indeed, a new classic fit to stand beside Brinton, Pettee, and Edwards—is Jack Goldstone's *Revolution and Rebellion in the Early Modern World* (Berkeley: University of California Press, 1991). I will have more to say about this study in chapter 22.

In addition to the works mentioned, I have profited greatly from reading Mark N. Hagopian, *The Phenomenon of Revolution* (New York: Harper & Row, 1974); Ted Robert Gurr, *Why Men Rebel* (Princeton: Princeton University Press, 1970); Samuel P. Huntington, *Political Order in Changing Societies* (New Haven: Yale University Press, 1968); Chalmers Johnson, *Revolutionary Change* (Stanford; Stanford University Press, 1982); and a host of more country-specific and regional studies of unrest.

2. Alexis de Tocqueville, *The Old Régime and the French Revolution* (Garden City, N.Y.: Doubleday & Company, Inc., 1955), p. 174.

3. Ibid., p. 175.

4. Ibid., pp. 176–77.

5. Gurr, pp. 46–56.

6. Hagopian, p. 174.

7. The 1906 strike at the Green Consolidated Mining Company at Cananea, Sonora, deteriorated into violence largely because of the panicky actions of some U.S. employees. Some twenty strikers were killed, and a number were sent to prison.

8. Crane Brinton (p. 260) comments that none of the societies affected by the "great" revolutions, "not even Russia, seems to have undergone changes as complete as those undergone by Turkish society since the wholesale, really revolutionary measures taken under Mustapha Kemal or by Japanese society during the Meiji Revolution—to say nothing of the MacArthur Revolution."

9. Tocqueville, p. 60.

Chapter 18

1. J. Fred Rippy, *Historical Evolution of Hispanic America*, 3rd ed. (New York: Appleton-Century-Crofts, Inc., 1945), p. 86.

2. Ibid., p. 64.

3. Richard M. Morse, "The Heritage of Latin America," in Louis Hartz et al., *The Founding of New Societies* (New York: Harcourt Brace Jovanovich, 1964), p. 142.

4. Ibid., p. 157.

5. J. M. Roberts, *The Pelican History of the World* (London: Penguin Books, 1987), pp. 596–97.

6. Percival Spear, *India: A Modern History* (Ann Arbor: University of Michigan Press, 1961), p. 213.

7. According to Eric Hobsbawm, "Emperors and empires were old, but imperialism was quite new. The word (which does not occur in the writings of Karl Marx, who died in 1883) first entered politics in Britain in the 1870s, and was still regarded as a neologism at the end of that decade. It exploded into general use in the 1890s. . . . In 1914 plenty of politicians were proud to call themselves imperialists. . . ." Eric Hobsbawm, *The Age of Empire* (New York: Vintage Books, 1989), p. 60.

Chapter 19

1. In rare cases, of course, a caste system may be so rigid as to obviate the very possibility of relative deprivation.

2. Robert Hughes, *The Fatal Shore* (New York: Alfred A. Knopf, 1987), pp. 164–65.

3. Percival Spear, *India: A Modern History* (Ann Arbor: University of Michigan Press, 1961), p. 43.

4. During the nineteenth century, Mexico had a number of different caste wars in the states of Oaxaca and Chiapas as well as the more famous and longer-lasting event on the Yucatán peninsula. A very readable account of the latter is Nelson Reed's *The Caste War of Yucatan* (Stanford: Stanford University Press, 1964).

5. Ibid., p. 47.

6. Spear, p. 8.

7. The military in some other third-world countries, especially in Central America, the Caribbean, and sub-Saharan Africa, does not have this proto-bureaucratic character but rather is itself an extension of the private sector with no other goal than that of feathering the nests of its members.

Chapter 20

1. My understanding of the nature of religion, although based largely on my own experience and observation, has been influenced by Sir James George Frazer, *The Golden Bough* (New York: Macmillan Company, 1960); Bronislaw Malinowski, *Magic, Science and Religion* (Garden City, N.Y.: Doubleday Anchor Books, 1954); Robert A. Lowie, *Primitive Religion* (New York: Liveright, 1970); William Howells, *The Heathens* (Garden City, N.Y.: Doubleday Anchor Books, 1962); Joseph Campbell, *Primitive Mythology* (New York: Viking Press, 1970); and a number of studies of specific societies. In a somewhat different manner, my ideas were also influenced by Herbert J. Muller, *The Uses of the Past* (New York: New American Library, 1952), and Donald Eugene Smith, *Religion and Political Development* (Boston: Little, Brown and Company, 1970).

2. Mark N. Hagopian, *The Phenomenon of Revolution* (New York: Harper & Row, 1974), p. 24.

3. Ibid., pp. 24–25.

4. Ibid., p. 25.

5. Ibid., pp. 28–29.

6. Michael Adas, *Prophets of Rebellion* (Chapel Hill: University of North Carolina Press, 1979), p. 158.

7. In addition to Adas's *Prophets of Rebellion* and Reed's *The Caste War of Yucatan* (cited in the previous chapter), a number of other works explain the range and nature of millenarian rebellion. Euclides da Cunha's nonfiction classic *Rebellion in the Backlands* (Chicago: University of Chicago Press, 1944) and Mario Vargas Llosa's fiction near-classic *La Guerra del Fin del Mundo* (Barcelona: Seix Barral, 1981) both treat the Canudos Rebellion of Antônio Conselheiro with great insight. Maria Isaura Pereira de Queiroz's *Historia y Etnología de los Movimientos Mesiánicos* (Mexico City: Siglo Veintiuno Editores, SA, 1978) gives an exhaustive anthropological and historical description of messianic movements around the world. Norman Cohn's *The Pursuit of the Millennium* (New York: Oxford University Press, 1970) and Eric Hobsbawm's *Primitive Rebels: Studies in Archaic Forms of Social Movement in the 19th and 20th Centuries* (Manchester: Manchester University Press, 1978) are also worth the reader's attention.

8. Folk Catholicism, even the more orthodox form practiced in the cities, is a descriptive but ultimately misleading term. Folk Catholicism is not a form of Catholicism. In fact, in some of its more extreme manifestations that elevate other spiritual beings to the level of Christ, it is not even a form of Christianity. It differs from orthodox Catholicism (say, that taught in the Catholic schools of the United States) far more than orthodox Catholicism differs from mainline Protestantism.

9. David Martin, *Tongues of Fire: The Explosion of Protestantism in Latin America* (Oxford: Basil Blackwell, 1990), pp. 57–58.

10. The most balanced account of Latin American Liberation Theology that I am acquainted with is Paul E. Sigmund's *Liberation Theology at the Crossroads: Democracy or Revolution?* (New York: Oxford University Press, 1990). For the "establishment" view, one may wish to read Deane William Ferm, *Third World Liberation Theologies: An Introductory Survey* (Maryknoll, N.Y.: Orbis, 1986), and Theo Witvliet, *A Place in the Sun: An Introduction to Liberation Theology in the Third World* (Maryknoll, N.Y.: Orbis, 1984).

11. From a colloquium presented by Mr. Ireland at the Woodrow Wilson International Center for Scholars on January 20, 1983.

12. Martin, p. 53.

Chapter 21

1. Buddhism, though clearly a universal religion, is not a world religion on the order of Christianity and Islam. It has no connected body of followers around the world.

2. It is perhaps indicative of the importance of the empire to Christianity that, whereas the Muslim prays in the language of Muhammad and the Jew in the language of Moses, the Christian (through much of West European history) has used the language of Caesar.

3. Herbert J. Muller, *The Uses of the Past* (New York: New American Library, 1952), p. 192.

4. This became less true in time. Religious scholars, teachers, lawyers, and judges came to have considerable influence even in orthodox Sunni Islam, while saints and mystics became important in the Folk Islam of certain regions. Nothing, however, that even remotely resembled the Christian clergy developed among the orthodox Sunnis.

5. The historical and religious differences between the Sunnis and the Shi'ites are very well explained in Michael M. J. Fischer, *Iran: From Religious Dispute to Revolution* (Cambridge: Harvard University Press, 1980), pp. 12–32.

6. The continuation of pre-Islamic traits in modern Shi'a Islam is well documented in Pio Filippani-Ronconi, "The Tradition of Sacred Kingship in Iran," in *Iran Under the Pahlavis*, ed. George Lenezowski (Stanford: Hoover Institution Press, 1978), pp. 51–83.

7. The position of the Muslim with regard to Western civilization is more problematic than that of the Latin American or East Asian. The Latin American, despite all his talk of the glories of his Indian heritage, sees himself as very much a part of Western civilization and can accept its bounties without mixed feelings. The East Asian, reared in the shadow of China and India, is used to cheerfully milking advanced foreign cultures for whatever they may have of value.

8. See Reinhold Loeffler, *Islam in Practice: Religious Beliefs in a Persian Village* (Albany: State University of New York Press, 1988).

9. Millenarian movements can, of course, arise in Sunni countries in response to the relative deprivation created by European encroachment. The stubborn revolts of the Sudan's Mahdi and Java's Dipanagara are cases in point. For such movements to have any chance of success, however, there must be a preexisting structure of tribal authority that the religious leader can appropriate. Such movements, unlike those of the Shi'ites, generally have little resonance beyond the original tribe or tribal alliance.

Chapter 22

1. Eric D. Larson, Marc H. Ross, and Robert H. Williams, "Beyond the Era of Materials," *Scientific American* 254, no. 6 (June 1986): 34–41.

2. Ibid., p. 39.

3. J. S. Nye, "Corruption and Political Development: A Cost-Benefit Analy-

sis," *The American Political Science Review* 61, no. 2 (June 1967): 417–27. See also Susan Rose-Ackerman, *Corruption: A Study in Political Economy* (New York: Academic Press, 1978), for a valuable though overly abstract discussion of the subject, and Hernando De Soto, *The Other Path: The Invisible Revolution in the Third World* (New York: Harper & Row, 1989), for a valuable though intellectually confused and (perhaps) overly concrete discussion of the same subject.

4. Huntington's conclusions about corruption are closer to my own. See Samuel P. Huntington, *Political Order in Changing Societies* (New Haven: Yale University Press, 1968), pp. 59–71.

5. First-world societies—the United States and Japan, for example—are often riddled with third-world-like corruption, but this does little harm, because the bureaucracy is generally left untouched. Presidents and congressmen differ little whether they are in Washington or Kinshasa; bureaucrats differ greatly.

6. See especially: Joan M. Nelson, *Access to Power: Politics and the Urban Poor in Developing Nations* (Princeton: Princeton University Press, 1979); Wayne A. Cornelius, *Politics and the Migrant Poor in Mexico City* (Stanford: Stanford University Press, 1975); and Janice E. Perlman, *The Myth of Marginality: Urban Poverty and Politics in Rio de Janeiro* (Berkeley: University of California Press, 1976).

7. Gary Fuller's only published paper on the subject that I am familiar with is: Gary Fuller and Forrest R. Pitts, "Youth Cohorts and Political Unrest in South Korea," *Political Geography Quarterly* 9, no. 1 (Jan. 1990): 9–22.

8. Jack A. Goldstone, *Revolution and Rebellion in the Early Modern World* (Berkeley: University of California Press, 1991), p. xxiii.

9. Ibid., pp. xxiii–xxiv.

10. Ibid., pp. 477–85.

Chapter 23

1. Janice E. Perlman, *The Myth of Marginality: Urban Poverty and Politics in Rio de Janeiro* (Berkeley: University of California Press, 1976), p. xvi.

2. For example, I vote in the state of Virginia. In any given election, I have a very good idea of who will win long before I cast my vote. I can either vote with the majority, or I can vote against the majority; either way my vote has no effect on the outcome.

As Mancur Olson puts it: "The gain to . . . a voter from studying issues and candidates until it is clear what vote is truly in his or her interest is given by the difference in the value to the individual of the 'right' election outcome as compared with the 'wrong' outcome, *multiplied by the probability a change in the individual's vote will alter the outcome of the election.* Since the probability that a typical voter will change the outcome of the election is vanishingly small, the typical citizen is usually 'rationally ignorant' about public affairs." (Italics in original.) From *The Rise and Decline of Nations: Economic Growth, Stagflation, and Social Rigidities* (New Haven: Yale University Press, 1982), p. 26.

Chapter 24

1. Mancur Olson, *The Rise and Decline of Nations: Economic Growth, Stagflation, and Social Rigidities* (New Haven: Yale University Press, 1982).

2. Ibid., p. 44. (Italics in original.)

3. Ibid., p. 75.

4. Many political scientists, who should know better, appear to believe that conflict somehow benefits good government. I am at a loss to understand how otherwise liberal scholars can support such a crude form of political Darwinism. Conflict is no more likely to produce good government than medieval trial by combat was to produce justice. In both cases, the stronger or the more unscrupulous win.

Chapter 25

1. What I call "empire"—a system of enforceable international law—should not be confused with "imperialism"—the stealing of other peoples' land. The former is based on law, bureaucracy, and equality, while the latter is usually (though not always) based on tribal greed and a sense of "national destiny."

2. This case, which is far more complex than I have described, is well covered in the *Wall Street Journal* of June 18, 1992. A large number of similar cases are cited in Robert B. Reich, *The Work of Nations* (New York: Alfred A. Knopf, 1991).

3. Reich, p. 3. (Italics in original.)

4. Although U.S. politicians will undoubtedly maintain that they have the right to take unilateral action in the international sphere, they will be increasingly hesitant to do so. The abject failure of Bush's *mano a mano* with Noriega means that no U.S. president is likely to take such unilateral action in the future. Nor is the U.S. government likely to kidnap any more minor drug figures from friendly countries in view of the universal scorn heaped so deservedly on the Justice Department as a result of the Álvarez Machaín case.

5. This scenario assumes that, during the next fifty or so years, the United Nations evolves away from politics and toward rational bureaucracy. This would entail the withering away of the General Assembly and the Security

Council and the total reorganization of most U.N. bureaucracies. At present, most U.N. entities have been either privatized for personal gain in true third-world fashion or politicized for ideological purposes in true second-world fashion. The minority of fine Weberian bureaucrats at the U.N.—often themselves from second- or third-world countries—must fight against the system that they are a part of.

Index